Education and Training of Personnel concerned with Environmental Issues relating to Industry

EF/92/22/EN

 European Foundation
for the Improvement of
Living and Working Conditions

Education and Training of Personnel concerned with Environmental Issues relating to Industry

by
Ecotec
Research and Consulting Ltd.

Loughlinstown House, Shankill, Co. Dublin, Ireland
Tel: +353 1 282 6888 Fax: +353 1 282 6456 Telex: 30726 EURF EI

Cataloguing data can be found at the end of this publication

Luxembourg: Office for Official Publications of the European Communities, 1992

ISBN 92-826-4852-4

© European Foundation for the Improvement of Living and Working Conditions, 1992.

For rights of translation or reproduction, applications should be made to the Director, European Foundation for the Improvement of Living and Working Conditions, Loughlinstown House, Shankill, Co. Dublin, Ireland.

Printed in Ireland

PREFACE

At a European Round Table on the Role of the Social Partners in Improving the Environment, 8-10 June 1988, the Foundation was invited to include in its four-year programme 1989-1992 a new theme on the firm in its local environment, focusing on SMEs and the southern Member States, in particular, and, as part of this theme, to examine education and training requirements and provisions regarding personnel concerned with environmental issues relating to industry. These proposals were later endorsed by the Administrative Board of the Foundation.

When undertaking this project in late 1989, the Foundation had just completed a study on education and training relating to hazardous waste (1988-89), and Directorate-General XI of the Commission was synthesising the findings of its extensive case study work, since 1983, on environmental training in specific areas in the European Community. It was clear from the outset, however, that although these activities provided a good basis for the Foundation's project, additional information was required on relevant initiatives taken by other services of the Commission and a vast number of other organisations. It was, therefore, decided as a first step to carry out a literature review of research findings relating to training and the environment and to combine it with a series of consultations with representatives of international and national organisations involved in promoting environmental management in SMEs. This enabled the contractor, ECOTEC Research and Consulting Ltd., to prepare a position paper indicating the key issues and to provide a framework for a postal survey during which regulatory agencies and other relevant public authorities, industrial federations, chambers of commerce, the social partners and other organisations in the Member States were approached. A draft overview report was then presented for evaluation at an international workshop at the Joint Research Centre in Ispra, in October 1990, at which representatives of the Commission, governments, the social partners and a number of national and international organisations discussed and developed ideas on substantive research issues. These ideas and suggestions were incorporated into the final report, together with the findings of ECOTEC's research for CEDEFOP (the European Centre for the Development of Vocational Training) on specific environmental management responses in the UK and the detailed environmental education and training requirements of SMEs. Moreover, regulatory agencies and the social partners in Italy were consulted on the research issues in order to relate the findings more closely to the southern Member States. A draft final report was sent to the participants at the international workshop for comments, and the comments received have been taken into account or directly included in the present report.

The procedure adopted when implementing this project has enabled the Foundation to present a more comprehensive and forward looking report than would otherwise have been the case. Thus, the present report not only describes and analyses the existing provision of education and training for the categories of personnel who are involved in environmental issues relating to industry, its inadequacies and the specific needs of regulatory agencies and SMEs, but it also points to the rationale for seeking short-, medium- and long-term improvements, the structures and mechanisms required, the crucial role of the various actors, including the social partners, and the particular responses and actions which will be necessary during the 1990s to achieve higher standards in the environmental performance of industry aimed at sustainable development. This comprehensive approach has been made possible because of the input of the vast number of public and private organisations and individuals listed in the annexes to the report, and the Foundation would like to thank these organisations and individuals for their contribution to the project.

This project has been followed by further studies relating to the environmental performance of SMEs in six Member States and undertaken as part of the Foundation's work programmes for 1991 and 1992. The findings of these studies, which have been carried out under the theme the firm in its local environment, will be available in 1993.

Jørn Pedersen
Dublin, November 1992

CONTENTS

EXECUTIVE SUMMARY **PAGE**

1.0 INTRODUCTION

1.1	Background	1
1.2	Study Aims and Objectives	2
1.3	A Definition of Environmental Management	3
1.4	A Definition of Training Needs	5
1.5	Method of Approach	6
1.6	Structure of Report	7

2.0 THE GENERAL NEED FOR TRAINING

2.1	Introduction	8
2.2	Awareness Raising in SMEs	8
2.3	Pressures for Environmental Management	10
2.4	An Analysis of Environmental Problems	19
2.5	An Analysis of Industrial Structure and Importance of SMEs	23
2.6	Overview of EC Regulatory Structures and Environmental Policy	26
2.7	The Relevance of Training in the Environment	32

3.0 THE NEED FOR TRAINING IN SMEs AND REGULATORY AGENCIES

3.1	Introduction	37
3.2	A Framework for Occupational Analysis	37
3.3	Definition of Occupations	40
3.4	Issues Emerging from the Case Studies	47
3.5	A Review of Training Needs	50
3.6	Education and Training Responses to Identified Needs	61
3.7	Company wide Responses to Environmental Management	64

4.0 AN OVERVIEW OF THE PROVISION OF ENVIRONMENTAL EDUCATION AND TRAINING IN THE COMMUNITY

4.1	Introduction	67
4.2	The Scope and Definition of Training	67

4.3	The Content of Training Provision	69
4.4	Method of Delivery	73
4.5	Scale of Provision	75
4.6	Conclusions	77

5.0 THE ROLE OF INTERNATIONAL ORGANISATIONS

5.1	Introduction	81
5.2	The European Commission	81
5.3	The International Labour Organisation	91
5.4	Organisation for Economic Co-operation and Developemtn (OECD)	95
5.5	UNEP	96
5.6	CEDEFOP	98
5.7	The International Chamber of Commerce	98
5.8	BAUM	100
5.9	Union of Industrial and Employer's Confederations of Europe (UNICE)	102
5.10	European Trade Union Confederation	102
5.11	Industry Associations	103
5.12	Co-operation Between the Social Partners	105

6.0 THE ROLE OF NATIONAL AND REGIONAL ORGANISATIONS

6.1	Introduction	107
6.2	A Review of Organisations	107
6.3	Private Sector Consultants	107
6.4	Training Agencies	109
6.5	Employers Organisations	110
6.6	Regulatory Agencies	113
6.7	Health and Safety Agencies	117
6.8	Research Institutions	117
6.9	Trade Unions	119
6.10	Business Support Channels	120
6.11	Co-operation Between SMEs and Regulatory Agencies	121

7.0 CONCLUSIONS

7.1	The Need for Improvements in Environmental Education and Training	122

7.2	The Training Needs of Regulatory Agencies	123
7.3	The Training Needs of SMEs	124
7.4	Environmental Education and Training Responses	125
7.5	The Possibilities for Co-operation Between SMEs and Regulatory Agencies	127
7.6	The Involvement of the Social Partners	128
7.7	General Comments on Improvements in the Provision of Services	129

ANNEXES

Annex A : References — 135

Annex B : Consultees — 143

Annex C : Survey Instruments — 191

Annex D : The International Workshop — 231

Annex E : Industry Case Studies — 239

Annex F : The Italian Mission — 253

Annex G : A Review of Environmental Training Provision in the UK — 257

Annex H : An Overview of Environmental Policy — 269

EDUCATION AND TRAINING OF PERSONNEL CONCERNED WITH ENVIRONMENTAL ISSUES RELATING TO INDUSTRY

EXECUTIVE SUMMARY

1.0 INTRODUCTION

Background

1.1 The Single European Act and the Fourth Environmental Action Programme make clear that the environment is an integral part of the European Community's economic, social, industrial and other policies. The Action Programme declares the European Commission's intention of making maximum use of contributions made by the European Foundation on the firm and its environment.

Study Objectives

1.2 The aim of this Phase I study is to identify, in general terms, the existing inadequacies and the scope for possible improvements, in the education and training of certain categories of personnel concerned with environmental issues relating to industry, thereby assisting the Foundation to inform medium and long-term policy development. Specifically, the objectives of the research programme are to:

- highlight the training needs of regional and local regulatory agencies;

- highlight the training needs of small and medium-sized enterprises (SMEs);

- indicate ways in which such needs could be more effectively met, so as to improve environmental management;

- identify the scope for good co-operation on environmental issues between SMEs and regulatory agencies;

- illustrate how the Social Partners can be more closely involved in the process of improving environmental management.

1.3 The study focuses on SMEs because it is largely recognised that they have limited resources to allocate to environmental management and lack the scale of operation to support the employment of environmental management specialists. SMEs, therefore, face particular constraints in preparing environmental management responses designed to improve their environmental performance.

1.4 The study also focuses on training and the environment and SMEs in Southern Member States. This focus reflects the growing realisation that the move towards higher environmental standards within the Community has particularly acute implications for the required improvement in environmental performance by SMEs in Spain, Portugal, Italy and Greece.

A Definition of Environmental Management

1.5 The study is concerned with the issue of the firm in its local environment and, for the purposes of this study, we have therefore focused on environmental problems caused by industry and the environmental management responses of SMEs. The responses of SMEs to control and manage these environmental problems we have termed environmental management, and define it as: the control and prevention of pollution to the different environmental media (water, air, land) via "end-of-pipe" technologies; the adoption and use of "cleaner" technologies which generate fewer emissions, via process modification and materials substitution; the recycling of waste products; and the management and disposal of pollutants.

Environmental management activities are undertaken by the polluting sectors (eg. water, chemicals, food processing and metals industries), the suppliers of goods and services for environmental management and other agencies mainly comprising regulatory agencies. Specifically excluded are activities which are chiefly concerned with health and safety and environmental conservation.

A Definition of Training Needs

1.6 The study uses the term training "need" as opposed to the "demand" for training services. This reflects our appreciation that there is a distinction between the determination of training requirements as a result of the need for improved environmental management (defined either by SMEs or by training and/or regulatory agencies), and the determination of training requirements as expressed in the demand, by SMEs and regulatory agencies for training services. The distinction arises because SMEs are often unaware of the improvement in environmental performance which is required and the consequent training requirements.

Method of Approach

1.7 The study combines existing research findings with original research undertaken as part of this study, to provide a synthesis of research at Community level, relating to training and the environment, in response to the study objectives. Key elements of the approach include an extensive literature review, a series of consultations with senior representatives of international and national organisations who have a role in promoting environmental management in SMEs, a postal survey of regulatory agencies, training agencies and Social Partners in each Member State, an international workshop to discuss and develop ideas on the substantive research issues, collaborative research with the European Centre for Vocational Training (CEDEFOP), and an extensive mission to Italy to inform the research findings as they apply to Southern Member States.

2.0 ENVIRONMENTAL TRAINING REQUIREMENTS

Training Needs

2.1 The study has identified a clear requirement for environmental training in SMEs and regulatory agencies. The lack of awareness amongst SMEs is identified as a major problem which needs to be addressed in developing environmental training responses. Training needs are required for personnel at all levels, and for a wide range of skills and competences. Training is also needed to facilitate the efficient implementation of environmental policy by SMEs and regulatory agencies and for the development of cost-effective company-wide environmental management responses.

Characteristics of Existing Training Provision

2.2 The main characteristics of existing training provision are considered with respect to the content, method of delivery and scale of provision.

Content of Provision

- SMEs generally regard external training courses as being more relevant than internal training provision.

- Environmental training continues to be extensively incorporated into training for health and safety, particularly in the case of internal training provision.

- Environmental legislation has had a significant effect on content, with particular emphasis on waste management and to a lesser extent on water pollution.

- Environmental management training is very limited, partly reflecting a lack of expressed demand, although some improvement is evident.

- Environmental education is developing, the effects of which are important in the longer term.

- The development of new training provision requires a clearer definition of environmental occupations and the requisite training requirements.

Method of Delivery

- The delivery of both internal training, using in-house trainers, and external training provision requires increased training provision. The trainers require training.

- The development of short external courses, targeted at senior managers, which are aimed at promoting awareness and developing corporate environmental responses, is likely to be a major method of delivery in the short to medium term.

- Consultants are likely to play a growing role in the provision of training.

- The development of provision by quasi-public organisations (employer organisations, research institutes) will require public finance.

Scale of Provision

- The scale of provision is partly determined by expressed demand. The essential requirement, to promote environmental awareness, is increasingly being recognised.

- Training services which are taken up are deficient in two ways, (i) management targeted provision is often too specialised and does not address the need to develop competences to prepare corporate environmental responses and (ii) technical level provision is often not sufficiently related to actual identified processes and applications.

- The scale of provision is directly related to the development of environmental legislation. Increasing awareness of SMEs and increasingly stringent environmental legislation will stimulate increased provision.

3.0 ENVIRONMENTAL TRAINING RESPONSES

3.1 This section provides a summary of the range of responses to the need for environmental training. It is important to recognise that environmental management is not the primary concern of those working in industry. As such it is necessary to be aware of the limitations which affect the ability of industry to respond to its environmental responsibilities. Training must be cost-effective and respond to the real demands of industry.

3.2 In order to move towards a position of greater responsibility and a greater capability in industry (for example in being able to identify the best available pollution control techniques) those working in potentially polluting industries will have to be encouraged to increase their awareness and expertise. In this respect the following requirements can be identified:-

- General programmes to enhance the environmental awareness of employees and employers.

- Greater provision of information and independent advice on available cleaner technologies, including advice on the efficiency and effectiveness of available pollution control techniques appropriate for specific industries.

- Similarly, there is a need to provide small developers and manufacturers of pollution control technologies with information on the market for their products and on (future) environmental policies, including any financial assistance schemes for which they might be eligible.

- A greater use of environmental databases and information systems on aspects such as environmental regulations and pollution control technologies.

- Promotion of 'in-house' training by the provision of technical back-up materials and facilities and flexible 'distance learning' information packages that can be used for study by the people concerned at their place of work or at home.

- Provision of short, very intensive courses both to keep staff up-to-date with technological and legislative developments and newly emerging environmental problems and also to fill certain gaps concerning specific technical and legal aspects of key environmental issues, especially regulations and the implementation of clean technologies.

- Greater dissemination of information on the types of courses that are available.

- Greater integration of environmental subjects into vocational training programmes and university degree courses in the traditional disciplines such as engineering, chemistry and also computing and electronics.

- Specialist advanced training in subjects such as pollution control technology, noise and air pollution control, risk analysis and environmental impact assessment. Such advanced training should have a strong inter-disciplinary element.

- Training in pollution control directed at small and medium-sized firms needs to enhance environmental awareness, to support 'in-house' training and to increase the provision of flexible information packages, the provision of information and independent advice, and short courses for vocational training.

- The potential also exists to utilise existing mechanisms for the provision of advice and information to enterprises. These would include local and regional development agencies providing advisory services; and also Commission supported initiatives.

3.3 The research, detailed above, makes clear the importance of addressing the requirements for environmental management at a company wide level. Management and technical competences are an essential element of successful corporate strategies aimed at securing improved environmental and commercial performance of SMEs.

3.4   The nature of a successful company wide response is illustrated in Figure 3.3 in the main report. This shows the range of management and technical competences which an SME requires and the vital role which the use of education and training services plays in ensuring the necessary environmental capacity of a SME to secure environmental performance.

3.5   A subset of the programmes and initiatives which the Commission support at Community level are those designed to support the business development of SMEs, through the setting up of business support networks. Examples of these networks include:

- Sprint;
- BC-Net;
- EBN;
- EIC;
- NETT.

3.6   These networks have a number of common attributes. First, they already exist to provide support to SMEs, and have mature network organisations. Secondly, the networks draw upon available business advisory services (financial, management, marketing, technical, personnel, training) to support SMEs in their development. Thirdly, they recognise the critical importance of supporting and encouraging innovative and technological development. Fourthly, they recognise the value of diffusing experiences between Member States and different companies. Fifthly, they recognise the potential benefits of encouraging SME collaboration between Member States. These attributes mean that these support networks are ready-made vehicles for the encouragement of environmental training, by stimulating awareness and supporting the provision of training services, in the context of improving the commercial performance of SMEs.

4.0   CO-OPERATION FOR ENVIRONMENTAL TRAINING

Co-operation Between the Social Partners

4.1   There are a large number of international organisations with an active role in improving environmental performance, primarily by assisting the stimulation of awareness and the encouragement of SMEs to undertake environmental training. It is clear that the Social Partners have a critical role to play in improving environmental performance. In relation to the role of, and co-operation between, the Social Partners, the International Labour Organisation (ILO) has a significant role to play through its tripartite structure and its commitment to the development of employment and training policy. The formal policy development which the ILO is currently undertaking with respect to environmental training represents an important opportunity for international organisations, particularly the Commission and the Foundation, to define, more closely, the ways of achieving greater co-operation between the Social Partners.

4.2 The role of the Foundation in developing policy aims and objectives therefore complements the work of the ILO and the other international organisations. Many of the very active organisations, eg the ILO and the ICC, have a worldwide perspective. The Foundation has an important role to play in ensuring that the policy development which these organisations stimulate is applied within the Community, and that models of co-operation, developed at a worldwide level, are applied and developed within the Community.

4.3 An essential part of the international response to secure improved environmental performance is the work of the Commission. The wide range of programmes and business support networks which are available to SMEs, provide an opportunity for the Foundation to secure a greater awareness amongst the Social Partners of the availability and value of these programmes, enabling the Foundation and international organisations to support Social Partners at a national and regional level.

Co-operation Between SMEs and Regulatory Agencies

4.4 Co-operation between SMEs and regulatory agencies provides a stimulus for the take-up and provision of environmental training. The potential for greater co-operation exists particularly at the regional, rather than the national, level. However, the regulatory agencies, because it is not their central responsibility, have difficulty in financing the development of environmental training beyond their existing informal information and advisory role.

4.5 There is, however, a wide range of national and regional organisations which have a role to play in stimulating the take-up and provision of environmental training. The effects which institutional traditions and developments have on the precise role played by the different organisations varies significantly. One needs to be careful, therefore, of identifying common roles and solutions for particular organisations. The process of policy development should, rather, focus on securing co-operation between SMEs and all national and regional organisations with the responsibility and commitment to secure improved environmental performance.

5.0 FUTURE ACTIONS AND ACTIVITIES

5.1 The executive summary has presented the main findings from the Phase I study. The study also identifies a range of actions, which should be considered in Phase II of the study, which would inform more fully the development of the Foundation's policy for the firm in its environment.

Areas of Activity

5.2 The Foundation has an important and continuing role in the development of environmental training, through close collaboration with the Commission and other organisations, particularly the Social Partners. There are a number of areas of activity which need to be developed in the light of this study.

- Advice on the development of environmental training provision, in collaboration with Commission Services, particularly:

    * The Taskforce on Human Resources

    * Directorate General for Environment (DGXI)

    * Directorate General for Enterprise, Commerce, Tourism and the Social Economy (DGXXIII).

- Support for further studies, in collaboration with CEDEFOP, to develop case studies of the occupational profiles of personnel concerned with environmental issues.

- Consultation with other international organisations, particularly the ILO and the ICC, to develop the most effective ways of securing co-operation between Social Partners, and advise on the most appropriate actions for the Partners, designed to encourage improved environmental performance by the respective memberships.

- Evaluate ways of developing Commission funded business support networks to encourage corporate environmental strategies and the take-up of environmental training.

- Assess the need for new institutional arrangements which are capable of evaluating the required company-wide environmental management response. The arrangement would embrace the need to develop information and expertise on the use of cleaner, waste minimisation production and pollution control technologies and to secure their diffusion and take-up by SMEs. The arrangements would respond to the increasing sophistication required of SMEs in the light of BATNEEC and multi-media environmental policy.

5.3 These areas of activity are reflected in concrete proposals, below, for Phase II; regional case studies and management training.

Regional Case Studies

5.4 The development of co-operation between the Social Partners and between SMEs and regulatory agencies needs to be encouraged at a regional level, since it is at this level that the largest impact on SME performance can be achieved. Phase II would examine, through detailed regional case studies in both northern and southern Member States;

* Key polluting sectors (with predominantly SMEs).
* Main pollution problems.
* Current responses of SMEs and regulatory agencies.
* Required responses (information, advice, technology transfer).
* Options for environmental training (evaluation of alternative methods).
* Contribution of the Social Partners and regulatory agencies.
* Role of business support networks.

5.5 The outputs of the case studies, combined with the overview from Phase I would constitute a comparative study where the problems, the needs, the present response, the current networks, and the possible options and solutions, as well as the approaches required would be identified in the Member States involved. The possibility of transferring successful training schemes from one region or Member State to another would be examined as would the possibility of integrating existing and new SME advisory schemes into environmental training.

Management Training

5.6 The detailed case studies will respond to the need to develop medium and long term policy. In this context one important set of research findings which should be followed up in Phase II relates to the value of management training. The critical importance of developing corporate responses requires that the management skills are allied to environmental competences. As noted in the Phase I study, environmental training is beginning to be incorporated into management school curricula. The Phase II study would :

- Examine the content of environmental management training in management and business school curricula;

- Evaluate, in the light of Phase I, the quality of the content against corporate management requirements;

- Examine the provision of advice to management schools of appropriate course content.

5.7 The development of environmental training for management would also be enhanced by further work aimed at defining the required management competences within the CEDEFOP framework. The Phase I study examined a limited range of occupations. This work could be extended into the regional case studies, (Sections 5.4 and 5.5 above), focused upon further definition of environmental management occupations at a senior level.

EDUCATION AND TRAINING OF PERSONNEL CONCERNED WITH ENVIRONMENTAL ISSUES RELATING TO INDUSTRY

1.0 INTRODUCTION

1.1 Background

The Single European Act and the Fourth Environmental Action Programme make clear that the environment is an integral part of the Community's economic, social, industrial and other policies. The Action Programme declares the Commission's intention of making maximum use of contributions made by the European Foundation.

The European Foundation for the Improvement of Living and Working Conditions is an autonomous Community body, established by the EC in 1975, designed to help solve the problems associated with improving living and working conditions. The European Foundation is responsible for a programme of activities focusing an new opportunities to improve living and working conditions in Europe. These programmes include activities for protecting the environment, the worker and the public, designed to address the question of the firm in its environment.

The European Foundation seeks to take an active stance, not simply reacting to problems, but anticipating events and adopting medium and long-term perspectives to design its activities to support political and strategic choices. In the area of the environment the Foundation is undertaking an examination of the firm in its local environment; analysing environmental developments and trends, (with 1992 through to the year 2000 in perspective). This study on training and the environment contributes to the work of the Foundation in this area.

The role of the Foundation tends to relate primarily to the early stages of the policy cycle associated with the development of policy aims and objectives, the forecasting and assessment of trends against these objectives and the identification of problems/opportunities requiring action. The Foundation is, therefore, well placed to adopt an "holistic" approach to environmental training issues and to perform a prospective role in identifying medium and long-term trends and policies. This study, undertaken by ECOTEC Research and Consulting Limited, responds to this approach.

1.2 Study Aims and Objectives

The aim of the study is to identify, in general terms, the existing inadequacies and possible improvements in the education and training of certain categories of personnel concerned with environmental issues relating to industry, thereby assisting the Foundation to identify medium and long-term trends and policies. Specifically the objectives of the research programme are to:

- highlight the training needs of regional and local regulatory agencies;

- highlight the training needs of small and medium-sized enterprises (SMEs);

- indicate ways in which such needs could be more effectively met, so as to improve environmental management;

- identify the scope for good co-operation on environmental issues between SMEs and regulatory agencies;

- illustrate how the Social Partners can be more closely involved in the process of improving environmental management.

The study focuses on SMEs because it is largely recognised that they have limited resources to allocate to environmental management and lack the scale of operation to support environmental management specialists. SMEs, therefore, face particular constraints in preparing environmental management responses. We adopt the EC definition of an SME as an enterprise employing less than 500 persons.

The focus on the role of agencies, particularly regulatory and employer and worker agencies, is designed to assist the Foundation in encouraging the use of appropriate existing channels of communication, to SMEs to promote improved environmental management, and to highlight areas where new channels are required.

The study also has a focus on training and the environment and SMEs in Southern Member States. This focus reflects the growing realisation that the move towards harmonised environmental standards in the Community has particularly acute implications for the required improvement in environmental management in SMEs in Spain, Portugal, Italy and Greece. These implications arise because there has traditionally been less emphasis placed on setting and observing formal environmental standards in these Member States. As a consequence, corporate environmental responses are less well developed.

Furthermore, Community Support Frameworks are currently being designed to encourage greater economic and business development in these Member States. Given the often fragile physical environment of these Member States, the risk of possible environmental damage from increased rates of economic growth in these Member States is substantial. This risk, therefore, places a particular emphasis on the need for environmental management skills and competences.

1.3 A Definition of Environmental Management

There is no simple way of characterising the environmental field. While the media (water, air, soil) are easily recognised characteristics, they do not provide an effective way of discussing training requirements. The field is very diverse and embraces all those issues which are concerned with the maintenance and improvement of the quality of the environment. It therefore incorporates many geographic variations in environmental conditions and problems, variations in economic development and structure, and in the extent of administration and legislation aimed at environmental protection.

The study is concerned with the issue of the firm in its local environment and, for the purposes of this study, we have therefore focused on environmental problems caused by industry and the environmental management responses of SMEs. Environmental problems caused by industry include:

- fugitive emissions and spillages;
- SO_x, NO_x and particulates emissions;
- industrial noise (both within and outside plants);
- emissions of toxic substances to the atmosphere;
- emissions of toxic substances to water bodies;
- handling and storage of hazardous substances;
- transport, treatment and disposal of hazardous wastes and sludges (including inter-media transfers of toxic sludges being generated by air or water pollution treatment techniques);
- the risk of industrial accidents.

The responses of SMEs to control and manage these environmental problems we have termed environmental management, and define it as:

- the control and prevention of pollution of the different environmental media (water, air, land) via "end-of-pipe" technologies;

- the adoption and use of "cleaner" technologies which generate fewer emissions, via process modification and material subsutition;

- the recycling of waste products; and

- the management and disposal of pollutants.

Environmental management activities are the responsibility of firms and industrial sectors which generate, or potentially generate (in the case of an accident or unforeseen problem) pollution. Major industrial sectors which exercise significant environmental management include power generation, the water industry, chemicals, engineering and metals industries and food processing. SMEs are more prevalent in the latter sectors. These sectors are consumers or purchasers of environmental goods and services which assist the company to prepare and implement environmental management responses.

These goods and services are supplied by the "environmental managment" industry. The environmental management industry encompasses a broad spectrum of firms engaged in a range of activities (eg, all types of engineering activities) producing a wide range of goods and services (eg., end-of-pipe equipment, integrated pollution control plant, waste management and consultancy services). For the purposes of this study the environmental management industry is defined as comprising those companies whose major or recognised activity is the provision of goods or services associated with pollution control or prevention. However, it should be recognised that environmental management skills are more focused in the provision of services for waste management and land remediation than in the provision of equipment for air and water pollution control.

Thus, at its simplest, environmental management activities can be divided between the "supply" side (the environmental management industry) and the "demand" side (the polluting sectors). For convenience, "supply" and "demand" will be used as terms to denote the environmental management industry and polluting sectors, respectively. There is also a third group of participants in environmental management mainly comprising legislative and regulatory agencies. This group includes national and regional/local regulatory agencies, responsible for particular environmental media or industrial pollution control and agencies responsible for industry health and safety regulation but which also have environmental management responsibilities. These agencies have a requirement for personnel with skills and qualifications similar to those required by the "demand" and "supply" sides of industry. This third group are important because, in addition to their regulatory role over industry, they provide an information and advisory source for companies.

This understanding of environmental management excludes two areas of activity: health and safety, and environmental conservation. The former activity is covered by a different set of legislation and regulations and is not directly related to the rationale for environmental protection. However, there are links between health and safety practise and environmental management. These are discussed in the report. Environmental conservation, whilst being concerned with environmental protection, is essentially concerned with activities such as countryside management and building preservation. These activities are not directly concerned with the prevention and control of pollution by industry.

1.4 A Definition of Training Needs

The primary focus of the study is to consider and identify the need for environmental education and training in SMEs and regulatory agencies, adding new research findings to existing results in order to prepare a synthesis of the research to date. This synthesis, in the light of a consideration of the existing and planned provision for environmental education and training, provides the basis for conclusions on the deficiencies in provision and the requirements for future provision.

The study uses the term training "need" as opposed to the "demand" for training services. This reflects our appreciation that there is a distinction between the determination of training requirements as a result of the need for improved environmental management (defined either by SMEs or by training agencies and researchers), and the determination of training requirements as expressed in the demand, by SMEs and regulatory agencies for training services. Research by ECOTEC in this and others studies suggest that SMEs, particularly, are unaware of their own need for training services and are unwilling, even when a need is perceived, to purchase training services. Thus a focus on the demand for training is likely to lead to an underestimation of the scale, and an inaccurate picture of the type, of training requirements.

A distinction also exists between expressed demand and latent demand; latent demand existing when SMEs and regulatory agencies perceive a need for training services but are unwilling to purchase these services and express their requirements in the market place. For the purposes of this study we define training needs as embracing unperceived requirements by SMEs and regulatory agencies and latent and expressed demand.

1.5 Method of Approach

The study combines existing research findings with original research undertaken as part of this study, to provide a synthesis of research at Community level relating to training and the environment, in response to the study objectives. Key elements of the approach include:

- an extensive literature review across the Community of research findings relating to training and the environment, (see Annex A). This review includes summary findings from those studies which have been funded under the EC ACE programme budget head concerned with employment and environment and which, is the subject of a separate report by ECOTEC to DGXI, (Reference 19).

- a series of consultations with senior representatives of international and national organisations who have a role in promoting environmental management in SMEs (see Annex B);

- a postal survey of regulatory agencies, training agencies and Social Partners in each Member State (see Annex C);

- an international workshop, held at the Joint Research Centre, Ispra, Italy with participants from a range of national and international organisations, to discuss and develop ideas on the substantive research issues (see Annex D);

- collaborative research with CEDEFOP, the European Centre for the Development of Vocational Training, to examine specific environmental managment responses in the UK and the detailed environmental education and training requirements of SMEs (see Annex E); and

- an extensive mission to Italy to consult and discuss the substantive research issues with government organisations, regulatory agencies and Social Partners in order to inform the research findings as they apply to Southern Member States.

These various elements, described above and in the annexes provided, have been brought together to provide the Foundation with a comprehensive, up-to-date and forward looking study, presented in the remainder of the report.

1.6 Structure of the Report

The need for environmental education and training is considered in the next section, paying particular attention to the environmental and economic factors which lead to variations in the scale and type of training needs between Member States and different regions. The specific needs for environmental education and training, discussing the detailed occupational and skills requirements, and the corporate environmental management responses are presented in Section 3.0. Section 4.0 provides an overview of the provision of environmental education and training in the Community, to give an indication of the nature and scale of provision. Sections 5.0 and 6.0 consider the roles of the different international and national organisations with potential to contribute to the improvement of environmental management. Section 7.0 provides our conclusions.

2.0 THE GENERAL NEED FOR TRAINING

2.1 Introduction

This section of the report examines the general need for training in the environmental field. This analysis considers the need for training, deriving from the pressures which exist to improve environmental management in SMEs. It also examines the environmental, economic and regulatory characteristics across the Community which lead to different environmental management problems and responses and, therefore, which influence the detailed nature of the requisite training services. The section also considers, on the basis of research in this and other studies, (for example those studies funded under ACE), the general rationales for environmental education and training.

This examination of the general need for training recognises the distinction between the need for training for improved environmental management, and the expressed demand for training services. To the extent that SMEs do not perceive a need for improved environmental management or consider that they have the necessary information, advice, skills and competences to undertake environmental management, the extent of expressed demand for training services is likely to underestimate the need for environmental education and training. This places a major emphasis on the importance of raising the awareness of the need for environmental management in SMEs.

2.2 Awareness Raising in SMEs

Consultations in this study emphasise that the increasing pressures for improved environmental management, which are discussed below, will only find expression in improved environmental standards if SMEs are able to recognise and respond to these pressures. Thus emphasis on awareness raising is a necessary pre-requisite for the improvement of environmental management and the articulation of demands for education and training services.

This study highlights two important elements in the process of awareness raising. Firstly, there is a requirement for concise, well presented information for dissemination which identifies the environmental pressures, the major management issues to be addressed and the commercial benefits to be gained from implementing good environmental management practise. Secondly there is a requirement for small seminars/workshops targeted at SMEs in specific sectors, held by government/regulatory agencies/Social Partners, in order to demonstrate the benefits of environmental management and to provide initial advice on preparing environmental management responses. This second element is vital if SMEs are to be convinced of the need for, and benefits of change.

The environmental management measures required for tackling environmental problems include improvements in the efficiency of production processes and greater process control (eg, for fugitive emissions and spillages), improved monitoring, product testing (eg, for chemicals) and application of currently emerging technological advances in the field of cleaner technologies including developments in areas such as microprocessors, sensors and biotechnologies. All of these have significant training implications since there is an under-supply of specialists trained in these fields.

Industrial firms need to make a greater use of currently emerging technological advances, especially their integration into production processes. There can be good economic reasons for this since, in some cases, this can lead to greater productive efficiency as well as lower pollution emissions. These technological advances can entail more sophisticated equipment and greater control over material flows. However, it is evident that there is a limited adoption of such cleaner technologies by many firms, especially small firms. This is due to their reluctance to alter their production process so as to reduce pollution emissions; the costs, and their lack of awareness and knowledge about available more efficient production and pollution control techniques (34).

Thus, ENI (30) reports the results of a survey of firms which found that 63% suffered from the lack of adequate information. The University of Amsterdam (64) reports that the currently available information is very dispersed and only really gets to the knowledgeable people in the larger firms. The small firms are much less able to obtain and utilise presently available information.

Incentive (37) states that priority should be attached to developing and applying improved measuring techniques and the establishment of data banks and expert systems for the storage and analysis of environmental data and information on production and pollution control techniques. There is a particularly important need for providing small firms with such information. Present advances in computer technology and "expert systems" provide a potentially valuable method of achieving this, which needs to be exploited further. Hence there is a need to promote not only the development of such environmentally beneficial technological advances, but also their application by firms, especially small firms.

The need for awareness raising activities has important implications, particularly for the Social Partners with their existing channels of communication with SMEs. This is considered in more detail in Section 6.0. There are also implications for existing, especially European, business support networks for SMEs. A good example of such a network is the European Business and Innovation Centre Network (EBN) which has a remit to assist the regional development of SMEs, by encouraging innovation and technology transfer. The core element of environmental management is the operation of production technologies and pollution control techniques. Improved environmental management is, therefore, likely to focus on technical change and adaption of existing processes and techniques. The EBN is well suited to provide support to SMEs in this respect. Further consideration of the use of European networks and international organisation to promote awareness is provided in Section 5.0.

2.3 Pressures for Environmental Management

The need for environmental management improvements stems from three main types of pressure; changes in environmental legislation, commercial pressures and technical change. This section provides a brief summary of these pressures.

2.3.1 Environmental Legislation

Legislation - Shifting Emphasis

Over recent years Community environmental policy has placed particular emphasis on air and water pollution and the control of point-sources within the Community. The emphasis in policy is now shifting towards waste management and contaminated land, as they become dominant environmental issues. For example, the European Commission has recently published a Waste Management Strategy which will shape Community Policy through the 1990s. The Strategy gives particular emphasis to the need to promote the use of clean, and low waste, technologies; to encouraging the use of recyclable products; and to the widespread use of valorisation techniques (recycling, material recovery, energy transfer). The Strategy also has to be viewed in the light of wider changes in the legal framework relating to pollution control, such as the Civil Liability Directive described below.

Thus, the waste management agenda in the 1990s will be significantly different to that in the 1980s, with ramifications throughout industry in terms of process engineering, waste disposal techniques etc. This in turn will demand a new set of services from the "supply-side", for example, in waste management and planning, and waste minimisation through process engineering with a subsequent requirement for new skills.

It is also recognised that the contaminated land problem has largely been ignored within the Community. Work by ECOTEC, for example, has shown that there are at least 60,000 potentially contaminated sites within the Community. At a European level, it is possible that legislation on this matter will be forthcoming in the medium term (say within 3-5 years), and in Denmark, the Netherlands and West Germany, legislation concerning liability for contaminated land already exists. Whether or not this takes the form of a European Superfund is uncertain. However, the increasing awareness of the contaminated land issue is likely to create a significant demand for both technical and project management services for site remediation and a need for SMEs to recognise the legal and financial implications of purchasing and owning contaminated land.

Legislation - Strict Liability

Over recent years, the liability of corporate bodies for the pollution they create has become an important issue in Europe, as the magnitude of the environmental problems has come to be appreciated. The problem is most acute for hazardous waste and contaminated land, where in both cases it is apparent that there is a legacy of industrial pollution as a result of previous economic activity for which the costs of clean-up are now being incurred, or will need to be incurred in the future. Often the original polluters are no longer in business, and even if they are, in most European countries there is no means of enforcing liability on them for clean-up costs "after the event". Thus, the problem of corporate liability for environmental damage is exercising the minds of legislators in the European Commission and at national level.

The two main areas where liability may arise are from the storage, transport and disposal of hazardous waste, and the clean-up of contaminated sites, and, as noted above, both of these are receiving attention in Europe. In a national context, it is generally those countries acknowledged to be in the "first division" with respect to environmental awareness (i.e Denmark, West Germany and the Netherlands) that have made the most progress in implementing liability measures.

The European Commission has recently proposed a Directive regarding the civil liability of waste producers for the wastes they generate. This aims to establish a uniform system of liability within Member States, to ensure, firstly that victims of damage receive fair compensation and, secondly, that industry's environmental costs resulting from waste are reflected in the price of the product or service giving rise to the waste. The Directive embodies these objectives within the principle of strict (i.e no-fault) liability as enacted in the Superfund legislation in the United States. Similar measures are already being introduced in the UK through the requirement for Duty of Care contained in the UK Environmental Protection Act, although this uses the mechanism of the criminal, as opposed to the civil law.

These measures will provide an incentive to SMEs for waste minimisation and to exercise greater control over the wastes which are generated. This will generate a demand in SMEs for significantly enhanced auditing and quality assurance competences with respect to their disposal activities.

Legislation - Increasing Standards

The change in emphasis in Community environmental legislation is also associated with a strengthening of environmental legislation providing for improved environmental standards. A good example of the legislative response to secure improved environmental standards is the new UK Environmental Protection Act (EPA). The EPA embodies the change in emphasis, discussed above, and illustrates the type of responses which Southern Member States may have to consider.

As far as industry and SMEs are concerned, the main effects of EPA will be:

i) The introduction of integrated pollution control (IPC) which introduces European policy relating to BATNEEC (best available technology not exceeding excessive cost); and

ii) The introduction of major amendments to waste disposal laws, including a Duty of Care on all those involved in the production, handling and disposal of waste.

In addition, other miscellaneous measures introduced under the Act will also influence the framework in which industry has to work with respect to environmental management.

Integrated Pollution Control

Integrated pollution control (IPC) is intended to provide a more comprehensive enforcement regime than has been the case to date. The indications are that the introduction of IPC will have a major impact on pollution control and waste management practices in industry. Together with other provisions in the EPA, such as a Duty of Care on waste producers for the wastes they generate, IPC will create a greater awareness of the overall social and financial costs of environmental protection, and so provide a stronger incentive to substantially reduce the quantities of waste generated. This can be achieved through the use of pollution control technologies, waste minimisation techniques and clean technologies.

The objectives of IPC are:

i) To introduce the principle of Best Available Techniques Not Entailing Excessive Cost (BATNEEC) regarding the control of pollution discharges to particular media, as is being adopted in EEC Directives;

ii) To introduce the principle of Best Practical Environmental Option (BPEO) regarding overall environmental impact, as recommended by UK Royal Commission reports;

iii) To meet Environmental Quality Objectives (E.Q.Os) as specified by EEC Directives;

In operational terms, there are three main elements of the IPC regime:

1) <u>Scheduling</u>: The scope of processes subject to Integrated Pollution Control will be layed down in Schedules similar to those currently in force for purposes of Best Practical Means (BPM). Initially, Scheduled processes will chiefly comprise those:-

   - currently under HMIP control regarding air emissons;
   - currently under Red List control regarding water discharges;
   - discharging significant quantities of Special wastes.

   Not all Scheduled processes will be under HMIP control; local authorities are also to be given powers to control air pollution from certain industrial processes, and the NRA will retain powers to control the discharge of certain substances to watercourses.

2) Prior Authorisation: All processes listed in the Schedules described above will be subject to a system of prior authorisation by HMIP before a new process is brought into operation or an existing one is substantially modified. The authorisation procedure will lead to the issuing of an IPC Authorisation which specifies the emission standards to be achieved, and possibly even the technologies to be used.

3) Residual Duties: Under the Bill there is a residual duty for the operator to use BATNEEC for all aspects of the process not specifically covered in the IPC Authorisation. BATNEEC will also be used to arrive at the Best Practical Environmental Option (BPEO) to minimise impact on the environment.

Although it will take some time, possibly up to 5 years, for all Scheduled processes to receive IPC Consents, the indications are that the introduction of IPC will have a major impact on pollution control and waste management practices in industry.

The extent to which IPC will change industrial practices will also dictate the extent to which it influences industry's costs. For example, there is some evidence from work in Europe (16) that industry's spending on pollution control changes with a shift from a single medium to a multi-media approach to setting environmental standards. Future issues to be explored here include an analysis of which sectors are most likely to be affected by such changes; what these changes will comprise; and the technological response industry will adopt.

In addition, company "image" is becoming increasingly important, see Section 2.3.2 below. The EPA will create a public register of information for each Scheduled process, giving details of the process, consented discharges, compliance record etc. Thus, a company's environmental record will be open to much closer public scrutiny which will provide a further incentive to achieve demonstrable emission reductions.

Duty of Care

Part II of the EPA introduces a "Duty of Care" on all those involved with the production, handling and disposal of waste to take reasonable measures to safeguard its transport, treatment and disposal. Such persons must take all reasonable measures:

i) to prevent any unlawful keeping, treating or disposal of waste by others;
ii) to prevent the escape of waste from either their control or that of anyone else;
iii) on transfer of the waste, to secure that the transfer is only undertaken by someone qualified to do so and that such agents receive a sufficient written description of the waste being transferred.

A code of practice is to be issued by the UK Department of the Environment (DoE) on how to discharge the duty (12). Breach of the duty will be a criminal offence punishable by a fine. Additionally, it is expressly provided that there shall be a civil liability for any damage caused by any deposits of waste prohibited under the new legislation. To date, however, there are no provisions for strict liability (i.e liability to pay for the costs of restoring damage to the environment), although such measures have been proposed in a draft EEC Directive.

Implications of the EPA For Training

The implications of the above measures for industrial training will vary across different industrial sectors. In some cases, IPC will result in increased investment in "end-of-pipe" pollution control equipment which may require a broader breadth of skills than has been available in the firm to date. Thus, the implications here are for new but specific skills relevant to particular equipment or technologies, and also for a general awareness of pollution control techniques so as to ensure that the techniques used comply with the principle of Best Available Techniques.

More importantly, it is apparent that in so far as IPC requires more efficient pollution control and waste management practices to be integrated across the production process it will substantially increase the need for an environmental awareness within mainstream training provision. However, whereas a particular end-of-pipe technology may be used across a range of industries, techniques such as waste minimisation and clean technologies are specific to certain industries and especially process industries (paper, food, chemicals etc). In this case the training requirements are specific to the industry, as opposed to the technology being employed, and so will be less transferable. Thus, the main demand here will be for process design and engineering skills which can be applied in a manner resulting in a net decrease in waste or pollution produced.

Significant implications are likely in the waste management industry. Here, the IPC and the Duty of Care provisions will require a very significant increase in the level of training provision across the industry. Under Duty of Care, waste management practices will have to take into consideration the likely effects on air quality (for example through landfill gas emissions), and on water quality (for example groundwater contamination by landfill leachate, or surface water contamination by run off): these have not been statutory requirements to date, although conditions may be specified in site licences.

With increasing attention being placed on waste disposal, through both UK and EEC legislation, it is recognised that the whole of the waste management industry needs to substantially improve its policies and practices, and training is being seen as an important part of this process. In the UK, the Waste Management Industry Training and Advisory Board (WAMITAB) has recently been established, by both public and private sector waste disposal operators, as a focus for improving the industry's professional standing through a more formal training structure. The Board aims to develop a Certificate of Proficiency (COP) and a Certificate of Technical Competence (COTC) within the NCVQ structure and to revise the Diploma in Waste Management as a route to chartered status for waste management professionals.

Overall, the EPA is predicted to lead to more stringent environmental regulations being imposed on industry: this in turn can be anticipated to lead to a greater emphasis being placed on environmental management within the firm, including higher expenditure on pollution control. However, the trade-offs between the benefits of improved environmental management and the costs of implementation are unclear, and therefore it is difficult to predict exactly how industry will react. For example, it is uncertain whether firms will perceive expenditure on pollution control to be more attractive than incurring the costs of the equivalent discharge permits. Similarly, increased expenditure on training in environmental management activities may not be perceived to have tangible financial paybacks for the SME.

2.3.2   Commercial Pressures

Corporate Awareness

It is apparent to ECOTEC, from involvement with environmental management markets over a considerable period of time, that corporate awareness of environmental issues has contributed to the development of environmental management over the last 2-3 years. Increasingly, industrial managers are coming to realise that a sound environmental record, both in terms of products and processes, is a powerful marketing and public relations tool, which can only work to the company's advantage in highly competitive markets.

Hence, although the situation varies considerably between countries and between industries, it is no longer true that legislation is the sole determinant in the requirement for environmental goods and services: often the intention is to pre-empt or surpass legislation rather than merely achieve compliance. This trend will continue, creating a demand for services such as environmental auditing and technical studies and the development of increasingly sophisticated environmental management responses.

Financial Incentives

With increasing awareness among industrialists of the potential for waste reduction and recycling and the positive effects this can have on unit costs, the prospect of substantial financial benefits from investing in pollution abatement, clean technologies, low waste manufacturing processes etc can be a significant driver in environmental management markets. This is over and above the impetus given by legislation, as noted above.

Institutional Change

Both general economic and technical change result in the long-term restructuring of industry and institutions which, together with the evolving legislative agenda, acts as a subtle environmental management. In the UK, the major structural changes are the privatisations of the electricity and water supply industries, while at a European level major adjustments are taking place as businesses restructure in advance of the Internal Market of 1992. The restructuring of the EC Structural Funds will also have ramifications for the spatial distribution of business. Many of the regions aided by such programmes have particularly susceptible environments and so are especially sensitive to further development.

2.3.3   Environmental Technology

The nature of environmental management is a function of both the production technology employed in a particular manufacturing process and the pollution control technology employed to deal with the resulting pollutants or waste streams. Historically these two aspects have been quite distinct, with pollution control technologies generally being "bolted on" to the end of the production process or unit. This so-called "end-of-pipe" technology is slowly being replaced by more integrated production systems which have integral pollution control systems, or replaced by "clean" technologies which do not produce the by-products and emissions which require control.

New Technologies

As far as end-of-pipe techniques are concerned, an analysis of the markets for goods and services associated with environmental management reveals several distinct technical trends, and these in turn will partially dictate the nature of the skills required by the "demand side" in implementing environmental management measures.

Within equipment markets, some of the major trends which have implications for future skills requirements are:

- improving equipment design and reliability;
- the development of new materials;
- the increasing use of biotechology for environmental management;
- the development of smaller modular pollution control plant.

In addition to changes in the nature of the technology, increased emphasis is being placed on the need for services within the environmental market. In particular, areas such as laboratory analysis, environmental monitoring, environmental auditing and regulatory assistance are in increasing demand. All of these are to some extent multi-disciplinary activities and hence have broadly based skill requirements, particularly at the professional and semi-professional levels. There are already indications that the availability of suitably experienced personnel is becoming a major factor limiting the growth of this sector.

Clean Technologies and Other Techniques

Apart from end-of-pipe techniques, there are four methods by which firms may manage their pollution/waste streams:

- material substitution;
- process modification;
- recycling;
- waste disposal.

The effects of this form of technological change on environmental management are not yet fully understood and are difficult to measure. In particular, the effect on the long term level of costs is ambiguous. The expenditure on the newer technology integrates or replaces pollution control systems and hence confounds the distinction between environmental and production management. This is an issue considered in the case-studies.

However, it is undeniable that industry is investing in newer, cleaner technology, in part because of the requirement for improved pollution control. To the extent that these changes are taking place, suggests that in future environmental management will be viewed as an integral part of production management, with a commensurate requirement that production managers and engineers understand the environmental impacts of production both upon the company and upon environmental quality. However, it is important to note that the requirements regarding clean technologies are sector-specific, and that from a technical and commercial point of view the main stimuli are likely to be the resultant energy and material savings and/or improvements in process efficiency.

2.4 An Analysis of Environmental Problems

This section provides a brief summary of the nature of environmental problems and characteristics in the Community, highlighting the spatial variations between Northern Member States and Southern Member States. These spatial variations serve to indicate the variations in the nature of the environmental management response required by SMEs and regulatory agencies, throughout the Community.

The spatial variation in environmental problems in the Community is illustrated in Figures 2.1 and 2.2. Figure 2.1 illustrates the extent to which the population and industry is served by waste water treatment facilities. High values on this measure indicate low levels of accessibility to waste water treatment. This problem is evident in Southern Member States. Figure 2.2 illustrates the extent to which solid wastes are generated and collected. High values on this measure indicate a low level of infrastructure, compared with the level of wastes generated, to handle solid wastes. The problem is again evident in Southern Member States.

2.4.1 Northern Member States

Major characteristics of these countries and regions include:

- urbanisation;
- industrialisation;
- high level of economic activity;
- declining industrial activity;
- relatively low environmental sensitivity.

Major environmental problems include:

- waste water treatment;
- contaminated soil;
- industrial waste.

In summary, these Member States have a high level of economic activity but a declining level of industrial activity. The sensitivity of the environment to industrial pollution in these Member States is generally lower compared with Southern Member States.

The major environmental problems relate to waste water and contaminated land, with a significant legacy of pollution from industrial sources, which has accumulated during the century. However, the adoption of clean technologies and recycling of wastes is comparatively well advanced.

FIGURE 2.1 EUROPEAN COMMUNITIES

Main Environmental Indicator: WATER I – Waste Water Treatment

(Index Values: EUR12/1985 = 100)

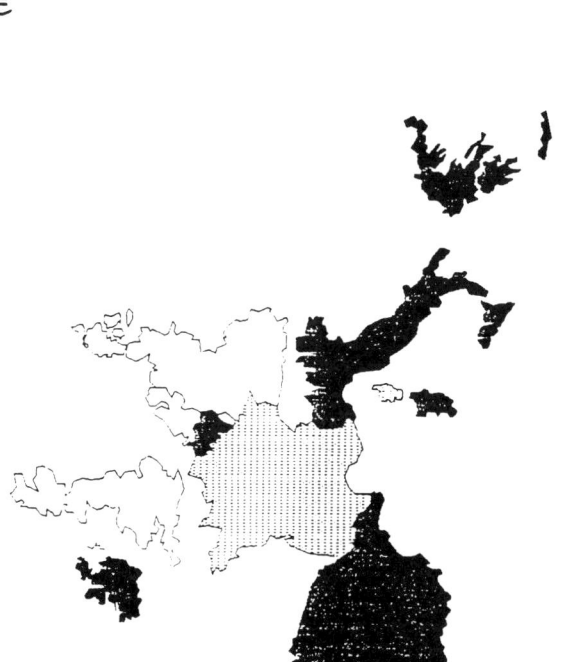

> 150
125 – 150
110 – 125
80 – 110
< 80

prognos '87

FIGURE 2.2   **EUROPEAN COMMUNITIES**

Main Environmental Indicator: WASTE I – Solid Waste Generation/Collection

(Index Values: EUR12/early '80 = 100)

> 150
125 – 150
110 – 125
80 – 110
< 80

prognos '87

2.4.2   Southern Member States

Major characteristics of these countries and regions include:

- rural communities;
- intense economic problems;
- rapid urbanisation and industrialisation of major centres;
- relatively high environmental sensitivity.

Major environmental problems include:

- waste management;
- water and coastal pollution;
- air pollution;
- soil erosion;
- limited environmental infrastructure and adoption of cleaner technologies.

In summary, these Member States have a low level of economic activity but a rapidly developing economy in major urban centres. The environmental sensitivity to pollution is high with very significant natural resources, requiring conservation. The major environmental problems relate to the handling and disposal of industrial and domestic wastes and water pollution, leading to significant marine and coastal pollution. Moreover, these Member States have a limited environmental infrastructure to deal with environmental problems and a comparatively low level of adoption of cleaner technologies in industry.

2.5   An Analysis of Industrial Structure and Importance of SMEs

The nature and scale of provision of the requisite environmental education and training for SMEs is, in part, determined by the industrial structure in each Member State; and the relative importance of SMEs in the individual national economies. The analysis of available secondary data suggests that in Southern Member States there is a comparatively larger percentage of the workforce employed in industry, compared with the Northern Member States. See Table 2.1. The exception to this is the employment structure in Germany.

TABLE 2.1 : RANKING OF THE IMPORTANCE OF INDUSTRY IN MEMBER STATES, 1988

Member State	Agriculture	Industry	Services	Total
	(Percentage of Civilian Employment by Sector)			
Germany	4.3	41.2	54.5	100
Portugal	20.7	35.1	44.2	100
Italy	9.9	32.6	57.5	100
Spain	14.4	32.5	53.1	100
Luxembourg	3.4	31.6	65.0	100
France	6.8	30.4	62.9	100
United Kingdom	2.2	29.4	68.3	100
Belgium	2.7	28.2	69.1	100
Ireland	15.4	27.8	56.8	100
Netherlands	4.8	26.5	68.7	100
Denmark	6.3	26.3	67.4	100

Source : Eurostat

Note : No data for Greece is available.

The distribution of employment between enterprises of different sizes also varies between Member States. The Southern Member States have a relatively larger percentage of total employment in SMEs. Moreover, the employment is concentrated in micro and small enterprises rather than medium sized enterprises. The relative importance of SMEs in the national economies in the South can be seen in Table 2.2.

This analysis has two implications for environmental education and training. First, to the extent that industry is relatively more important in the economy the generation of industrial pollution is likely to be greater. This suggests that future industrial pollution problems are more likely to occur in Southern Member States, although the legacy of pollution resulting from previous industrialisation remains centred in Northern Member States.

TABLE 2.2   RANKING OF PERCENTAGES OF TOTAL EMPLOYMENT
             BY MICRO, SMALL, MEDIUM AND ALL SMEs IN
             MEMBER STATES, 1986

Member State	Micro	Small	Medium	All SMEs
	(Percentage of Total Employment)			
Spain	41.4	36.5	14.1	91.9
Italy	40.3	33.2	9.4	82.8
Portugal	38.1	27.8	14.5	80.3
Luxembourg	26.4	29.9	19.5	75.7
Belgium	31.0	26.1	14.6	71.5
United Kingdom	23.3	24.0	22.9	70.0
Germany	18.3	27.4	18.7	64.2
Netherlands	19.5	26.0	16.0	61.3
France	19.5	26.3	15.4	60.9
EUR-12	26.9	28.3	16.7	71.9

Source : DGXXIII : Enterprises in the European Community

Definitions : Micro   : 0 - 9 employees
               Small   : 10 - 99 employees
               Medium : 100 - 499 employees

Secondly, the relative importance of SMEs, especially small enterprises suggests that there are comparatively greater problems in Southern Member States associated with communicating, supporting and developing the business community. In the context of this study the particular problems of awareness raising that is associated with SMEs can be seen to be a particular issue in Southern Member States.

2.6 Overview of EC Regulatory Structures and Environmental Policy

This section presents a brief overview of the environmental policies of the twelve Member States, complementing the earlier discussion associated with environmental pressures. The overview highlights the relative priority that has been given to environmental issues in the development of national environmental legislation. Annex H provides a more detailed discussion of the environmental policy framework in each Member State.

Those countries which have developed the most comprehensive environmental policies are the Northern European countries: for example, Denmark, West Germany and the Netherlands. These are the most advanced in this respect, having formulated comprehensive environmental policies over the last two decades and having placed a high priority on the integration of environmental policies with economic and industrial policies. Belgium, France, Ireland and the United Kingdom are characterised by less rigorous environmental policies but, nonetheless, have a tradition of environmental protection practices. The Southern European countries, Italy, Spain, Greece and Portugal lag behind in terms of the development of environmental policies. Spain, Portugal and Greece have only recently joined the European Community and are expected to experience difficulties in complying with, increasingly stringent, EC environmental Directives. This is exemplified by requests for dispensation (eg, Portugal regarding the EC drinking water and bathing water directives).

This brief discussion serves to illustrate the different environmental policy "tradition" of Northern and Southern Member States, which acts as a framework for the development of responses to improve environmental performance. To illustrate the nature of the environmental institutional framework in the South we provide a more detailed description of the framework as operated in Italy. Prior to this we briefly consider the extent of implementation of EC environmental policy and the enforcement structures to secure greater implementation.

The extent to which environmental policy has been implemented and enforced is also important in shaping the response of SMEs to the requirement for improved environmental performance. In this respect there has been a general failure of EC Member States to comply with, and enforce environmental directives. This is highlighted by the number of violations currently under investigation by the commission (31.12.89). These violations are summarised by environmental sector in Table 2.3.

TABLE 2.3 : FAILURES TO IMPLEMENT EC ENVIRONMENTAL LEGISLATION BY ENVIRONMENTAL SECTOR

	Water	Air	Waste	Chemicals	Noise	Nature	Total
Belgium	11	3	18	8	2	7	46
Denmark	2	-	-	-	1	2	5
France	15	3	2	1	-	20	41
Germany	8	4	2	3	-	11	29
Greece	10	4	5	2	3	20	45
Ireland	7	2	3	2	-	7	21
Italy	9	4	10	2	3	12	40
Luxembourg	6	2	2	-	1	2	12
Netherlands	6	2	2	3	3	8	24
Portugal	2	1	4	-	-	7	14
Spain	12	2	10	4	-	29	57
UK	18	5	3	3	-	4	31
Total	**104**	**32**	**62**	**25**	**13**	**129**	**382**

Source : European Commission

In 1984, there were only 11 cases of environment related complaints but, by 1989, this had risen to 460. Spain, with 57 reported violations under investigation, leads the current "blacklist". Spain is followed by Belgium (47), Greece (45), France (41), Italy (40) and the United Kingdom (31), whilst Denmark has the 'cleanest' record with only 5 reported infringements.

In an attempt to rectify the situation the commission has adopted a number of measures to coerce Member States to comply with environmental pollution standards. We summarise here the litigation measures which have been taken. Supportive measures with financial aid are discussed in the context of the role of the EC in developing environmental training, in Section 5.2.

The Commission has agressively pursued a policy of taking Member States to court for failing to implement EC Directives. It is currently taking action on 352 cases of failing to implement environmental legislation. The status of these actions is summarised in Table 2.4.

TABLE 2.4 : STATUS OF LITIGATION WITH REGARD TO NON-ENFORCEMENT OF EC ENVIRONMENTAL DIRECTIVES

	Warning Letter	Warning with Grounds for Action	Referred to Court	Total
Germany	13	8	8	29
Belgium	27	8	7(+4)	46
Denmark	5	-	-	6
Spain	45	9	3	57
France	28	5	7	41
Greece	37	6	3	45
Ireland	16	5	-	21
Italy	17	18	7	40
Luxembourg	9	2	1	12
Netherlands	18	5	2	24
Portugal	10	4	-	14
UK	18	8	6	31
Total	242	75	44	352

Source : European Commission

The Environment Commissioner of the European Community (EC), Carlo Ripa di Meana, has condemned EC Member States for their overall failure to implement environmental Directives, and has suggested that environmental aid could be withheld from countries which are persistently failing to comply. Mr Ripa di Meána has also recently (March 1990) called for greater powers to enforce EC laws in Member States. This would involve an extension of the powers of the Court of Justice.

In order to help co-ordinate and enforce environmental measures, the European Council of Ministers (May 1990) has agreed the Regulation (COM(89)303) which was required to bring the European Environment Agency into legal existence. The Agency is to record and assess environmental data, as proposed by the Commission, and is to assist and advise the Commission co-ordinating the activities and training of environmental protection officials at a national level.

The European Parliament postponed its vote on the creation of the Agency at the beginning of March 1990, declaring that the definition of the Agency's functions, as proposed by the Commission, would have to be revised if the Agency were to be effective. The Parliament wished to see a body with more enforcement and inspection powers, a move rejected by the Commission which claimed that it could not delegate such powers to an independent body. In the end, the Council of Ministers opted for the compromise clause drafted by Environment Commissioner Carlo Ripa di Meana, whereby the activities of the Agency are to be re-examined and revised after 2 years. The clause provides for a possible extension of the Agency's activities in a number of fields, but not for it to be given its own independent "power of inspection" for environmental matters, as proposed by the Parliament. The proposed areas are:

- granting of powers to monitor the implementation of European Community (EC) environmental legislation in co-operation with the Commission and existing competent bodies in the Member States;

- promotion and utilization of techniques and intensification of the transfer of such techniques within the EC and with third countries;

- development of criteria for the evaluation of Environmental Impact Assessments necessary for the application of Directive 85/337/EEC and its possible revision; and

- preparation of labels and the definition of criteria which justify them for products, methods, goods, services and programmes which are non-pollution and conserve natural resources.

In its 1990 budget the Parliament included funding of ECU 5 million ($3.8 million) for the start-up of the Agency, which is also to be open to non-EC States entering into a formal agreement with the EC.

The Regulation COM(EQ) 303, as well as establishing the EEA, also established the European Environment Monitoring and Information Network. The proposal for a Council regulation contains details of how the EC environment network should operate. The EEA and the monitoring and information network are together referred to as 'the system'. The aim is to provide the Community and Member States with technical and scientific support, to enable them to achieve the goals of environmental protection and improvement established by the treaty of Rome.

The system's tasks are set out as follows :

- Provision of objective information for formulating and implementing effective environmental policies. Such information should be available to the Community, Member States and participating third countries.

- Provision of technical information to the Commission, to help identify environmental action, and formulate environmental legislation.

- Stimulation of environmental modelling and forecasting techniques, to assist preventive action.

- Assistance with harmonisation and comparability of EC environmental data, with integrating such information into international monitoring programmes.

- Other tasks defined by the management board in agreement with the Commission.

The system's principal areas of work will be the gathering of information on the quality of the environment, the sensitivity of the environment and the pressures on the environment. Information will be used to implement EC policy, in addition to assisting programmes drawn up at international, national regional and local levels. Priority areas will be air quality, water quality, soil quality and land use.

2.6.1   The Institutional Framework in Italy

2.6.1.1   Role of Central Government

Traditionally, the responsibility for public activities relating to the management and protection of the environment in Italy has been divided between eight different ministries thus presenting a highly fragmented regulatory structure. In July 1986, however, as environmental issues came to the political fore, the Ministry of Environment (Ministerio dell'Ambiente) was set up with the objective of centralising activities relating to environmental protection. The Ministry's responsibilities are limited to the following media; water pollution, air pollution, solid wastes and national parks. Regarding these media there is considerable overlap between the responsibilities of the Ministry of Environment and other central Ministries. For example, the Ministry of Environment works in conjunction with the Ministry of Public Health with regard to atmospheric pollution, noise pollution and drinking water. The Ministry of Environment is obliged to liaise with other administrations with regard to the following;

* national development plans which have a significant environmental impact;
* land policy;
* land and soil protection;
* plans for the use of water resources; and
* general plans for the protection of the seas.

Consultations undertaken as part of our Mission to Italy (see Annex F), suggest that although Italy has established a Ministry to deal explicitly with the environment, the traditional division of responsibility between a number of Ministries prevails; namely the Ministry of Public Health, the Ministry of the Merchant Marine and the Ministry of Industry. The issue is further complicated by the devolvement of many of the regulatory and policy functions to the Regions, Provinces and Municipalities.

2.6.2.2   The Role of Regional Governments

The Italian Constitution gives the Regional Governments wide powers with regard to environmental protection. Under Article 101 of Law 616 of 24 July 1977, certain administrative functions relating to soil, atmospheric, water, heat and noise pollution and public health and hygiene came within the remit of the Regions. The Regions were additionally empowered to carry out water purification and waste disposal functions. Many of the regulatory functions, industrial inspections and the enforcement of pollution control, have been further devolved to Italy's 100 Provinces (Province) which have responsibility for inspecting factories and waste treatment and disposal facilities, and to the 8000 municipalities (Comuni) which have responsibility for monitoring emissions from heating plants and for air and noise pollution. This decentralised structure has resulted in there being wide discrepencies in environmental standards throughout Italy, reflecting the different environmental practices and policies adopted by the Regions. Given that the Italian legislative system is highly fragmented and responsibilities for pollution control are often shared between a large number of parties, it is clear that this decentralised system, rather than providing a mechanism by which local governments have the power to protect their local environment, has resulted in a fragmentation of real power which, compounded by a lack of co-ordination, has resulted in ineffective control.

An assessment of the level of public expenditure allocated to the environment is difficult due to the large number of different agencies involved in public spending in this area. According to the Ministry of the Environment "Report on the State of the Environment 1989" (51), in 1988, 6500 billion lire was allocated to the administration of natural resources. The regional government spent an estimated 1500 billion lire in 1988 which, together with the expenditure of the provinces and municipalities, gives an estimated expenditure of 10 trillion lire which is approximately 1% of Italy's GNP (30).

Overall, there has been a rapidly increasing awareness of the environment in Italy reflected by, for example; an increasing number of prosecutions under more stringent pollution control laws rapid growth in the number of firms operating within the environmental management market, and the founding in 1989 of a new environmental research institute by the employer's organisation Confindustria.

2.7 The Relevance of Training in the Environment

This section articulates the main rationales for improving the provision and take-up of environmental education and training, based upon the research in this and previous studies, see especially (19).

- First, and crucially, training has an essential role to play in the effective and efficient implementation of environmental policy and instruments. The studies carried out suggest that there are insufficient numbers of trained personnel to implement current or proposed policies. Furthermore, that in some Member States and regions of the Community there are also gaps in existing training provision. Training is vital in assisting the Community's labour market to adjust and respond to the need for trained personnel in the environmental field. Demographic changes will not make this situation any easier, as competition for qualified workers increases in the coming decade. Training will help to ensure that there will be sufficient personnel with appropriate levels of skills and competence to put into operation and to enforce current and emerging environmental legislation.

- Second, training is vital in the Community's capacity for adapting and responding to scientific and technological change. It is central to the process of improving environmental awareness, and also improving competence in the planning and management of the environment, as a response to these changes. The nature of environmental problems with which the Community must deal is changing as the rate of technological development accelerates and new and different pollutants emerge which create new pressures on the environment. Therefore, the Community's responses to, and competence to deal with, these pressures, must also adapt and improve by: becoming more anticipatory and preventative rather than reactive; developing and operating more environmentally sensitive practices in industry; developing and adopting new technologies to reduce environmental pollution; and by developing more sophisticated approaches to environmental management. Responding to environmental problems as they occur necessarily means that the environmental damage is already done. Cleaning up pollution is more expensive, economically as well as environmentally, than prevention Environmental policies are required which are designed to prevent pollution and environmental degradation arising. Implementing such policies will depend in part on new and adapted technologies.

- Third, training very effectively assists in the dissemination of information and the diffusion of new technologies. There are wide regional variations in the Community; in the sophistication of pollution control technology and management; in the amount of research and development; in the application of legislation to protect valued environments and control pollution; in the distribution of pollution itself; and of valued ecological resources. At the same time there are also variations in the levels of knowledge, expertise, vocational skills, and technological and training resources. There are considerable environmental, economic and social benefits to be derived from activities which initiate collaboration, exchange, and the movement towards common standards of environmental protection.

- Fourth, the Treaty of Rome as amended by the Single European Act, now incorporates a recognition that the maintenance and improvement of the environment is an important objective of the European Community. The completion of the Internal Market in 1992 and beyond is expected to give rise to increased economic growth and pressure for development. It is clearly important that the

Community, in its Member States and regions, has the capacity to integrate environmental safeguards into the planning of change to ameliorate the environmental impacts consequent upon economic, infrastructural and demographic changes. Such an integration of economic and environmental objectives is a prerequisite for achieving sustainable development and training has a key role to play in promoting such integration in relation to both public and private sectors (62).

- Fifth, training will help to realise the potential of environmental protection and enhancement to support economic and social objectives in the regions of the Community. In parallel with the completion of the Single Market, and in recognition of the need to maintain social cohesion across the regions of the Community, the reforms of the Structural Funds will result in significant shifts of development and investment, both public and private, to many regions which have fragile or degraded environments. Again, this process calls for integrated and more environmentally aware approaches to the application of the structural funds.

By ensuring that the Community has the requisite skills and manpower to preserve and enhance the environment, training in the environmental field can contribute significantly to improving the efficiency and effectiveness of both the Commission's and Member States' instruments to promote regional economic development. Thus training will, for example, increase the Community's capacity to preserve the valued and often fragile environments of the Less Favoured Regions which have both economic and ecological value, and also the capacity to undertake the repair and restoration of the frequently damaged and degraded environments of the Community's Industrially Declining Regions, which is a prerequisite for their economic revival and halting their depopulation.

- Sixth, training is an important part of the process of raising environmental awareness which in turn helps to create conditions in which:-

    * the political will is strengthened to develop policy for, and resource, environmental protection;

    * public sector agencies acknowledge and act upon their responsibilities to enforce legislation and to properly manage public sector facilities at the local and regional level;

* private sector industry accepts its responsibilities in relation to pollution control and its local environment, and manages its activities so as to minimise environmental damage paying, where necessary, for technologies and processes which prevent such damage;

* the public and citizens of the Community call for and support actions to improve and protect the environment and recognise the benefits of additional costs arising from such actions.

In this way, awareness is an important determinant of demand for environmental protection and enhancement, but also for related training since it has been the case in the past that increased awareness of environmental issues has led to new legislative controls or practices which drive a demand for new skills and competences.

- Seventh, the potential exists to create significant numbers of new jobs in environmental protection and waste management and training will help to realise this employment potential.

- Finally, therefore, training emerges as an essential component in the dynamics of environmental protection, forming a vital link between the various components which include: the preparation, monitoring and enforcement of policy, legislation and programmes; and the development and adoption of new clean technologies and environmentally sensitive management practices in industry and in society. Training cannot be viewed in isolation. Instead it should become a central consideration to be addressed and included in legislative and programme development.

In summary, the rationales for training are to:

- Reduce the shortage of trained personnel;

- Improve the level of skills and competences;

- Support the effective implementation of environmental policy;

- Respond to changing environmental problems and priorities;

- Respond to the need to develop environmental legislation and policies;

- Encourage environmentally sensitive managment of natural resources;

- Respond to the greater integration and multi-disciplinary approaches to environmental management;

- Promote the diffusion of environmental knowledge, technology and management throughout the Community;

- Encourage greater environmental awareness among the Communities citizens, industrialists and policy makers;

- Help to improve the effectiveness of regional development instruments;

- Help to realise employment potential in the environmental field.

3.0 THE NEED FOR TRAINING IN SMEs AND REGULATORY AGENCIES

3.1 Introduction

This section of the report examines in detail the training needs of SMEs and regulatory agencies. The analysis draws upon two separate information bases. The first information base comprises a number of case studies, prepared in collaboration with the Foundation, CEDEFOP, and the UK Training Agency examining the nature of environmental management as conducted by SMEs and regulatory agencies in the UK. These case studies, undertaken within a framework proposed by CEDEFOP, examine the detailed manner of environmental management responses and the requisite skills and competences.

The second information base comprises the range of studies undertaken throughout the Community which have examined training needs for environmental management. The European Parliament, in 1982, provided financial support for Community Operations in the Environment (ACE). The ACE programme was partly used to fund studies which assessed, by descriptive analysis, the need for training to conserve and improve the environment. These studies represent an important element of the information base. The research undertaken in this current study, particularly the survey of Social Partners and regulatory agencies, adds to this information base.

3.2 A Framework for Occupational Analysis

The framework for occupational analysis which has been used in this study, to examine training needs, is taken from the work undertaken by CEDEFOP, the European Centre for the Development of Vocational Training. The framework is consistent with the new Standard Occupational Classification developed by the UK Training Agency. CEDEFOP have prepared the framework to enable a detailed analysis of all occupations on a standard basis. The use of this framework in this study has two benefits. It ensures that the analysis in this report is broadly comparable with occupational research which might be undertaken in other studies. Secondly, to the extent that the CEDEFOP framework is adopted by Member States it will ensure that the analysis in this report is broadly comparable with any subsequent research. This latter benefit is considerable given the anticipated requirement for future occupational research in this area.

The framework consists of two parts: classification and definition. Each part is then sub-divided into two further elements, providing a total of four elements to the framework. This framework, illustrated in Figure 3.1, allows detailed occupational profiles to be prepared on a consistent basis and defined according to a set of employment tasks.

The four elements to the occupational analysis are discussed in further detail below.

3.2.1 Functional Areas of Work

Functional areas of work are large aggregates of productive or service functions which do not necessarily, but sometimes, follow the logic of the economic sectors. For example, administration and clerical occupations, or metal working.

3.2.2 Occupational Families

In each functional area of work there are groups or "families" of occupations. It is these families which relate to the tasks associated with particular jobs, for example, the operation of machines. The new UK Standard Occupational Classification (SOC), details various occupational families, from very large occupational families (the major groups) through to small families (the unit groups).

3.2.3 Core Tasks

The definition of occupations, in both the CEDEFOP framework and the SOC, is based upon the employment tasks associated with the job. For example, in the occupational family "operation of machine" the following tasks can be identified: study of the design of the workpiece; control the mechanism; monitoring; etc.

3.2.4 Modules of Competence

For each core task the competences required to exercise the occupation may be defined on the basis of three criteria:

- qualifications or knowledge required;

- competences or skills required; and

FIGURE 3.1   A FRAMEWORK FOR OCCUPATIONAL ANALYSIS

ELEMENT

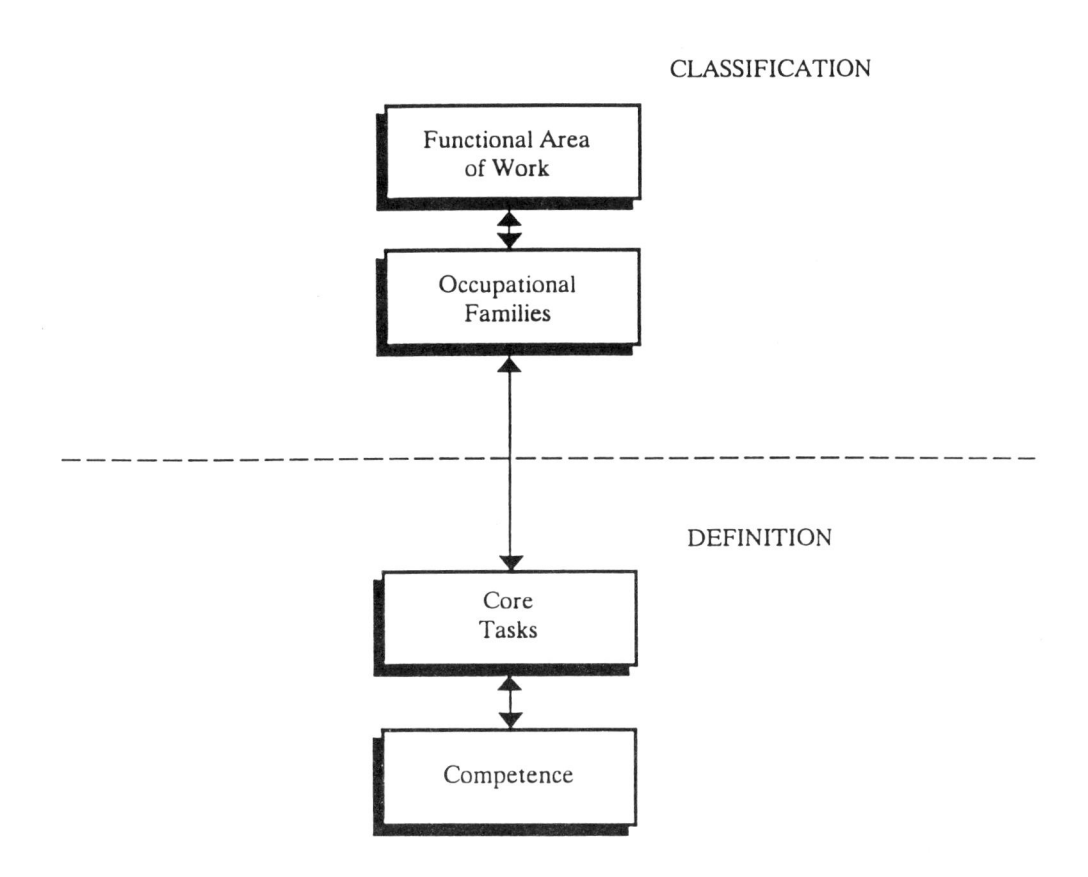

CLASSIFICATION

- Functional Area of Work
- Occupational Families

DEFINITION

- Core Tasks
- Competence

SOURCE : CEDEFOP (1990)

- social or attitudes of behaviour required.

By defining these modules of competence the nature of the job can be defined, giving rise to the production of job titles and an appreciation of training received and required.

In the context of this study, the use of the framework to clarify occupations associated with environmental management must be based upon the generalisation of results from the definition of tasks and competences, unless it is partially informed by available secondary data. The following section (3.3) focuses upon the definition of the tasks and competences of occupations associated with environmental management, based upon detailed discussions with companies in the following industrial sectors; chemicals, metals and the water industry. Detailed summaries of the case studies are presented in Annex E.

3.3 Definition of Occupations

3.3.1 Introduction

The case studies identified a range of occupations which involved some responsibility for environmental management. The case studies examined almost 40 jobs in detail to identify specific tasks and competences which were related to environmental management. Actual core environmental management tasks and competences associated with eleven of these jobs are presented in Figure 3.2. These selected jobs exemplify the range of tasks and competences associated with environmental management. Figure 3.2, therefore, provides a summary of the occupational analysis, within the analytical framework, in so far as this research programme has allowed.

3.3.2 Core Tasks

Core tasks associated with environmental management can be considered separately for managers and operatives. Management tasks broadly relate to production management and to monitoring and analysis. Production management tasks include:

- maintaining awareness of relevant environmental legislation;
- developing process changes for compliance with environmental standards;
- setting, and ensuring compliance of the plant with, environmental standards.

FIGURE 3.2 Occupational Analysis for Environmental Management

INDUSTRIAL SECTOR	JOB TITLE[1]	CORE TASKS (JOB SPECIFIC)[2]	SUGGESTED OCCUPATIONAL GROUP[3]	CORE TASKS (SOC)[4]	TYPICAL ENTRY ROUTES AND ASSOCIATED QUALIFICATIONS[5]	SKILLS AND COMPETENCES[5]
CHEMICAL INDUSTRY	Senior Chemist for the Environment	Developing sampling and analytical techniques; carrying out process research into waste minimisation; investigating new methods of treating waste-streams; supervision of laboratory personnel; attending the company's environment committee.	Minor Group: Natural Scientist SOC 2(a)20/200	Analyse and research physical aspects of chemical structure and change within substances and develop chemical techniques used in the manufacture or modification of natural substances and processed products. Other concerns are the development of experimental procedures and setting up and analysing the results of experiments.	Chemistry degree.	Graduate chemist; 10 years experience as an industrial chemist; understanding of micro-biology; strong skills in analytical chemistry. Understanding of the manufacturing process and a comprehensive knowledge of pollution control technologies.
	Energy Effluent Manager	Responsibility for running the boiler-house; providing site services; responsibility for waste disposal; liaising with the regulatory bodies; providing technical input into waste disposal research; management duties.	Minor Group: Production managers in manufacturing, construction, mining and energy industries SOC 1(a)11/110	Plan, organise, direct and co-ordinate the activities and resources necessary for production in manufacturing industries and the maintenance of engineering items equipment and machinery.	Degree in Chemistry or Chemical Engineering.	Ten years experience in a related field; energy, water or waste management. Extensive knowledge of environmental legislation, particularly waste disposal and local consent levels. Understanding of energy issues (plant and efficiency), man management skills and an understanding of waste disposal techniques.
	Effluent Plant Operator	Operation of the effluent plant; analyses temperatures, flow rates and nutrients; routine testing, sampling and analysis.	Minor Group: Chemicals, paper, plastics and related process operatives SOC 8(a)82/820	Operates the plant to process chemicals and related materials by crushing, milling, mixing and seperating or by chemical heat or other treatment.	Academic qualifications are not normally required. Training is provided primarily on-the-job.	Numeracy and literacy; basic understanding of the operation of the bio-treatment plant; knowledge of the drainage system ie in order to contain spillages; knowledge of consents; process limits ie feed-rate and temperature; interpretation of results from simple analysis.

41

INDUSTRIAL SECTOR	JOB TITLE[1]	CORE TASKS (JOB SPECIFIC)[2]	SUGGESTED OCCUPATIONAL GROUP[3]	CORE TASKS (SOC)[4]	TYPICAL ENTRY ROUTES AND ASSOCIATED QUALIFICATIONS[5]	SKILLS AND COMPETENCES[5]
METALS INDUSTRY	Technical Director	Overall responsibility for all technical aspects on-site. Responsibility for process development, responding to legislative changes and providing documentation on emission levels; checking daily monitoring and liaising with group managers regarding environmental targets.	Minor Group: Production managers in manufacturing, construction, mining and energy industries SOC 1(a)11/110	Plan, organise, direct and co-ordinate the activities and resources necessary for production in manufacturing industries and the maintenance of engineering items equipment and machinery.	Degree in metallurgy, chemical engineering or physics.	Ten years experience and a detailed understanding of the operation of the plant; knowledge of environmental legislation; awareness of technical and financial constraints of production; knowledge of pollution control techniques;strong inter-personal, man-management,interpretation and report writing skills.
	Environmental Services Engineer	Responsibility for identifying the need for new kit and writing the necessary tender documents. Undertaking the conceptual design work to improve the environmental performance of the plant and to ensure compliance with legislation; liaising with regulatory bodies and the public; providing technical advice to plant managers.	Minor Group: Associate professional and technical occupations nec SOC 3(a)39/399	Establishes principles and techniques to improve the quality, durability and performance of materials. Designs new systems and equipment with regard to cost market requirements and feasibility of manufacture. Devises and implements control systems to monitor operational performance and efficiency of the system and materials.	Degree in Chemical Engineering (a candidate with an appropriate level of expertise would be considered without a degree).	Competent engineer with a comprehensive knowledge of th manufacturing process. Good understanding of: environmenta issues, legislation and engineering; knowledge of pollution control, waste management and effluent control technology.
	Tips Controller	Supervision of operative staff; hiring and deployment of machinery; recording the amounts and types of waste; planning waste disposal at the site and responsibility for off-site waste disposal; liaising with external bodies involved with waste disposal.	Minor Group: Other operations nec SOC 9(b)99/999	Miscellaneous tasks not elsewhere classified.	No formal qualifications required. Post holder is expected to have extensive experience in the industry.	In-depth knowledge of waste; broad understanding of the manufacturing process; some, civil engineering background (to assist in the design of the tips) experience of working with mobile tools; high level of inter-personal skills.
	Operative	Monitoring the chemical content of the waste stream (pH,nitrates, temperature); carries out maintenance and operation of the equipment; operation of recovery and separation equipment; supervises the incineration of ammonia.	Minor Group: Metal making and treating process operatives SOC 8(a)83/839	Sets up, assists with and operates piercing, rolling and extruding equipment; assists with the operation of galvanising equipment; operates continuous plant to remove dirt, scale and other surface impurities and performs other metal processing, forming and treating tasks.	City and Guilds certificate in Coal Carbonisation and by-product recovery.	Comprehensive knowledge of the plant operation; knowledge of hazardous chemicals and knowledge of safe working procedure; knowledge of the chemical processes involved in the plant; knowledge of the parameters within which the plant must operate.

INDUSTRIAL SECTOR	JOB TITLE[1]	CORE TASKS (JOB SPECIFIC)[2]	SUGGESTED OCCUPATIONAL GROUP[3]	CORE TASKS (SOC)[4]	TYPICAL ENTRY ROUTES AND ASSOCIATED QUALIFICATIONS[5]	SKILLS AND COMPETENCES[5]
WATER INDUSTRY	Principal, Environmental Quality	Reviewing and reporting on water quality performance; identifying and implementing programmes to ensure maintenance and improvements of the quality of water supply; implementing measures to ensure compliance with EEC and UK legislation; negotiating consents with the Water Authority; identification of training requirements.	Minor Group: Production managers in manufacturing, construction, mining and energy industries SOC 1(a)11/110	Plan, organise, direct and co-ordinate the activities and resources necessary for production in manufacturing industries and the maintenance of engineering items, equipment and machinery.	A degree in either chemistry or biology. A member of the Institute of Water and Environmental Management (IWEM) or the Royal Society of Chemists.	Knowledge of: environmental pollution control technology, legislation and directives; experience of programme implementation; planning and negotiating skills; computer literacy; inter-personal, man-management, report writing and presentation skills.
	Chartered Civil Engineer, Flood Defence	Designing and preparing drainage plans; carrying out pre- and post- work surveys; liaising with legal and estates sections in order to prepare matters; undertaking cost benefit analyses; liaising with third parties in advance of works (land-owners, planning authorities).	Minor Group: Engineers and technologists SOC 2(a)21/210	Undertakes research and advises on water and waste water treatment processes and other civil engineering matters. Determines and specifies construction methods, organises and plans projects and establishes control systems to monitor operational efficiency.	Chartered engineer with at least 10 years work experience. Formal training in environmental management is not required.	The ability to undertake a wide range of tasks; financial contractual and engineering; good technical knowledge; strong inter-personal and negotiating skills; knowledge of legislation, particularly in relation to land drainage; economic modelling ability; man-management skills.
	Senior Scientific Officer	Development of analytical techniques; responsibility for the quality of analysis and the turn-around and through-put of analysis; responsibility for maintaining stocks; on 24hr call to respond to pollution incidents; writing reports; attendance at management meetings.	Minor Group: Natural Scientist SOC 2(a)20/209	Analyse and research physical aspects of chemical structure and change within substances and develop chemical techniques used in the manufacture or modification of natural substances and processed products. Other concerns are the development of experimental procedures and setting up and analysing the results of experiments.	A degree in chemistry and/or a Masters;five years laboratory experience. Membership of the Royal Society for Chemists. Limited provision of post-entry training.	experience of analytical chemistry; a high degree of literacy and numeracy; good report writing, communication, and inter-personal skills; dexterity with instruments; detailed knowledge of EC and UK legislation; knowledge of new technologies; good understanding of the Health and Safety aspects of chemical analysis.
	Scientific Assistant	Duties include solvent extraction, sample preparation, filing, clerical duties and the manipulation of samples (adding agents and treating samples for a variety of tests).	Minor Group: Scientific technicians SOC 3(a)30/309	Sets up apparatus for experimental, demonstration or other purposes; undertakes tests and takes measurements and readings; performs calculations, records and interprets data.	A Levels in science subjects. There is no requirement for previous work experience. Post-entry training is given a high priority. Training is provided primarily on-the-job, supplemented by the use of manuals /short courses.	Skills required include: organisational skills, initiative, communication skills and an ability to follow instructions.

NOTES
(1) Job title of post examined in the case studies.
(2) Core tasks as defined in the case studies.
(3) Occupational group as suggested on the basis of the job title and core tasks and defined by the Standard Occupational Classification.

Monitoring and analysis tasks include:

- sampling and analysis of waste streams;
- liaison with regulatory agencies;
- preparation of applications for consents and licences.

Implicit in these tasks is an awareness, on the part of the management, that the plant has an impact on the environment. These tasks are typically additional to the core tasks associated with the mainstream production management and scientific analysis associated with the production process. Only in the largest firms are there senior managers and scientists who have a full-time responsibility for environmental management. However, the monitoring and analytical tasks are considered to be growing in importance and scale, as a result of both the increase in environmental standards and control of new substances and the increasing requirement for environmental audits.

Typically these environmental management core tasks would represent in the order of 25% of the time of the job, although in large plants a full time post may be created. In some instances the development of these environmental management tasks is related to existing responsibilities for health and safety or quality control/quality management.

The tasks of operatives do not require any general environmental awareness although frequently the tasks involve operating within a set of parameters in order to avoid exceeding consent limits or violating environmental regulations. The tasks generally relate to the operation of plant and equipment and increasingly to sampling and monitoring of waste streams. More senior operatives (supervisors) may be involved in the collation of environmental data and be responsible for on-the-job training. A wide variation exists in terms of the proportion of the time of a job associated with environmental management, depending on company policy and on the particular type of plant.

3.3.3 Competences

Competences associated with environmental management can again be considered separately for managers and operatives. Managers will require:

- at least a degree level education in science/engineering;
- management competences (personnel/financial/communications);

- at least five years industry experience.

Thus the main competences relate to the scientific, engineering background and managerial and industrial experience. These competences are either gained before entry into the job or through on-the-job training. Environmental management competences are supported through some off-the-job education and training, using a variety of means: exhibitions, conferences, seminars and short courses. Post entry training of middle management is quite rigorous although senior management training is reported to be fairly minimal.

The competences required by operatives are basic production/process engineering skills. These occupations are associated with little or no pre-entry qualifications although City & Guilds is often encouraged post-entry. Laboratory based staff have some basic scientific training, perhaps to 'A' level. However, subsequent to the implementation of Total Quality Management the level of competences required of operatives is expected to rise and it it expected that this requirement for higher standards will be met by increased post-entry training.

The main form of post-entry training is one in which an operative to understudy a more experienced operative or receives less formal on-the-job training. This training would be expected to be more formalised in larger firms compared to smaller firms.

3.3.4   Training Requirements

The occupational analysis indicates that environmental management skills relate to a wide range of occupational families. Thus there are environmental management skills to be acquired and applied at the senior management level, middle management level, supervisory level and operative level.

The discussions with industry associations, undertaken as part of the case studies, also reveal that there are issues of awareness as well as technical competence. Environmental awareness includes an appreciation, by the different occupational families, of the impact of the company's production activities on the wider environment.

In the light of the case studies there are three main areas where training is required. Firstly, there remains a major deficiency in the level of awareness in industry of the requirement for environmental management This lack of awareness relates to an ignorance of: environmental legislation and commercial pressures for enhanced environmental management; how the operation of the plant impacts upon the environment; and the most effective strategies for implementing environmental management initiatives. This lack of awareness is more prevalent amongst smaller firms.

Secondly, an increasing proportion of management time is being spent on the preparation of applications for consents, discharge permits, operating licenses, etc. This process can be legally and technically complex. The rapid changes in legislation mean that companies are pressed to keep abreast, and to understand the implications, of new legislation. The increasing requirement to monitor and measure the environmental impact of the plant, requiring new analytical techniques means that scientific and engineering skills and knowledge need to be continually kept up-to-date.

Thirdly, preparing specific pollution control and waste minimisation and recycling initiatives in response to the generation of waste streams and pollution can be a technically complex process. The lack of exchange of information between plants, as to the technical environmental management responses, increases the requirement on individual companies to find their own solutions. External advice and support, however, needs to be specifically tailored to the operating circumstances of a given company. This in turn means that training courses aimed at improving technical responses need to be highly specific.

As part of the discussion of core tasks, above, it was noted that these tasks are typically additional to main-stream tasks. Thus, apart from the very largest firms, industry does not employ full-time "environmental specialists". This has implications for the training response. Typically, the plant manager/technical director, together with the company chemist/scientist will require the skills noted above. In addition, many of the future skill requirements which might be expected in the light of possible changes in legislation and technologies, will also need to be satisfied by staff at technical director/senior chemist level.

Finally, individual jobs within companies and regulatory agencies were examined to identify core tasks. These have been compared with the core tasks as detailed in the UK Standard Occupational Classification (SOC). On this basis the identified jobs associated with environmental management have been related to minor groups of occupational families within the SOC to allow a preliminary classifiction of occupations associated with environmental management.

The occupational families defined at a minor group level which perform environmental management functions are:

- Production managers in manufacturing, construction and energy industries. (SOC minor group no: 11)
- Specialist managers (12)
- Natural scientists (20)
- Engineers and technologists (21)
- Scientific technicians (30)
- Other associate professional and technical occupations, nes (39)
- Metal machining, fitting and instrument making trades (51)
- Metal forming, welding and related trades (53)
- Plant and machine operatives (80).

Broadly, the occupations associated with environmental management, identified within the case-studies, fall into one of the above occupational families.

3.4 Issues Emerging From the Case Studies

The detailed analysis of the case studies, reported above, has also raised a number of general issues which have implications for the development of training responses.

3.4.1 Sectoral Considerations

The existence of particular skills requirements prompts a consideration of whether these requirements are centred upon particular industries. The development of integrated pollution control (IPC) suggests that there would be a general requirement across all industry and throughout the full production process for environmental management skills. However, the development of future environmental policy, with specific production processes effected by new legislation, will lead to a sectoral focus in requirements. A good example, is the increasing identification of training requirements in the waste management industry, following new legislation covering waste disposal.

A sub-set of sectoral considerations relates to the size and ownership of the company. Smaller companies face particular difficulties for two reasons: firstly, they have limited resources to ensure that sufficient up-to-date information on environmental and technical issues is maintained; and secondly, they are unlikely to be able to employ specialists with responsibility for environmental management, leaving environmental management functions to be added to mainstream company functions.

Foreign companies operating subsidiaries in the UK may have differing requirements, to the extent that UK subsidiaries are expected to comply with environmental management practices of the parent company which operate to standards which are stricter than UK standards. A good example is the practice by US subsidiaries of operating to US environmental standards in the UK, even though these are more demanding of the company than UK standards.

Plants which operate as part of a group of companies may have access to group training resources and thus the training for environmental management may be different compared with a plant operating independently.

3.4.2   Training the Trainers

A major source of information and advice on environmental management issues is derived from contact with the regulatory agencies. However, there is increasing concern, given the introduction of IPC, that the regulatory agencies will be required to adopt an increasingly arms-length relationship with industry. More broadly, the provision of environmental education and training is a relatively under-developed area and there has been some concern expressed in this study that there are not sufficient training providers who have the appropriate skills. This concern reflects, in part, the highly specialised nature of the training requirements, with industry requiring, process specific environmental management training. The reduction in the informal information exchange which currently takes place with regulatory agencies will place greater emphasis on the requirement to develop suitable training resources.

3.4.3   Requirements of Specialist vs Generalist

The discussion, above, highlights the requirement for both general skills, including awareness, and specialist skills. To the extent that new education and training provision will be developed, the distinction between generalists and specialists requires some clarification. This issue has been discussed with firms in this study.

Training for environmental management is required at two broad levels; management training and operative training. Management training will have a broader base, being concerned with awareness, philosophy, management attitudes etc, compared with operative training. Operative training will focus on specific technical tasks.

Higher education provision for environmental management is required for industrial managers. However, industry views technically competent graduates (eg, in chemistry or engineering) with an understanding of environmental aspects, as being preferable to "environmental scientists" who have a broad range of environmentally related skills (eg, knowledge of policy/legislation, technologies, environmental impact assessment etc). This implies that in developing education policy in this area, the emphasis should be placed on post-graduate education.

City & Guilds education and training is often undertaken by operatives with environmental management tasks, particularly in process engineering. The move towards a broader based City & Guilds education, away from specific craft related training, is in keeping with the requirement to add additional skills associated with environmental management to mainstream process engineering skills.

3.4.4   Role of the Supplier

The specific training requirements, particularly of operatives, are often met by the supplier of environmental management goods and services. This is the case where the new skills relate to new plant or production processes. Suppliers provide this training as part of the sales package. This service is important because it means that the move towards cleaner technologies is less likely to be constrained by the absence of the necessary technical skills. It also means that the reduced distinction between production and environmental management need not inhibit the acquisition of the necessary skills.

3.4.5   Health and Safety Practices

There is frequently a close relationship between existing health and safety practices and compliance with health and safety regulations and environmental management practices. Good examples relate to the handling of hazardous materials, eg, chemicals and some waste metals. This relationship means that certain tasks which could be undertaken to comply with environmental legislation are already being undertaken and training supplied accordingly, in order to comply with health and safety practices.

A number of consultees also made the point that the current development of attitudes towards environmental management and the greater attention being given to defining and meeting environmental management tasks mirrors the process which industry has previously been through with respect to health and safety practices. This in turn may be expected to lead, eventually, to the position where attention to environmental management, by all members of a company workforce, will become implicit and automatic.

3.4.6   Total Quality Management

The increasing attention being focussed on total quality management (TQM) by industry leads companies to examine the extent to which they produce wastes and the benefits from waste minimisation initiatives. As a consequence environmental management functions are being identified and new competences are being satisfied. TQM is, therefore, aiding the development of environmental management in industry.

3.5   **A Review of Training Needs**

The review examines training needs and the type of training personnel require in three sectors; manufacturing industry, waste management and the regulatory agencies.

3.5.1   The Need for Trained Personnel for Environmental Management in Manufacturing Industry

Trained personnel are required within the polluting industrial sectors to ensure that their pollution problems are overcome efficiently and effectively and that environmental standards are complied with. Imperial College (2) demonstrated that the lack of skilled personnel and technical knowledge was an important constraint upon the adoption of pollution controls in 10% of the firms surveyed in the UK, and was a particularly important constraint in the case of small firms. It also revealed a need for developing and applying improved measuring and monitoring techniques to inform assessments of pollution levels and remedial action in industry. This involves the establishment of data banks and expert systems for storage and analysis of environmental data, as well as information on production and pollution control techniques, particularly in relation to the information needs of small firms. Present advances in computer technology and expert systems provided a potentially valuable method of achieving this.

ISFOL (40) examined training needs for the Italian Ministry of Environment and concluded that industry needed to develop training in environmental management in order to develop responses, particularly relating to technical innovation. The importance of incorporating environmental management activities into existing production techniques, modifying existing plant to achieve improved environmental performance and changing the production processes is highlighted. The training needs which these changes generate are considered to be extensive with a requirement to recognise new professions. The report highlights the requirement to combine scientific, technical competences with a knowledge of legislation and an awareness of advancements in technology.

In Germany, the water and air pollution control laws stipulate that major polluting firms must appoint an environmental protection officer responsible for: ensuring that the firm complies with the relevant environmental regulations; preparing annual environmental reports to the authorities; influencing the selection, development and implementation of new technologies and products so as to ensure that they are compatible with the environment; and increasing employees' awareness of the (potential) environmental impacts associated with their activities. This environmental protection officer should have completed studies in engineering, chemistry or physics and should have two years practical experience in a suitable plant or one year in the case where the officer has specialist knowledge in environmental studies.

Incentive (37) also suggests that there is a need within individual firms for such an officer specifically responsible for environmental protection matters. Such an officer should have a broad range of skills and expertise coupled with a technical background so that he can tackle the variety of environmental and workers' health and safety issues arising in his company. He should promote and co-ordinate environmental information and training programmes for all levels of staff. He should be good at communicating with personnel within the company and with outside bodies such as the regulatory agencies. He should be capable of drawing upon outside groups for technical assistance and information about developments in pollution control technologies. Hence, this entails a combination of scientific, technical, legal, management and communication skills.

In contrast, Imperial College (2) reports a survey of 22 UK firms from different industries which showed that pollution control in industry has tended to be performed by factory managers with training in a specific discipline (mostly chemistry, various types of engineering and other sciences) rather than by specialist environmental scientists. Similarly, the ENI report (30) states that few of the Italian firms they examined have a special environmental expert. There are three major reasons for this.

- Firstly, many companies feel that they do not have enough purely environmental work to justify employing someone to work specifically on environmental matters. This is supported by the case studies presented in the previous section.

- Second, and possibly more important, many companies' career and training structures involve their personnel working in different parts of their operations so that they can then gain an overall working knowledge of the company. Engineering or science graduates are considered to be more appropriate for this. Thus the environmental controller in most firms tends to be someone with a thorough working experience of all the company's operations and with good contacts within and outside the industry. This point is substantiated by a survey of 100 firms in France which found that 85% of the environmental protection officers in these companies had been promoted from within the company (47). The case studies, reported in the previous section, also supports this view.

- Third, industries increasingly view pollution control as an integral part of the production process. This is facilitated by pollution control measures being undertaken by someone with a sound knowledge and experience of the company. This general position is likely to remain in the future, although there may be a slight change in the specific types of graduates sought by firms, with an increased demand for electronic engineers likely because of the greater sophistication involved in the present advances in monitoring, production and pollution control technologies. Some firms are currently experiencing difficulties in finding sufficient numbers of trained staff to operate these new technologies (2).

For most small and medium-sized firms, the increased environmental activities would be undertaken by a company manager trained in one of the traditional disciplines and with experience of the company's operations. These activities would embrace not only pollution control but also workers' health and safety (24).

Such firms, that cannot support full-time specialist staff devoted to environmental protection, would draw upon external sources (eg, regulatory agencies and private and public research, consultancy and advisory organisations) for advice and technical support in respect of specific pollution control problems. ENI (30) estimated that 2,000-4,000 trained personnel were required over the five year period 1983-88 to cover staff turnover and growth by private environmental research, consulting and advisory organisations in Italy. Of this total, 500-1,000 would be highly qualified environmental specialists. In 1983 almost 7,000 people were employed by these organisations in Italy (30). The types of specialist skills required by the pollution control equipment suppliers include: electronics; computing; chemical; mechanical and electrical engineering physics; process control; water treatment; chemical analysis; and microbiology (2). The study notes that there is currently a shortage of electronic engineers and computer specialists.

Personnel will also be required to perform environmental impact assessments and risk analyses, within SME's. Such people must be capable of not only following the set procedures for EIAs but also of performing (or organising the performance of) technical studies which identify the potential impacts, estimating the likelihood of these impacts occuring, assessing the significance of these impacts, proposing appropriate control measures and of ensuring that these measures are integrated into the firm's planning of the project. Such tasks might fall within the responsibilities of the general environmental managers described above, as has traditionally occurred in the past. Nevertheless, these activities would also involve personnel in the firms' investment planning and review divisions so that good liaison with these personnel would be necessary. Moreover, the environmental impact and risk assessments and control studies require the use of expertise for which firms will have to turn to consultants if they do not possess appropriately qualified staff. ENI (30) suggest that, in the light of the Seveso Directive, there is an increasing need for the development of industrial risk analysts as a new profession concerned with controlling the risks of industrial accidents and substantial pollution incidents.

The review of training needs for environmental personnel in industry, described above, indicates a particular requirement for the following specific types of trained personnel:

- more skilled technicians and operators with flexible capabilities and a broad knowledge of several areas of their (increasingly sophisticated) production processes and an awareness of the potential environmental impacts;

- handlers of hazardous substances who are knowledgeable about the nature of these substances, the potential for major accidents and the necessary precautionary measures;

- qualified engineers and staff in the heating, ventilation and air conditioning industry;

- specialists in the areas of noise and air pollution control;

- toxicologists/biological specialists for the testing of chemicals;

- experts in data processing and systems analysis for the development of environmental data banks and information systems;

There is also a need for greater environmental awareness amongst industrial employees from the shop floor upwards. This is particularly relevant with respect to fugitive emissions and pollution resulting from incorrect operation of equipment (eg, leaks and spillages). This last aspect is of increasing importance because of the toxic nature of many of the substances used in manufacturing operations which means that care is needed to prevent discharges of these substances and to ensure the effective operation of control procedures.

3.5.2   The Need for Trained Personnel for Waste Management

A major sector requiring specialist skills is the waste management industry. The discussion of environmental pressures (Section 2.3) indicated the growing requirement for a highly skilled and competent waste management industry.

In all Member States there is a particular need for training in the collection, disposal and monitoring of hazardous waste. More vocational training is needed for those working in the hazardous waste field. The design and implementation of training programmes provides an opportunity for national governments to introduce a method of certification for adequately trained waste handlers. This would be an important step in seeking to control the quality of operators in the field, and in reducing the environmental hazards which arise from accidents and malpractice. The necessary training establishments are most needed, and should be situated in highly industrialised areas where waste, and particularly toxic waste problems, are most severe. In support of the Toxic and Dangerous Waste Directive (78/319/EEC) which requires Member States, as a matter of priority, to help prevent toxic waste through recycling and recovery, practical experimentation and demonstration units for new technologies should be encouraged in these areas.

Assessments undertaken for the Commission, show that the absence of adequate controls on the collection and disposal of domestic and industrial wastes can create significant local environmental impacts (eg. in the form of leachate contaminating surface and groundwaters, contamination of soil, fires, smells and unsightliness of sites and air pollution from incinerators). There is therefore, a need to ensure proper planning, siting, engineering and management of controlled landfill sites. This is a Community-wide need but is particularly marked in the regions of southern European countries where municipal waste services are less developed. In Greece, for example, there are many cases of significant environmental problems being caused by many uncontrolled waste disposal tips (3).

In those countries and regions of the Community where waste management procedures are less likely to require any major increase in manpower needs, there is nonetheless a need to improve and broaden training in relation to; the potential environmental problems arising from poor disposal practice; the transportation, treatment and disposal of hazardous waste; the potential for the recycling of waste; and the better planning and subsequent management of disposal and treatment facilities. Available evidence suggests that the current training programmes for waste management are limited. For those countries with established waste management legislation and procedures, existing training comprises preparatory training for new recruits, frequently provided by individual private sector companies, with additional, "on-the-job" training and day release schemes to colleges. For example, such training is provided by the Institute of Waste Management in the UK for operations of waste disposal sites. In many countries, however, the provision of training is far less systematic. Training for existing employees in waste disposal authorities needs to improve and to embrace environmental conservation. In France for example, the level of training provided for the 31,000 employees in waste disposal is reported to be minimal (69). Regarding SMEs, within the hazardous waste industry there are few training programmes for small hazardous waste operators. A very small proportion of workers receive formal training, due both to the lack of appropriate courses, and the reluctance of small operators to use them. Among the Member States, the FRG has the most extensive system of worker training relating to the handling and movement of hazardous wastes. German companies working in the field are required to appoint a qualified "agent in charge", who assumes responsibility for safety.

In the less developed regions which are currently embarking upon new waste management legislation and procedures, the lack of suitably trained personnel is a serious barrier to rapid and effective implementation in relation to overall monitoring and planning of solid waste management. In these areas, waste disposal and management requires controls, facilities and standards. There are already insufficient numbers of adequately trained personnel to ensure proper planning and management of disposal sites and to prevent contamination of the environment from drainage. In Italy, for example, an additional 15,000 specialists are estimated to be needed for waste management (68). A similar need exists in Greece where waste collection and disposal is an urgent environmental problem and is estimated to require 1,300 local waste advisors to provide a short term solution to the problem (3). As a short to medium term solution to the environmental problems posed by inadequately controlled disposal, advisors could be trained and attached to local authorities in the less developed regions. In these countries, existing training is particularly inadequate with regard to:

i) Training environmental managers, on the methods and techniques for dealing with the sources of domestic and industrial toxic wastes, disposal techniques, and pollution control measures (70).

ii) Training environmental specialists on detailed theoretical and practical skills relating to domestic and toxic waste management, including sources of toxic wastes, elements of toxicology, environmental problems caused by toxic wastes, monitoring, site selection and land use planning, and recycling and disposal techniques.

Finally, it is important to acknowledge the responsibilities of those in industry in relation to investment in the recycling and re-use of specific waste streams, and in low-waste technologies. For example, in the FRG some 190,000 tonnes of heavy-metal - containing hydroxide sludges are generated each year by the galvanising industry, and 180,000 tonnes of paint sludge from industrial paint spraying. Opportunities exist, and more must be found, to reduce these wastes.

Trained personnel are required for all aspects of solid waste management. These personnel include:-

i) Managers and supervisors to undertake the planning and evaluation of waste treatment facilities. At the regional level this requires the ability to carry out thorough technical, economic and environmental evaluations of the most efficient waste collection and disposal system appropriate to local conditions.

ii) Specialists in the design and construction of facilities for waste collection, recycling and treatment disposal, which are capable of dealing with both existing and new types of industrial and domestic wastes by incorporating technological developments in the methods for handling such waste, including toxic waste.

iii) Managers and specialists are also needed to undertake the day to day management of waste disposal facilities. Specialists are needed to support the management and operation of waste management systems capable of dealing with differences in the quality and composition of wastes, which are frequently related to the production processes in the industry from which they arise.

iv) Technicians to undertake the monitoring and inspection of waste treatment and disposal facilities while in operation and when subsequently no longer used.

In relation specifically to special hazardous or toxic wastes, the need to transport, treat and dispose of increasing levels of such waste requires additional specialists, particularly chemists and civil engineers, biologists, geologists and land surveyors. Such personnel are required throughout the Community (71,31,69).

In those regions of the Community currently implementing waste management legislation and procedures, the need for those trained personnel indicated above is more extensive, and includes both environmental managers and specialists in both the public and private sector. In Italy, for example, the disposal of most toxic industrial waste is undertaken by private firms which provide little training (70). Personnel are also required in these countries for the collection and disposal of domestic waste. For example, it has been estimated that in Italy an additional 4,000 managers of domestic waste handling facilities are needed (68). The greater exchange of experience and information, particularly from the more developed to the less developed regions, on waste management procedures and technological and legislative developed in domestic and toxic waste would also help to reduce the gaps in the current level of expertise in domestic, industrial and special wastes management.

Finally, it needs to be remembered that in order to effect low waste solutions at source in industry new skills will have to be assimilated in polluting industries.

3.5.3   The Need for Trained Personnel in the Regulatory Agencies

As a result of growing environmental awareness in Europe, various environmental laws have been enacted at both the national and community level. In order both to attain the desired environmental goals efficiently and implement these regulations effectively, there is a need for public sector environmental personnel capable both of handling a wide range of environmental protection activities and of ensuring that there is an efficient co-ordination of the diverse regulations concerning the different environmental media which are implemented by the various (levels of) public authorities.

This calls for two main types of trained personnel:-

i)   Environmental Managers skilled in administration, management and planning who are knowledgeable about a wide range of environmental protection measures and capable of understanding inter-media issues. These people would not directly run control facilities. Instead they would draw on a range of technical, legal and economic knowledge and expertise in order to plan and co-ordinate environmental protection programmes and to assist in strategic decision-making about environmental policies. This requires a broad and balanced knowledge of environmental technology, economics, policies and laws coupled with management and communication skills to be able to draw on particular technical experts for information on specific issues.

ii)   Environmental Specialists - The second group comprises environmental specialists with a technical background who would be running particular control facilities (eg, a sewage treatment plant or a waste treatment facility) or providing technical expertise on specific environmental problems (eg, research and monitoring and scientific analysis of environmental pollution). This entails a more in-depth technical training in certain fields but would nevertheless still require multi-disciplinary knowledge.

In addition, the environmental personnel in the public sector need to have good technical support services such as libraries, data banks and information systems. This latter aspect points to the need for both the environmental managers and specialists to have information science skills.

According to two Italian reports, (72,30), there is at present an acute shortage of trained staff in the various public bodies in Italy responsible for environmental protection and management. In addition, there is a lack of the technical equipment and back-up facilities required for the present staff to perform effectively their wide ranging tasks. A synthesis of the Italian Studies, (73), states that this shortage will prevent the public bodies in Italy from effectively implementing and enforcing environmental legislation in Italy.

The Econpublica report (72) assesses the level of additional trained personnel required to implement the existing environmental legislation in Italy, along with certain EEC directives concerning wastes and also the additional personnel resulting from a reorganisation of the environmental administration in Italy (a transfer of responsibility for some environmental management activities to the regions). This legislation includes:

- water pollution control and water supply;

- land (including treatment of domestic and industrial solid wastes);

- noise;

- air pollution control;

- control of major environmental hazards and accidents.

In order to implement this environmental legislation effectively in Italy, the report (72) estimates that 10,700 additional trained environmental personnel would be required.

At present, the environmental specialists in the public sector in Italy comprise mainly holders of diplomas or graduates, mostly in architecture and engineering, followed in descending order by mathematics, science, law and economics. Most of the additional personnel required are also expected to come from the same sort of disciplines. However, there will be a particular need for administrators skilled in planning, co-ordination and management and for specialists to provide the technical support required for the effective formulation and implementation of environmental regulations. At present there are particularly significant gaps in respect of these two types of expertise. Thus, Econpublica (72) confirms that few environmental staff in the public sector in Italy have received sufficient training in planning and co-ordination.

These additional personnel requirements in Italy would be full-time workers, with the exception of certain local mountain communities where there would be a need for part-time environmental personnel with a less specialised training. Similarly, the establishment of a decentralised network of such local environmental advisers attached to remote communities in Italy and Greece has been proposed in the reports by Anagritur (1) and Balafoutas (3).

Balafoutas (3) notes that there are many small local communities in Greece, where 90% of the communities have less than 1600 inhabitants. He states that the officials (eg mayors) in these local communities in Greece lack awareness of the environmental problems that can be caused by inadequate environmental management and lack information about available control measures and how these should be operated eg, waste disposal and sewage collection and treatment systems.

He advocates that there is a need for a network of technical environmental advisers attached to the local communities, who could advise the local mayors on the environmental problems in their area and help them to select, implement and operate control systems that are appropriate to their local circumstances and needs. He suggests that a total of about 5,900 such advisers are required for the 6,038 communities in Greece. These advisers would cover the management of the following environmental problems: water supply; sewage treatment; solid wastes; planning; streets and traffic; air pollution; parks and recreation; municipal information and impact studies. This network would comprise of a combination of generalist advisers and more specialist advisers. The more specialist advisers would be required for the larger communities in the areas of solid wastes, sewage treatment and water supply; while, for the (groups of) smaller communities each of the following areas would be the responsibility of a single adviser: sewage treatment and water supply; planning, streets, traffic and air pollution; parks and recreation; municipal information and impact studies. 1,300 waste manager advisers are required along with 900 advisers on sewage systems, 900 advisers on the provision of clean water supplies and 500 providing advice for small communities (of less than 500 people) operating septic tanks. These advisers would be young engineering graduates (up to 30 years of age), preferably from the area in question, who would have completed a further training in environmental management, in particular the problems and needs of rural communities.

3.6   **Education and Training Responses to Identified Needs**

This section provides a discussion of the range of responses to the training needs, discussed above. It is important to recognise that environmental conservation is not the prime activity of those working in industry. As such it is necessary to be aware of the limitations which affect the ability of industry to respond to its environmental responsibilities. This includes firstly the constraints on managers', engineers' and others' time. Training needs to be flexible therefore and to fit in, realistically, with time availability.

Secondly, the cost constraints which arise from the need to be competitive are also limiting. This applies, to the cost of both pollution control plant and equipment and of the training needed to manage this equipment properly. Training must therefore be cost-effective and respond to the real demands of industry.

In order to move towards a position of greater responsibility and a greater capability in industry (for example in being able to identify the best available technology) those working in potentially polluting industries will have to be encouraged to increase their awareness and expertise. In this respect the following requirements can be identified :-

- General programmes to enhance the environmental awareness of employees and employers. The type of information provided needs to vary: company directors require more information about environmental legislation and policies and to be made more aware of the economic instruments used, eg, polluter pays principle, and of the fact that pollution prevention can pay for itself; managers require technical material and information about environmental regulations and environmental impact assessments (e.g. legislative requirements for EIA and the manner in which the assessment should be performed); supervisors require more purely technical information along with some information about relevant environmental regulations; and operators require technical, plant specific information to induce them to implement better process control and 'good housekeeping' measures.

- Greater provision of information and independent advice on the clean technologies industry, including: efficiency and effectiveness of available pollution control techniques that are appropriate for specific firms; names and addresses of clean technologies suppliers; and the provision of consultancy services on integrating clean technologies into production processes. This information should be particularly directed towards the needs of small and medium-sized firms. Possible sources of this information and advice include the regulatory authorities, trade associations, public and private research and consultancy organisations.

Recognising this need the Commission has helped to establish **NETT (European Network for Environmental Technology Transfer)**. Based in Brussels, NETT is a collaborative network of producers, industrial users, university research departments and others concerned with environmental protection and waste management, see Section 5.2.

- Similarly, there is a need to provide small developers and manufacturers of pollution control technologies with information on the market for their products and on (future) environmental policies, including any financial assistance schemes for which they might be eligible (26). This should provide the individual firms with access to the available information and with contacts with potential collaborators or customers, and specific technical and marketing advice regarding their products and also general guidance as to how to perform and better manage innovations and entrepreneurial activity so as to overcome the barriers (e.g. technical, marketing, financial) encountered by small firms.

- A greater use of environmental data bases and information systems on aspects such as environmental regulations and pollution control techniques.

- Promotion of 'in-house' training by the provision of technical back up material and facilities and flexible 'distance learning' information packages that can be used for study by the people concerned at their place of work or home. Such packages would be particularly valuable for employees in small firms and for technicians and supervisors.

- Provision of short, very intensive courses both to keep staff up-to-date with technological and legislative developments and newly emerging environmental problems and also to fill certain gaps concerning specific technical and legal aspects of key environmental issues, especially regulations and the implementation of clean technologies. These courses should comprise short one to four day courses on specific subjects. The provision of such courses is particularly important given the preference of industry, especially small and medium-sized firms, to use personnel trained in the traditional disciplines to perform their pollution control activities.

- Greater dissemination of information on the types of courses that are available.

- Greater integration of environmental subjects into vocational training programmes and university degree courses in the traditional disciplines such as engineering, chemistry and also computing and electronics. Industry prefers this approach to that of creating a new faculty specifically for environmental specialists.

- Specialist advanced training in subjects such as pollution control technology, noise and air pollution control, risk analysis and environmental impact assessment. Such advanced training should have a strong inter-disciplinary element. The environmental impact assessment courses should concern the practical performance of EIAs entailing identification of environmental impacts and their evaluation in practices and the implementation of appropriate control measures.

- Training in pollution control directed at small and medium-sized firms needs to enhance environmental awareness, to support 'in-house' training and to increase the provision of flexible information packages, the provision of information and independent advice, and short courses for vocational training. More specialist training on the control of pollution should be targeted at larger firms which, potentially, have greater emissions.

- The potential also exists to utilise existing mechanisms for the provision of advice and information to enterprises. These would include local and regional development agencies providing advisory services; and also Commission supported initiatives including:

    * Business Co-operation Network (BC-NET)
    * Network for Environmental Technology Transfer (NETT)
    * European Business and Innovation Centres (BIC's)
    * Euro Info Centres
    * COMETT - Community Programme in Education and Training in Technology.

3.7 **Company Wide Responses to Environmental Management**

The final part of this section of the report dealing with training needs considers company wide responses to environmental management and training needs. The research, detailed above, makes clear the importance of addressing the requirements for environmental management at a company wide level. Management and technical competences are an essential element of successful corporate strategies aimed at securing improved environmental and commercial performance of SME's.

The nature of a successful company wide response is illustrated in Figure 3.3. This shows the range of management and technical competences which an SME requires and the vital role which the use of education and training services has in ensuring the necessary environmental capacity of an SME to secure environmental performance.

FIGURE 3.3 Strategies and Programmes for Corporate Development

Environmental Corporate Policy

Environmental corporate policy is particularly difficult to establish because it requires a response which can :

- Combine emerging legislation and policy development with customer and investor demands.
- Address not only the product itself but also the the opportunities for management and technological changes in the production process and/or the supply stream.
- Adapt to changing market and commercial conditions.

Successful Strategies

A successful strategy requires the following actions :

- *Look ahead and anticipate change.*
    * monitor political and scientific debate
    * monitor customer expectations
    * integrate expectations of change into investment decisions
    * assess future capacity of existing plant
    * modify products in the light of expected change
    * develop products for new market opportunities

- *Minimise environmental costs.*
    * cut environmental cost component for product users
    * cut company's own environmental production and management costs
    * reduce environmental liabilities and risks
    * identify new environmental beneficial cost saving options

- *Establish an environmental capacity*
    * establish appropriate management systems
    * integrate environmental concerns into management performance criteria
    * sensitise staff to current and future trends
    * develop appropriate personnel capacities
    * develop appropriate communications tools

4.0 AN OVERVIEW OF THE PROVISION OF ENVIRONMENTAL EDUCATION AND TRAINING IN THE COMMUNITY

4.1 Introduction

This section provides an overview of the provision of environmental education and training services in the Community. The overview provides information on the content, the method of delivery and the scale of provision, supporting general observations. The purpose of this overview is to provide an indication of the character of supply to inform study conclusions. The institutional infrastructure for the delivery of training services is the subject of separate observations in Sections 5.0 and 6.0.

Provision in each Member State has not been characterised. The mission to Italy placed particular emphasis on identifying training provision and we have, therefore, provided a separate analysis for Italy.

4.2 The Scope and Definition of Training

Training is taken to mean the process of helping to bring a person to an agreed standard of proficiency, skill or knowledge, by practice and/or instruction, and the provision of information. Use of the term training in this study is taken in its widest sense to incorporate both experience, education and awareness.

Environmental training is taken in this study to include those activities which help to develop skills and competences to improve the environmental performance of industry. As such training services are aimed at developing:

- an understanding of the environmentalist philosophy concerning matters such as resource sustainability and the recycling of materials;

- a general awareness of current environmental issues;

- an understanding of the existing and potentially harmful effects of the company's operations, on the external environments (including EIA);

- the skills required to control or avoid these effects;

- an appreciation of the economic and social costs of the environmental effects of a company's operations and the costs and benefits of proposed actions or solutions;

- the motivation to respond to the five points above.

Environmental training in industry consists of both formal and informal education and training. The methods used are listed below:

- Formal methods include:

    * the inclusion of environmental subjects in college curriculum;
    * vocational courses and on-going training programmes;
    * in-house training courses (including relevant induction training);
    * short courses provided by external institutions;
    * day or block release training;
    * evening classes;
    * distance learning;
    * practical courses and placements.

- Informal methods include:

    * on-the-job experience;
    * films, videos, talks;
    * seminars, conferences;
    * educational campaigns;
    * leaflets, circulars, information on the company's environmental policy, advertising material from firms offering services or equipment, publications such as journals, Trade Association bulletins, field visits, outings;
    * discussions with consultants, Trade Unions, Industrial Associations.

These methods are used to enhance the level of skills for, and awareness of, environmental management by instruction and education, generally using formal methods, and by practice and experience, generally using informal methods.

4.3 The Content of Training Provision

The content of in-house training courses in France placed greatest attention on workers health and safety legislation and, to a lesser extent, noise. Relatively little attention was given to environmental issues such as waste, air and water pollution. However, research indicated that firms were generally satisfied with these courses (47).

The content of external courses in France was considered to be more relevant to the needs of environmental management, being concerned with water pollution, noise and environmental legislation. The majority of firms using these courses (66%) considered that they were adequate but the remainder considered that a programme of more intensive and practical courses, particularly in the areas of clean technologies was required. Companies also placed emphasis on courses providing training on health and safety issues, and did not place much weight on the distinction between environmental management and health and safety issues (47).

A review of training provision in the UK, (24) identified water and waste management as areas where training was most advanced although the recent increase in general environmental awareness seminars was highlighted. The main failure of the training content was the lack of specific and targetted courses responding to specific environmental management issues in industry.

In countries with established waste management procedures there is a greater provision of training for waste management personnel. The content is tailored to new recruits, providing preparatory training, and existing personnel providing "on-the-job" training and refresher, day-release, courses at technical colleges. However, there is concern, even in these countries, that training is inadequate and that the content of training needs to focus more on management competences required to manage waste disposal activities.

The development of environmental training targeted at senior managers in industry and at future industry managers has, to date, been limited. However senior management training, covering those areas of competence required to develop company wide responses (see Section 3.7 above), is beginning to develop. Courses being developed by the International Institute for Management Development (IMD) are a good case in point.

Environmental training for future, industry and regulatory agency employees, provided in degree and post-graduate courses in the UK, has been reviewed by ECOTEC. This work suggests that the main emphasis is on environmental legislation, technology and economics. In the light of industry requirements Universities are incorporating environmental components into traditional courses with, for example, environmental issues being taught as part of chemical and engineering degree courses. Further details of this review are given in Annex G.

In general terms this overview highlights the lack of courses, particularly courses for personnel in industry and the regulatory agencies, which provide for the extension of individual competences to include the necessary combination of specialist technical knowledge and an overall view of the inter-relationships between the diverse problems involved in environmental protection. The content of existing courses is either too highly specialised and does not provide a sufficiently broad understanding of other disciplines, or they are too general and fail to respond to the detailed needs of personnel with respect to particular industrial processes.

The review of course content highlights the particular absence of courses for industrial risk analysis. The need, especially following the Seveso Directive, for greater control, both by industry and regulatory agencies, over the risks of industrial accidents and pollution incidents requires advanced training comprising techniques for risk assessment, information on relevant legislation and responsibilities of agencies and the incorporation of risk assessments in industry management (30).

In Italy the content of environmental training provision covers water purification, environmental protection, energy, waste management, environmental impact assessment, and other courses covering, for example, air pollution control. The relative focus on these different elements in overall provision is summarised in Table 4.1. This indicates that the greatest provision of courses is for environmental protection and water purification, accounting for half of all courses. Details of the course content are summarised below:

- Water Purification

    * Plant management;
    * Technology;
    * Disposal of toxic wastes;
    * Environmental legislation;
    * Water analysis.

TABLE 4.1 : THE CONTENT AND SCALE OF ENVIRONMENTAL TRAINING PROVISION IN ITALY

| | Type of Course [1] | | | |
Content	FP	Agg	University	Total
	(Number of Courses)			
Water Purification	30	11	-	41
Environmental Protection	37	6	3	46
Energy	17	3	2	22
Waste Management	14	7	-	21
Environmental Impact	6	8	-	14
Others [2]	12	14	10	36
Total Courses	116	49	15	180

Source : V. Cogliati (1988)

Notes : [1] FP = Formazione Professionale
Agg = Aggiornamente

[2] includes; air pollution control and sanitation planning.

- Environmental Protection

    * land management;
    * water pollution;
    * soil pollution;
    * air pollution;
    * energy issues.

- Energy

    * energy management;
    * energy technologies;
    * energy conservation.

- Waste Management

    * legislation;
    * recycling;
    * scientific/engineering;
    * technology.

- Environmental Impact Assessments

- Various Other Courses

    * atmospheric pollution control;
    * sanitation planning.

The Italian mission, as well as detailing the content of training provision also identified a number of consistent views amongst consultees relating to the quality of the training provided. Consultees suggested that the quality and value of a high proportion of the courses offered fell below expectations. In particular, the consultees noted that courses provided by research institutes and private training organisations are of a higher quality than those provided by the Regions/State. However these former courses are often too technical and frequently targeted at management level without sufficient emphasis on general environmental awareness issues [10]. The consultees suggested a number of contributory factors.

- First, clearly defined profiles of environmental occupations do not exist, although some are in the the process of development [40]. Thus course content has to be developed with only partial recognition of the required competences of personnel.

- Secondly, given that environmental management embraces a wide range of disciplines there is difficulty in getting the correct balance, in the content of the course, between different disciplines.

- Thirdly, research into the nature of environmental problems and, therefore, of the required environmental management responses is very limited. Consultees stressed the link between research and the quality of training, and the importance of applying research findings to the benefit of industry. Initiatives are now being launched to improve the relationship between universities and industry in Italy.

- Fourthly, there is no central point of information on environmental training provision or a central agency responsible for co-ordinating the development of environmental training. Thus the application of common standards and the development of common accreditation systems has not taken place.

4.4 Method of Delivery

The range of methods available to deliver training services has been summarised above, Section 4.2. The method of delivery, for the purposes of this discussion is considered with respect to internal/external methods, and to public/private methods.

4.4.1 Internal/External Methods

Most firms tend to train their personnel "on-the-job" and "in-house", supplemented by the collection of information from trade associations and trade journals (2, 47). The use of internal methods are used primarily in smaller enterprises, and to train more junior personnel, operatives and technicians (2). This places a requirement on public programmes, which are designed to encourage greater take-up of provision, to target those medium-sized firms with a personnel/training manager, and provide training and training materials for application by in-house training managers; ie, training the in-house trainers.

The most significant external methods are, currently, the provision of short courses aimed at different levels of personnel, but mainly with an emphasis on technical issues and conferences/seminars, targeted at more senior company personnel, which are more likely to have an emphasis on awareness raising. The future development of external methods are likely to centre upon the development of more focused short courses aimed at senior and middle management designed to integrate wider management and specific technical competences. External methods are also likely to develop around the use of environmental consultants as SMEs seek to use flexible and customised training services.

4.4.2 Public/Private Methods

Training services are provided through a combination of publicly funded and organised courses and private services operated for profit. The traditional structure of state organised training has become less appropriate in both Northern and Southern Member States. In both the UK and Italy, for example, there has been a significant increase in the number of private sector training providers.

The distinction between public and private sector provision is blurred by the increasing public sector provision which is fee earning and the quasi private sector provision offered by industry associations, which again, is fee earning. The development of training services which are of relatively low cost to SMEs, compared with the cost of professional private sector suppliers, is particularly important. This places a considerable emphasis on the focused and co-ordinated use of skills in local colleges and universities to benefit SMEs. The institutional responses to this requirement are discussed in Sections 5.0 and 6.0.

In Italy the mission identified a growing "labyrinth" of training provision. The traditional provision of training, using secondary and tertiary educational institutions, has now changed to a position where services are provided by a wide range of organisations; assessorate of education, assessorate of professional training, private training organisations and research institutes.

Extensive research by Cogliati (10) to unravel the "labyrinth" indicates (Table 4.1 above) that training courses are generally delivered in three separate ways. The majority (60%) of environmental training courses in Italy, in the sectors described in Section 4.3, are delivered as "Formazione Professionale" (FP), i.e. professional training courses delivered by public and private sector training organisations. FP courses are generally of 500-800 hours duration and are usually provided by the State at a regional level, free of charge to the participant. Each course would typically have 20 places.

The second method of delivery is by the use of Aggiornamente courses, which are short intensive courses, typically lasting for no more than 80 hours. Aggiornamente courses account for a quarter of the courses provided in Italy, provided, for a fee, by private training organisations and by "assesoratis" which are state departments within the Regions.

The third method of delivery is by the universities, which provide graduate courses, post-graduate specialist courses and "suate dirette a fini specizli". University provision is relatively under-developed compared with the other methods of delivery but a number of universities are planning to introduce new graduate courses in environmental disciplines. These include Genoa and Trieste. The provision of specialist postgraduate courses is increasing. For example, both Pavia and Genoa Universities now provide postgraduate courses in environmental legislation and in the management of environmental resources.

"Suate dirette a fini specizli" courses do not lead to a degree qualification, but to a vocational qualification which is of a higher level than an FP qualification. Applicants need only have a school diploma. Courses are generally two years in length. These courses are assessed to be more flexible than degree courses. Organisers of these courses work directly with government bodies and private industry, and hence course content is able to respond to the skills requirements of industry. This type of training provision is also increasing.

The relative importance of the public and private sectors in funding the provision of courses in Italy is shown in Table 4.2. Two thirds of the identified courses are funded by the public sector. The private sector funds about a quarter (23%) of courses. Universities provide 8% of courses.

The importance of public funding varies between courses offering different subjects. For example, the public sector funds over 90% of courses in energy. However, the number of courses for environmental impact assessment provided by the public sector is almost matched by the private sector.

4.5   **Scale of Provision**

The scale of environmental training provision in the Community is difficult to estimate because it partly depends upon the level of expressed demand at a given time and the degree to which "spare" capacity exists because latent demand has not been translated into expressed demand. Moreover, the important issues is not the absolute level of provision but how far the scale of provision is sufficient to respond to the training needs of industry and the regulatory agencies.

There are two issues: how far is there provision for training which is not exploited by SMEs and regulatory agencies; and to what extent does new provision need to be developed? Reports of surveys suggest that firms, whilst recognising the benefits of environmental training, are unwilling to allocate time and money to training (2). The lack of demand is also recognised as being the result of inadequate information on the availability of courses and sources of advice (2). To the extent that these factors are important, enhancement of the scale of provision will not lead to increased take-up of training services.

TABLE 4.2 : THE SOURCES OF FUNDING OF ENVIRONMENTAL TRAINING COURSES IN ITALY

| | Sources of Funding for Courses ||||
Course Content	Public	Private	Universities	Total
Water Purification	31 (76)	10 (24)	-	41 (100)
Environmental Protection	39 (85)	4 (9)	3 (6)	46 (100)
Energy	20 (91)	-	2 (9)	22 (100)
Waste Management	13 (62)	8 (38)	-	21 (100)
Environmental Impact	8 (57)	6 (43)	-	14 (100)
Other[1]	12 (33)	14 (39)	10 (28)	36 (100)
Total Courses	**123 (68)**	**42 (23)**	**15 (8)**	**108 (100)**

Source : V. Cogliati (1988)

Notes : 1 includes air pollution control and sanitation planning.

Evidence collected in this study emphasises the importance of the factors above but also indicates that the level of demand is constrained by the lack of appropriate provision. Surveys reveal that industry believes that environmental training provision is inadequate and unsuited to the needs of industry, lacking flexibility and relevance (2, 47). The discussion on training content also addressed these deficiencies. Thus the training response, as already discussed in Section 3.0, must address the need to market services and develop more appropriate services.

Whilst the study has not quantified the existing level of provision in each Member State, the survey of training providers conducted as part of the study has identified the large range of training and other agencies, national and regional, with some responsibility for environmental training for industry and regulatory agencies. Annex (H) provides the Foundation with the necessary basis for further research and development in this area.

The analysis in the study has so far focused on provision at a national or Community level. Research by Cogliati (10) has begun to examine the regional variations in provision, see Table 4.3. To the extent that provision is tailored to local firms one would expect to find a concentration of provision in those regions which encounter particular industrial pollution problems. However, although there are significant concentrations in industrial regions, (Lombardia, Emilia Romagnia), there are concentrations in less industrialised regions (Abruzzo, Marche) and limited concentrations in industrialised regions (Lazio). This suggests, that the existing regional provision is not a reasonable indication of training need and indicates that the regional development and supply of courses is ad-hoc and unplanned.

This is a significant finding. The Italian consultees were of the view that the scale of provision was inadequate and did not respond to the needs of the SMEs or regulatory agencies. This finding is supported in earlier research (30). The ad-hoc regional provision is an indication that the supply and demand for training provision is out of balance.

4.6 Conclusions

The main conclusion from this overview are considered with respect to the content, method of delivery and scale of provision.

Content of Provision

- SMEs generally regard external training courses as being more relevant than internal training provision.

- Environmental training continues to be extensively incorporated in the training for health and safety, especially in internal training provision.

- SMEs generally require the services of external training sources as they do not have resources to supply in house training.

TABLE 4.3 : THE REGIONAL PROVISION OF ENVIRONMENTAL TRAINING IN ITALY

Region	Water Purfication	Env Protection	Energy	Waste Management	Env Impact	Other	Total
Piemonte	2	4	1	1	-	2	10
Liguria	-	-	-	-	-	2	2
Lombardia	7	1	-	2	3	9	22
Veneto	-	-	-	-	-	1	1
Trentino	1	-	-	-	-	2	3
Emilia Romagna	6	6	3	4	4	6	29
Toscana	-	2	2	1	3	3	11
Umbria	1	3	3	-	-	1	8
Marche	2	4	2	1	-	1	10
Lazio	1	2	-	-	-	2	5
Abruzzo	5	3	-	5	-	-	13
Molise	1	1	1	-	-	1	4
Campania	1	2	-	2	2	3	10
Puglia	3	9	7	-	1	1	21
Basilicata	1	1	1	-	1	-	5
Calabria	1	-	-	-	-	1	2
Sicilia	2	1	-	-	-	-	3
Sardegria	7	7	2	5	-	1	22
Italy	41	46	22	21	14	36	180

(Number of Courses)

Source : V. Cogliati (1988)

- Environmental legislation has had a significant effect on content, with particular emphasis on waste management and to a lesser extent on water pollution.

- Environmental management training is very limited, partly reflecting a lack of expressed demand, although some improvement is evident.

- Environmental education is developing, the effects of which are important in the longer term.

- The development of new provision requires clearer definition of environmental occupations and the requisite training requirements.

Method of Delivery

- The delivery of both internal training, using in-house trainers, and external training provision requires increased training provision. The trainers require training.

- The development of short external courses, targeted at senior managers and which are aimed at promoting awareness and developing corporate environmental responses, is likely to be a major method of delivery in the short to medium term.

- Consultants are likely to play a growing role in the provision of training.

- The development of provision by quasi-public organisations (employer organisations, research institutes) will require public finance.

Scale of Provision

- The scale of provision is partly determined by expressed demand. The essential requirement, to promote environmental awareness, is increasingly being recognised.

- Training services which are taken up are deficient in two ways, (i) management targeted provision is often too specialised and does not address the need to develop competences to prepare corporate environmental responses and (ii) technical level provision is often not sufficiently related to actual identified processes and applications.

- The scale of provision is directly related to the development of environmental legislation. Both increasingly awareness of SMEs and increasingly stringent environmental legislation will stimulate increased provision.

5.0 THE ROLE OF INTERNATIONAL ORGANISATIONS

5.1 Introduction

This section introduces the major international organisations which will be instrumental in improving the environmental performance of SMEs and regulatory agencies through the Community. These organisations are in a position to stimulate the awareness of SMEs of the need for improved environmental performance and the subsequent training requirement. They are also in a position to advise and encourage the extension of the existing provision of environmental training.

The discussion in this Section serves two purposes. First, it provides the Foundation and other interested readers with an introduction to the different organisations, identifying their objectives and their role in improving environmental performance. Secondly, it provides the basis for subsequent policy development by identifying the potential areas of overlap and areas left uncovered and the potential for co-ordination between organisations to secure, as efficiently as possible, improvements in environmental performance.

5.2 The European Commission

The Commission have a legitimate interest in training, firstly because unless training provision and delivery is adequate, then EC environmental legislation will not be effectively implemented and environmental standards will not be met, and secondly because environmental standards are of central importance to policies relating to economic and social development in the Community. To these ends the Commission has formulated an environmental education policy; details are provided in Annex H.

Given this legitimate interest and concern, the Commission therefore has the following roles to play in ensuring that training supports environmental policy:-

(i) Stimulating others to action at the national, regional and local levels, to fulfill training requirements, many of which have been identified in this report. This includes raising awareness within the Community of the necessity for training to meet the skill requirements associated with new and emerging environmental policy in the Community.

(ii) Identifying and monitoring gaps in training and training needs, particularly in relation to new and emerging environmental policy as expressed in EC Regulations and Directives, and in those areas of the Community where skills shortages slow down the pace of environmental enhancement. Such activity needs to be forward looking and preventative, anticipating potential training deficiencies.

(iii) Maintaining and ensuring high standards and quality in training provision, sufficient to ensure adequate standards in environmental management and protection, and promoting comparability of training and environmental standards, thus supporting the transfer of expertise throughout the Community.

(iv) Taking a policy lead in ensuring that other EC policy areas reflect environmental concerns and needs, and provide support for environmental training, particularly where environmental enhancement and training supports other policy objectives, including those of social, agricultural and regional development.

(v) Supporting training where there is a unique EC dimension, or where there are very specialised and limited requirements for skills at the EC level, or where initiatives can make a significant contribution to the objectives of environmental training provision in the Community.

(vi) Achieving a greater degree of integration of environmental concerns within other policy areas is the responsibility of all the social partners and should be pursued at the international, national and regional levels. The Commission should seek to ensure this integration in relation to EC policies, programme and operations. This responsibility rests with those Commission services responsible for the policy areas concerned. Of particular importance in this respect are the following:

* Directorate General for Environment (DG XI)

* Directorate General for Regional Affairs (DGXVI)

* Directorate General for Employment and Social Affairs (DGV)

* Task Force on Education Training and Youth Policy

* Directorate General for Science, Research and Development (DGXII)

* Directorate General for Energy (DGXVII)

* Directorate General for Enterprise, Commerce Tourism and Social Economy (DG XXIII)

The Commission could continue to support training in the environmental field in two ways. First, by supporting, through a dedicated training budget, particular kinds of training initiative which meet the objectives of training in the Community and which meet specific criteria. Secondly, by incorporating environmental training initiatives within its support frameworks for social, agricultural and regional policy and for training and research and development. The Commission, therefore, has a major role to play in securing improvement in the environmental performance of SMEs across Europe. The range of initiatives which are available to meet this end are summarised below. Further details are given in (19).

5.2.1   Initiatives for Environmental Training

The following kinds of initiative could be supported by the Commission from a budget dedicated to training in the environmental field:-

* Exchange programmes between Member States, the regions, and non-EC countries which facilitate the transfer of experience and knowledge.

* Information dissemination and networking which facilitates the movement of information and the transfer of technologies between Member States.

* Conferences and seminars which bring together from different Member States, those involved not only in training, but also those involved in environmental management, and in policy and legislative formulation, in order to raise awareness and stimulate action.

* Pump-priming activities in relation to projects which can make a significant contribution to the long term development of a Community training infrastructure such as centres of excellence, particularly where these serve more than one Member State, or training materials capable of EC wide application and dissemination.

* Studies which assess training needs, particularly in relation to gaps in our knowledge, and in relation to training for new EC legislation.

* Demonstration and pilot schemes which have the potential to stimulate action at Member State level, and/or which are focused on environmental issues which have an EC dimension.

5.2.2 Community Programmes

The Commission could also give its support to training in the environmental field through other policy and programme areas and to include the training dimension to environmental enhancement into the political agenda. These are illustrated below.

5.2.2.1 Structural Funds

Within the context of the reforms to the structural funds, there are two-way benefits to be derived from a greater commitment in the use of these funds for environmental, including training, activities and support:

The Less Developed Regions (ERDF, ESF, FEOGA) - Objective 1

The less developed regions of the Community are rich in natural resources and provide important recreational tourism and scientific resources. Without proper environmental management these resources will be depleted with the consequential effects not only on the environment, but also on the long-term sustainability of the regional economies due to damage to farming, forestry, tourism and other industries associated with them.

As this programme has revealed, the less developed regions also lag behind in terms of skilled manpower in the environmental field, access to environmental technologies, and the development of management approaches which are appropriate to the needs of such regions in relation to their level of financial and technical resources.

It is therefore in the interests of the less developed regions, and in accordance with the objectives of the Commission as regards the application of the structural funds, that environmental protection and enhancement is supported in these areas. This support will only be effective if training (in the broad context used here) is also provided.

Recognising the need for concerted environmental action in the Less Developed Regions, the Commission has recently adopted two new Community initiatives; ENVIREG and MEDSPA (See Section 5.2.2.2).

The Declining Industrial Regions (ERDF and ESF) - Objective 2

The challenge posed by converting those regions, employment areas and urban communities in industrial decline includes that of dealing with the environmental degradation to be found within them. This means reversing the trend of urban decay, removing the dereliction of former industrial areas now decommissioned, dealing with contaminated land, and upgrading the working and lived-in environments in order that enterprises and communities are attracted to them again.

The environment is a key component in the future prospects for these regions. As such, support for these regions should include support for environmental activities including the development of training initiatives concerned with: mechanisms for dealing with derelict and contaminated land; the restoration of the built environment; the provision of open space and recreational areas; and renovation and maintenance not only of buildings of historical interest, but also the main housing stock.

Combating Unemployment (ESF) - Objectives 3 and 4

Both the young and the long-term unemployed, the particular targets of Community policy in relation to the unemployed, stand to benefit from activities linked to the environment. These benefits are both direct and indirect. Directly they can gain both short and long term employment, as well as experience to develop their competence at work thus improving their employment prospects. Indirectly, because environmental protection and management can help conserve economic resources (for example in relation to less developed regions) and can help to regenerate economic activity (for example in relation to declining industrial regions) the prospects for the unemployed are also improved.

This is not to say of course that environmental protection in itself creates large numbers of net additional jobs - although it is undoubtedly creating new industries in clean technologies, environmental monitoring, etc. Nor however, should the role of environment in relation to employment be underestimated.

Agricultural Adjustment and the Development of Rural Areas (FEOGA, ESF, ERDF) - Objective 5b

The adjustment of agricultural support mechanisms will produce fundamental changes in the nature of agricultural production and in land use. Farm economies will come under increasing pressure as will those of workers in associated industries. Equally, there will be challenges in finding ways to manage the land for the purposes of conservation amenity and landscapes. New farming techniques must be developed and diffused. Within this context, the role of training to prepare for these changes, and to find solutions to some of the problems posed is apparent.

5.2.2.2 ENVIREG and MEDSPA

Two recent Commission initiatives are directly concerned with environment.

ENVIREG, a Community initiative of regional measures geared to environmental problems, was proposed by the Commission in 1989. It has been allocated an indicative total of 500 million ECUs for the period 1990-1993 and will be financed from the Structural Funds. The programme will concentrate on all coastal areas of Objective 1 regions and the Mediterranean regions in Objective 2 and 5b areas.

The following operations will be eligible:

- sewage disposal and treatment infrastructures in urban centres, generally with a population of less than 100,000;

- the treatment of solid waste in the same urban centres;

- port facilities intended to prevent hydrocarbon pollution;

- the protection of biotopes.

The Commission will also assist efforts to solve the problems caused by toxic and dangerous industrial waste in all Objective 1 regions. ENVIREG is administered by the Directorate General for Regional Policy, DG XVI.

MEDSPA is administered by the (Directorate General for Environment, Nuclear Safety and Civil Protection) (DG XI) and is concerned with the Protection of the Mediterranean Environment and applies both to Community and non-Community countries. The MEDSPA programme includes; demonstration projects which link upstream R + D to downstream investment or large scale applications; projects designed to raise public awareness; and technical assistance.

5.2.2.3 Research and Development

There is a very important link between training, specifically those kinds of training activity described here, and research and development. This is because training is central to the process of improving the utilisation of results in that:-

* training helps co-ordination and co-operation through exchange and increased dialogue

* training increases information dissemination relating to scientific and technological research

* training encourages mobility of academic and industrial research staff

* training encourages technology transfer.

Training therefore needs to accompany the Commission's and other R & D programmes in the environmental field. This includes firstly "Community Operations in the Environment" **(ACE)** such as **ACE** Clean Technologies (Directorate General for Environment, Nuclear Safety and Civil Protection (DGXI)). Also, within the **Framework Programme on Research and Development,** it includes the programme for

Science and Technology for Environmental Protection **(STEP)** which came into force in late 1989 and runs until 1992 with the objective of providing scientific and technical support for the Community's environmental policy, particularly preventative policy (Directorate General for Science Research and Development - DGXII)). Finally, there are, within the Framework Programme, other research and development programmes with important environmental components; for example research into energy derived from waste within the **JOULE** Programme; and **REWARD** (Recycling Waste Research and Development).

5.2.2.4   Enterprise

First, this includes operations in support of an enterprise policy for the Community. On the one hand, the formation of new businesses dealing in environmental technologies/activities is to be encouraged and training can help in this process. Thus enterprise in relation to environmental protection should be encouraged and supported where possible, with training, help and advice. The mechanism for delivering support will be the new Business and Innovation Centres (BIC's).

On the other hand, greater environmental awareness within industry is a fundamental step towards industry taking responsibility for the pollution it causes. Information and its dissemination are the key factors here, and one mechanism for helping to disseminate information are the **Euro Info Centres** in each Member State.

Environment should therefore be a component in training and support for enterprise; in terms of information provision on products, legislative controls, etc; in terms of management and vocational training for SME's; in terms of technology transfer and innovation; and in terms of the commercial uptake of R + D from research into the productive sector.

5.2.2.5   Tourism

The link between tourism and environment has already been made, specifically in relation to the less developed regions, but this link is highly relevant to the Community as a whole. Operations in the field of tourism could usefully incorporate training which focused on the synergy between environmental protection and quality, and the economic potential of tourism.

5.2.2.6   Training and Education

The potential also exists of course to introduce more environmental schemes within existing training programmes supported by the Commission and the **Task Force on Education, Vocational Training and Youth Policy.** Some actions have already been suggested. In 1989 the Youth Exchange Scheme **(YES)** has included 34 bilateral, 4 trilateral and 7 multinational exchanges with an environmental theme and the Young Workers Exchange Programme also include an environmental project. Both the **ERASMUS** programme for university students and the **COMETT** programme for education and training in technology have also supported exchanges between universities, and universities and industry, concerned with environmental research and technologies.

5.2.3   European Investment Bank

The EIB is the main financial institution of the European Community, concerned with financing economic development both within and beyond the Community's borders. Concern for the conservation of natural resources and environmental protection has long been characteristic of the EIB's leading activities. Since 1984, all projects submitted to the Bank have been subject to a detailed appraisal regarding the environmental consequences of the proposed investment. Increasingly, the EIB is financing projects specifically concerned with environmental protection.

EIB lending for environmental purposes has increased in recent years. The Bank is currrently engaged in a joint initiative with the World Bank to combat environmental pollution in the Mediterranean. The Integrated Mediterranean Programme is reviewing the investment needs and priorities in water supply and effluent treatment, industry and energy, agriculture and land-use, and shipping pollution. In addition, the study is concerned with identifying financial and administrative constraints, providing cost estimates and making recommendations on sources of international finance for a comprehensive regional environmental protection programme. The study aims to set the context within which the Bank will finance projects within the region.

These figures relate to projects where environmental considerations have played a determining role in the decision of finance. Including projects for which environmental considerations were important but secondary in the decision to finance, as is the case for investment in geo-thermal and hydro-electric power plants, district heating, road schemes and noise reduction at airports, the lending figure for projects with an environmental component would be significantly higher.

The Bank has its own Technological Advisory Board which advises on such aspects as the abatement of industrial air emissions, the quality of the natural aquatic environment, and conservation and landscaping. As such, the Bank is a major client for EIAs, ecosystem surveys and monitoring and analysis.

Within the European Community loans of ECU 1.7 billion were advanced in 1989 for projects concerned with environmental protection and quality of life, compared with ECU 1.2 billion ($1 billion) in 1988. Of this, ECU 899 million ($691 million) was for water and wastewater treratment schemes in Italy, Spain, UK, West Germany, Ireland, Denmark and Greece; ECU 651 million ($500 million) went to air pollution and the treatment of municipal and industrial wastes; ECU 178 million ($137 million) was given over to enhancing the urban environment.

5.2.4   Business Support Networks

A subset of the programmes and initiatives which the Commission support at Community level are those designed to support the business development of SMEs, through the setting up of business support networks. Examples of these networks include:

- Sprint (primarily support to business advisors who are encouraging technology transfer between SMEs);

- BC-Net (a computerised network of European business advisors);

- EBN (European business and innovation network, developing regional centres to provide business support to SMEs developing innovative technology based projects);

- EIC (Europen Information Centres providing information to SMEs on a wide range of matters);

- NETT (a network for environmental technology transfer between subscribing members).

These networks have a number of common attributes. First, they already exist to provide support to SMEs, and have mature network organisations. Secondly, the networks draw upon available business advisory services (financial, management, marketing, technical, personnel, training) to support SMEs in their development. Thirdly, they recognise the critical importance of supporting and encouraging innovative and technological development. Fourthly, they recognise the value of diffusing experience between Member States and different companies. Fifthly, they recognise the potential benefits of encouraging SME collaboration between Member States.

These attributes mean that those support networks are ready made vehicles for the encouragement of environmental training, by stimulating awareness and supporting the provision of training services, in the context of improving the commercial performance of SMEs.

Moreover, these networks provide the basis for the Social Partners to consider ways of encouraging the improvement in environmental performance amongst their Member companies and their member workforces. The need to recognise the limited resources of SMEs to develop training, and the importance of developing company-wide environmental management responses, and the value of technical innovation in their responses, place a premium on the attributes possessed by these networks.

The Social Partners can encourage and coordinate the use of these networks amongst their members and play a pivotal role in stimulating the improved environmental performance of SMEs, see Sections 5.7. to 5.11.

5.3   The International Labour Organisation

The International Labour Organisation (ILO) was founded in 1919 to advance the cause of social justice and to contribute to universal and lasting peace. The ILO's structure is unique in that representatives of workers, employer and government participate in the International Labour Conference and the Governing Body of the ILO as well as in many of its regional meetings. The ILO has established codes of international labour standards in the form of Conventions and Recommendation relating to a wide range of social issues: freedom of association, employment and training policy, conditions of work, social security, industrial relations.

5.3.1 The Role of the ILO

A great deal of ILO's work consists of the provision of advice and technical assistance to individual countries in the fields of training and employment.

The ILO's involvement in environmental training has been undertaken in the framework of its traditional programmes, mainly in the developing countries, and has been fairly limited. However, the ILO considers this to be an area which could be expanded within its wide range of national and regional training programmes.

Currently the ILO does not have a formal environmental training policy. However, an interdepartmental Working Group is currently preparing a strategy to inform policy and is examining the role which the ILO might potentially play. The following issues will be addressed by the Group:

- the priority to be given to developing training programmes directed at anticipatory or preventative activities rather than alleviative programmes

- the need to develop a training programme for worker organisations comparable to those devised for employer organisations;

- the need to develop support activities to ensure that environmental specialists at the national and regional level are fully aware of _general_ training issues and problems which might apply to environmental training;

- the integration of environmental issues into training activities related to other ILO programmes, eg, co-operatives, labour intensive public works projects.

In the ILO publication, Environment and the World of Work (39) significant emphasis was given to the role of training in the context of the achievement of environmentally sound and sustainable development. The paper highlights that employers will be affected by changing skills requirements related to environmental management and the appreciation of new environmental technologies, processes and procedures.

Given the number of international organisations involved in the environment the ILO has sought to define clearly its responsibilities in relation to the environment and environmental training (39). One of the ILO's current objectives is to strengthen employer and worker organisations so that they can deal more effectively with these issues themselves, eg, the ILO/UNEP programme which aims to support environmental activities within the employer organisations. A similar programme is about to be launched for worker organisations throughout the world. The programme will reinforce the ongoing activities of the Worker Education Programme aimed at integrating environmental considerations within many of its traditional training programmes. In order to support the development of environmental education and training the ILO is developing a new environmental training strategy. The ILO is aiming to integrate environmental training into its training activities related to other ILO programmes, for example at the Turin Centre and the International Institute for Labour Studies.

The ILO is currently undertaking a study of environmental training. The study will carry out seven case studies from the industrialised countries, some European, in order to examine how environmental training is integrated into general training programmes and more specifically to assess the effectiveness of environmental training both in terms of labour market effectiveness and the affect on the environment. The study will look at the provision in industry and in government institutions. The study, which is funded by the German Government, is scheduled to be completed at the end of 1991.

The ILO also aims to increase its activities in the collection and analysis of information regarding the relationship between employment and the environment. Actions may include the establishment of a multi-disciplinary research team which has the remit to analyse the potential employment and training effects of environmental problems and policies currently under discussion. The ILO could also provide a forum for tripartite technical meetings and meetings of experts to facilitate a detailed examination of sector-specific environmental impacts. There have been recent examples of joint statements on environmental policy being established by Trade Unions organisations and employer organisations (eg, The Netherlands, Italy) which suggests that this is an area in which the ILO's tripartite structure provides an appropriate forum in terms of seeking compliance on many of the key issues.

5.3.2 The ILO and its Tripartite Role

The ILO's unique tripartite structure also provides an opportunity for the views of the Social Partners to be reflected in other international forum and thus to be taken account of in environmental policy discussions. The ILO, through its tripartite structure, has an opportunity to play an active role in raising general environmental awareness and it intends to collaborate more closely with other bodies working in the field of environmental training.

In its report, Environment and the World of Work (39), the ILO discussed the role to be played by a number of key actors;

5.3.2.1 The Role of Governments

The report (39) determined the key role to be played by government organisations, namely the Ministries of Labour and Employment, as being the provision of support for the assessment of manpower and training needs. Once skill shortages have been identified, Ministries may be able to promote a co-ordinated approach to the provision of training at all levels: within enterprises (formal and on-the-job training) and local communities as well as regionally and nationally. It recommends that Ministries should encourage training institutions to integrate environmental considerations into all vocational and management training programmes. This would have practical and cost effective implications for environmental protection in the future. The report also advocates the incorporation of general environmental awareness into public service training as well as into inspection and monitoring services. It stresses that requirements of governments to monitor and enforce environmental legislation, standards and guide lines will require new technologies and new administration and management techniques which will be met through training.

5.3.2.2 The Role of Employers Organisations

The report (39) cited employers and their organisations as being key partners in the growing effort to protect and rehabilitate the environment. Given the growing awareness of "corporate environmentalism", it is essential that employers are given adequate training in order to ensure the achievement of environmental policies. It also believes that employer organisations should play an important role in promoting environmental awareness among these members, through the provision of information and training and that they should integrate environmental training, especially for managers within their traditional training activities. The ILO also believe that employer organisations have a role to play in the exchange of information both between members and with other employer organisations, regionally and internationally.

5.3.2.3 The Role of Workers Organisations

Given the relatively recent recognition of the link between the working environment and the external environment and given the employment impacts of environmental policies, workers and their organisations have become increasingly involved in environmental issues and environmental training both at enterprise level, as well as through their national, regional, international and sector based organisations. At enterprise level, the ILO (39) considered that regarding environmental training, workers should participate in the design and development of training programmes for workers and management to provide environmental awareness and the skills necessary to meet environmental objectives; in particular, Health and Safety representatives or environmental representatives should receive adequate environmental training.

5.4 Organisation for Economic Co-operation and Development (OECD)

The Organisation for Economic Co-operation and Development was established on 30 September 1961 in Paris. Its objectives are to help member countries promote economic growth, employment and improved standards of living, and to help promote the sound and harmonious development of the world economy. An Environment Committee and various specialised groups are responsible for the economic and policy aspects of OECD's work on environmental affairs. Their work has led to agreements setting out guiding principles on the international trade aspects of environmental policies, and other agreements have been adopted concerning the use of environmentally dangerous chemicals, noise, waste, pollution, energy production, coastal management, the transboundary movement of hazardous waste and accidents including hazardous substances, transfrontier pollution and the polluter-pays principle.

5.4.1 Business and Industry Advisory Committee to OECD (BIAC)

The Business and Industry Advisory Committee was founded on 9 March 1962 in Paris to represent business and industry at OECD and to express opinions at OECD on all questions of common interest. BIAC's activities in the environmental field are co-ordinated by the BIAC Environmental Committee, the BIAC Chemicals Committee and task forces on accidents involving hazardous substances, and on hazardous wastes.

The majority of BIAC's input on the question of environmental management and training takes places through the participation of company representatives in OECD Workshops and Conferences.

BIAC has frequent informal consultations with the OECD Secretariat on OECD programmes and holds formal consultations with OECD Committees or working groups on the occasion of OECD meetings. Some of the recent OECD activities (1987-1988) on which BIAC has been consulted include: the systematic investigation of existing chemicals; chemical testing and assessment; chemicals export notification; accidents involving hazardous substances; the transfrontier movement of hazardous wastes; economic techniques and instruments in environmental policy.

5.4.2   Centre for Educational Research and Innovation

The OECD Centre for Educational Research and Innovation is currently undertaking a project on Environment and School Initiatives. Its objective is to evaluate current provision of environmental education within and across OECD member countries. The Programme aims to formulate environmental education policy on the basis of this evaluation.

5.5   UNEP

UNEP's Industry and Environment Office (IEO) office was set up in 1975 in order to bring industry, government and non-governmental organisations together to work towards environmental sound forms of industrial development. It seeks to:

* define and encourage the incorporation of environmental criteria in industrial development;

* formulate and facilitate the information of principles and procedure to protect the environment;

* promote the use of safe, low and non-waste technologies;

* stimulate the exchange of information and experience on environmentally sound forms of industrial development throughout the world.

The IEO seeks to provide access to practical information to industry and to develop co-operative, on-site action and information exchange, backed up by regular follow-up and assessment. It encourages all sectors of industry to adopt and implement environmentally sound policies at all levels in the enterprise. IEO's work programme is divided into four principal divisions: the publications of technical guides; technical co-operation; training; and information transfer. In addition, the IEO seeks to promote environmentally sound forms of industrial development through, for example, the introduction of awards for environmental achievements by industrial concerns, and meetings designed to promote industrial action on environmental issues at the highest level.

In 1989 and 1990 it has been concentrating its training activities in the field of:-

- Hazardous waste management; workshops in Western Asia and Asia and the Pacific;

- Prevention and response to technological accidents in the framework of an Awareness and Prepareness for Emergencies at Local Level (APELL) programme workshops in Bahrain, Brazil, Latin America and the Caribbean.

In addition:

- In co-operation with ILO and with industry associations in developing countries, it is continuing to organise training activities for business leaders;

- In co-operation with UNIDO, training activities on industry and environment issues have been developed in the University of Tampere (Finland) and in the USSR;

- Together with Tufts University (USE) and INSEAD (Institute European d'Administration des Affaires), UNEP/IEO organised a seminar in 1990 on the integration of the environmental dimension in the business schools.

- More generally, at headquarters, the Environmental Education and Training Unit (EETU) is organising activities to increase general awareness of environmental issues, and this might include industry targets.

5.6 CEDEFOP

The European Centre for the Development of Vocational Training (CEDEFOP) was set up in Berlin in 1976. It assists the Commission of the European Communities in the development of initial and continuing vocational training. It also acts as a European forum for institutions and experts concerned with vocational training, enabling them to exchange ideas and experiences and harmonise conceptual and particular initiatives.

CEDEFOP is currently working in conjunction with the European Commission to establish a European directory of occupational profiles. Within the framework of this programme CEDEFOP will undertake a number of studies on the development of occupational groups in the Member States and on existing and emerging occupational profiles. CEDEFOP is also carrying out a programme on the comparability of vocational training qualifications for the EC. In 1990, in recognition of the importance of environmental protection and thus environmental training, CEDEFOP launched a pilot study designed to examine the degree to which, and the way in which, environmental problems and the environmental challenge are reflected in the occupational profiles and qualification requirements of personnel in the metal and chemical industries (25). CEDEFOP expects to increase its research activities in the field of environmental training.

5.7 The International Chamber of Commerce

The International Chamber of Commerce was founded in 1919 to establish a permanent non-governmental organisation of world business. The ICC represents the business community at international level though the promotion of world trade based on free and fair competition and the harmonisation of trade practice and terminology.

5.7.1 The Commission on Environment

The International Chamber of Commerce is very actively involved in environmental issues. It set up its Commission on the Environment in 1978. Its aim are to:

- provide a world-wide forum through which representatives of all business and industrial sectors can meet to exchange views on environmental issues and developments;

- represent the business community at UNEP and other international agencies concerned with environmental issues;

- formulate environmental policies on technical issues.

Hence the Commission on Environment has two roles:

1. to assist the business community to make a constructive contribution to the solution of environmental problems; and

2. to ensure that business views are taken into account by the intergovernmental organisations concerned with the environment.

The Commission on the Environment has a membership of approximately 100 businesses from 30 industrialised and developing countries. It is currently organising a second World Industry Conference on Environmental Management (WICEM II) which is to be held in Rotterdam in April 1991. The Commission on Environment in conjunction with other international organisations is also active in providing environmental guidelines to industry which act as codes of conduct which are applicable to industry in all sectors and countries. These guidelines have been revised in 1990 and now include a waste supplement. The Commission also arranges conferences on the environment and has launched initiatives to promote the level of public information that is available from companies regarding their environmental performance. It has also prepared a paper on environmental auditing.

5.7.2   International Environmental Bureau

The International Environmental Bureau (IEB) was set up in 1986 with the objective of assisting SMEs in developed countries and companies generally in the less developed countries to improve their environmental performance. The IEB aims to disseminate information regarding technologies and management techniques aimed at solving environmental problems and thereby encourage the adoption of these successful innovations by the business community. Principally, it functions as a trans-industry clearing house for environmental **management** information. The IEB complements the policy work of the Commission on the Environment.

5.8 BAUM

In West Germany a number of well known industrial companies have got together to form the German Environmental Management Society (BAUM : The Bundesdeutscher Arbeitskreis fur Umweltbewubtes Management). Its objectives are to adopt the Integrated System of Environmental Business Management through an on-going exchange of information and to encourage the practical introduction of environmental protection measures in member firms. The Integrated System of Environmental Business Management was developed by a German company, Winter & Sohn, manufacturers of diamond tools in Hamburg which declared environmental protection as one of its corporate aims. It incorporates all sectors of company activity:

* apprentice and adult training and re-training
* programme policy
* research and development
* materials management, production and research
* new plant construction.

BAUM has decided to concentrate initially on the question of low pollution material management with a view to persuading companies to take as their procurement criteria, not just quality, service, price and delivery time, but also the issue of environmental acceptability.

BAUM's aim are:

* to strengthen the businessman's sense of environmental responsibility;
* to pass on environmental business know-how;
* to organise exchanges of information from firm to firm;
* to co-ordinate pilot and research projects;
* to extend suppliers environmental liability;
* to develop a career profile in business ecology;
* to complement the work of other institutions.

BAUM is a member of INEM (the International Network for Environmental Management) which is a global network of independent business organisations devoted to environmental education and problem solving. INEM's role is to provide a support network to help industry adopt a more pro-active response to environmental issues. Through INEM, BAUM is linked to other national members such as ARBRE (Association pour le Respect de Bioecologie dans les Realisations des Enterprises) in France and TREE (Technology Research and Enterprise for the Environment) in the UK which was established in 1990.

Coventry Local Authority in the UK has established a Pollution Protection Panel which now operates under the auspices of TREE. The Panel is represented by local industry and the regulatory authorities and facilitates communication between the authority, industry and the regulatory authorities.

SMEs, in particular, are in need of better information on pollution control and therefore benefit from increased information from control authorities. Local authority schemes such as Pollution Prevention Panels can act as a catalyst for the promotion of environmental good practice and information exchange. The objectives of the Panel are:

- to prevent pollution of land, water and air, including noise pollution, by the most practically effective and economic means;

- to establish liaison between industry and the public authorities dealing with pollution control;

- to disseminate information relating to environmental pollution;

- to establish a body of experience and expertise from which members can obtain advice;

- to provide interpretation of current legislation and advice on proposed legislation;

- to develop mutual trust between industry and the public authorities dealing with pollution control by treating all information in strict confidence;

- to represent local industry to government by responding to consultation documents.

5.9 Union of Industrial and Employer's Confederations of Europe (UNICE)

The Union of Industrial and Employer's Confederations of Europe was established in 1985 and recognised as official spokesman for European business and industry vis-a-vis the European institutions. It is composed of 33 member federations from 22 European countries with a permanent Secretariat based in Brussels. UNICE's purpose is to promote the common professional interests of the firms represented by its members; to provide the framework within which member organisations can co-ordinate their European policies; to ensure that European decision-makers take UNICE's policies and opinions fully into account. It has a special Expert Commission on Environment.

5.10 European Trade Union Confederation

The European Trade Union Confederation environmental policy emphasises the Prevention Principle determining that industrial and social policy should be aimed at the protection of the environment rather than at enacting responses to environmental damage. The ETCU is an advocate of the Polluter Pays Principle and is committed to the implementation of "state-of-the-art" technology with regard to best available technologies. The ETUC calls for measures to allow workers to effectively influence the environmental impact of investments and the reorganisation of production processes at plant, company, regional, national and European level. In this context the ETUC states that the worker should be granted the right to pursue further education activities in the environmental protection field. Furthermore the ETUC stipulates that industry should increase the number of personnel responsible for environmental protection and that trade union representatives be able to to approach independant experts so that an assessment of company's environmental policy and environmental impact can be made. Trade Unions policy statements of this type serve to raise priorities relating to the environment and provide a mechanism by which to change the environmental culture within an industrial plant or company. It also provides a means by which its members may be regularly involved in the development of national and international environmental policies.

5.11   Industry Associations

5.11.1   Lead Development association (LDA)

The Lead Development Association was founded in 1946 and is supported principally by lead mining companies and lead metal producers. It is non-profit making and exists to promote the use of lead in all forms and to represent the lead industry at national and international levels. The Association maintains an up-to-date library and provides technical advice on all aspects of lead, including health and safety and environmental issues.

5.11.2   The European Chemical Industry Federations (CEFIC)

The European Chemical Industry Federation is the recognised voice of the European Chemical industry - an industry which employs more than 2 million people and accounts for one third of world production. Located in Brussels, CEFIC is the forum through which the European chemical industry co-ordinates its positions and approaches vis-a-vis the international bodies and authorities which have an influence on its business environment. Formed in 1972, it now has as members, the National Chemical Federations of 15 European countries, and represents the interests of 34 major companies working in various sectors of the chemical industry. Issues which CEFIC tackles on its members' behalf include international trade, environment, health and safety, transport and distribution of chemicals, energy and raw material supplies, information and statistical surveys, and many others of areas of interest to the European chemical industry.

CEFIC considers the protection of the environment to be an integral part of good business practise. In response to the Environmental Guidelines for the World Industry established by ICC (see Section 5.7) the CEFIC has prepared its own guidelines in order to assist chemical companies translate the principles into practise. CEFIC has emphasised the requirement for companies to provide the public with information regarding the potential environmental impacts of the companies operations. Specifically CEFIC recommends that every chemical plant should apppoint a person or persons responsible for contact with the public and external bodies and that this person should be appropriately trained in environmental issues and in communication skills. CEFIC also recommends that chemical plants should implement communication programmes which might include environment news releases, educational visits or the mailing of fact sheets. All of these initiatives demand an environmental awareness by personnel throughout the company in order that the company may respond adequately to the environmental concerns of the community.

CEFIC's primary activities in relation to environmental eduction and training are: issuing guidelines on best practise for industry; promoting environmental good practice; and providing information on environmental legislation and policy, health and safety and general environmental issues. CEFIC has established an Environment Protection Committee and a number of Working Parties which are active in contributing to EC Policy Formulation and implementation. For example, the Working Party for the Protection of Water represents the chemical industry view in the development of Directive 76/464/EEC.

The Working Party on Air Pollution contributed to the implementation of Directive 84/360 for the reduction of air pollutant emissions by particularly focusing on the concept of "Best Available Technology". Regarding Waste Management, CEFIC has been active in preparing guidelines on industrial waste management and in 1989 organised a seminar on the management of liquid organic-halogenated wastes.

The main type of training provision is the organisation of seminars and conferences on regulatory development and adaption to new requirements and CEFIC has increasingly become involved in the preparation of codes of practice and guidelines for industry.

CEFIC, therefore, has a major role to play in promoting environmental good practice amongst its members and in the provision of formal advice and information. It also plays a major role in policy formulation at EC level and thus provides a forum by which the views and concerns of the chemical industry are considered.

5.11.3   International Iron and Steel Institute (IISI)

The International Iron and Steel Institute was the first of the international industry associations to deal solely with one industry. It was founded in 1967 in New York with headquarters in Brussels. IISI is a non-profit-making research organisation dealing with various aspects of the international steel industry. Its aims are to provide a forum for free and open discussion of steel industry problems; to undertake research as directed; to collect, evaluate and disseminate statistics and information; to effect and maintain liaison with other organisations relating to steel; and to promote the use of steel. The Standing Committee on Environmental Affairs was formed in 1973.

5.11.4 International Petroleum Industry Environmental Conservation Association (IPIECA)

The International Petroleum Industry Environmental Conservation Association is an association of petroleum companies and petroleum industry associations founded in March 1974. Its remit includes the examination of environmental and health and safety issues in the content of their impact on the petroleum industry. Its principal purposes are to act as the industry's forum for considering these matters and to be its focus for interaction with UNEP and, selectively, other inter-governmental and international organisations active in this field.

5.12 Co-operation Between the Social Partners at International Level

This section has identified a large number of international organisations with an active role in improving environmental performance; this generally involve the raising of environmental awareness, thus encouraging companies to undertake environmental training.

It is clear from the previous discussion that the Social Partners have a critical role to play in improving environmental performance. In relation to the role of, and co-operation between, the Social Partners, the International Labour Organisation (ILO) has an important job to play through its tripartite structure and its commitment to the development of employment and training policy. The formal policy development which the ILO is currently undertaking with respect to environmental training represents an important opportunity for international organisations, particularly the Commission and the Foundation, to define, more closely, the ways of achieving greater co-operation between the Social Partners.

The important role of the Foundation in developing policy aims and objectives therefore complements the work of the ILO and the other international organisations. Many of the very active organisations, eg the ILO and the ICC, have a worldwide perspective. The Foundation has an important role to play in ensuring that the policy development which these organisations stimulate is applied within the Community, and that models of co-operation, developed at a worldwide level, are applied and developed within the Community. Furthermore, whilst there does not appear to be any major areas of omission from the policy debate there is considerable potential for overlap, between the organisations. To the extent that the Foundation takes an "holistic" approach to environmental training issues, there is scope to clarify and co-ordinate policy development in this field.

An essential part of the international response to secure improved environmental performance is the work of the Commission. The wide range of programmes and business support networks which are available to SMEs, provide an opportunity for the Foundation to secure a greater awareness amongst the Social Partners of the availability and value of these programmes, enabling the Foundation and international organisations to support Social Partners at a national and regional level. Moreover, the clear recommendations for action, made in Section 5.2, for the Commission implies a major role for the Foundation in developing and formulating these actions into realisable policy objectives.

6.0 THE ROLE OF NATIONAL AND REGIONAL ORGANISATIONS

6.1 Introduction

This section of the report provides a review of the potential role which the various national and regional organisations have in developing environmental training and improving the environmental performance of SMEs. The analysis draws upon the discussions at the international workshop (Annex D), the observations made by consultees during the mission to Italy (Annex F), the response to the survey of different organisations in Europe (Annex C) and the wider experience of ECOTEC.

6.2 A Review of Organisations

The research by ECOTEC in this study has considered the range of different organisations who can directly contribute to the development of environmental training in industry and in the regulatory agencies. Training and regulatory agencies and Social Partners were asked in the survey to consider the range of organisations and to give their view as to which organisations offered the best opportunity for improving the environmental performance of SME's.

The views canvassed to date, which are summarised in Table 6.1, suggest that the most significant opportunity lies in using training agencies to develop environmental training. Regulatory agencies are not seen as providing the best opportunity for developing environmental training.

It should be stressed that this ranking is presented only as a guide to the collective views which have been expressed to ECOTEC. As such it disguises the individual views expressed and the quite different ranking which some individual consultees suggested. We consider below the potential role of the different organisations.

6.3 Private Sector Consultants

Private sector consultants are taken to include not only training consultants but also management and environmental consultants. In this section we differentiate between environmental training and management services provided by private sector

TABLE 6.1 :   ORGANISATIONS AND THEIR RELATIVE IMPORTANCE FOR DEVELOPING ENVIRONMENTAL TRAINING

Organisation	Ranking
Private Sector Consultants [1]	1
Training Agencies [2]	2
Employer Organisations	3
Regulatory Agencies	4
Health & Safety Agencies	5
Research Institutions	6
Trade Unions	7
Business Support Channels (Banks, etc)	8

Source : ECOTEC Survey

Notes :   [1]:   This includes management and training consultancies and all services provided outside of the formal public sector provision

[2]:   This includes only the formal public sector provision of education and training services.

consultants and services provided for a fee by quasi-independent non-profit making institutes, which are usually research based. These latter services are considered with respect to research institutes, in Section 6.8.

The role of private sector consultants is clearly seen as being very important in developing environmental training and in providing environmental management services, including, for example, environmental audits, monitoring and analysis services and strategic management advice. In the context of improving the environmental performance of SME's, with their observed reluctance to develop in-house responses and the often limited public sector provision of environmental training, private sector consultants have a major role to play.

There are a number of issues associated with the developing role of the private sector in responding to the requirement for improved environmental performance by SME's. Firstly, to the extent that the private sector provides environmental services to the SME, there is a requirement for the private sector to possess the relevant skills and competences. The range of skills and competences which are required have already been discussed in relation to the skills requirement for environmental management and the necessary company-wide responses, in Section

3.0. These are demanding and will require the private sector to acquire new skills. Thus, there remains a training requirement, not of SMEs but of consultants.

Secondly, the requirement to train consultants is currently being met through informal training (seminars/conferences) and the recruitment of new post-graduate/graduates with environmental management competences. This places emphasis on the long-term requirement for the development of environmental education. In the short term there is considerable uncertainty over whether consultants have available or can quickly develop the appropriate skills.

Thirdly, while consultants may advise firms on environmental management responses in the short term, the need for SMEs to develop in-house competences for environmental management will require direct training of SME personnel. There is anecdotal evidence from consultees that private sector training provision is increasing, and is particularly aimed at more senior management personnel. This provision is likely to highlight the need for training in the development of company-wide responses and stimulate the take-up of environmental training.

Fourthly, private sector consultants have a role to play in stimulating the appropriate networks of expertise in support of the necessary technology transfer which is an integral part of improving the environmental performance of SMEs. The need for new structures to enhance the relationship between SMEs and regulatory agencies, particularly at a time when the relationship is becoming more formalised, by adding information and training in the application of new technology and existing technology developed in other industries, is evident in the light of the analysis in Sections 3.0 and 4.0. The need for these new structures is also considered with respect to the role of the Social Partners and Business Support Networks, in Section 5.2.

6.4   Training Agencies

The most obvious organisations with a role to play in developing environmental training are the formal national and regional training agencies, which have the necessary remit and infrastructure. Existing training services can be developed to incorporate the development of competences for environmental management.

However, there are a number of issues relating to the more formal development of training services, which are partly informed by the Italian mission and which need to be addressed if training agencies are to develop their role in this area. Firstly, there is only initial and preliminary research to define those competences required by personnel in SMEs and the regulatory agencies. The collaborative work with CEDEFOP, reported in Section 3.0, represents one of the most detailed pieces of work to-date in this respect. In order for training services to develop, a clear picture of the necessary competences is required.

Secondly, whilst there are moves towards the development of common vocational qualifications, which are extensively developed in countries such as Germany but hardly recognised in Southern Member States, there are still very few commonly agreed standards for the required competences for environmental management. Moreover, the necessary accreditation systems for securing the agreed standards have still to be developed.

Thirdly, the multi-disciplinary nature of environmental management means that the development of training courses needs to draw upon a wide range of expertise. This has implications for the time and resources which are required to develop suitable training services. Thus the longer term development of training services may well complement the service being developed by private sector consultants.

Thus training agencies have a major programme of work to undertake in order to develop comprehensive environmental training services. The training agencies, particularly regional agencies, also have some responsibilities for encouraging the take-up of training services. For example, the Training and Enterprise Councils (TECs) in the UK have an important role to play in stimulating the awareness of SMEs and encouraging the take up of training services.

6.5 Employers Organisations

Employer organisations have an important role to play in the development of environmental training. There are a number of functions, building upon their spatial and sectoral coverage, which they can perform. Firstly, they can raise the awareness of their members to the need for, and benefit of, improved environmental management. Secondly, they can facilitate the exchange of information, between members, on the development of environmental management practices. Thirdly, they can co-ordinate and anticipate the training requirements of their members. Fourthly, they can assist in the development of accepted and accredited training provision. These functions may have a particular value if they build upon a level of trust and mutual understanding between members and the organisations.

The Mission to Italy identified training providers amongst the employer organisations. Generally, all the organisations felt that they provided an appropriate mechanism by which to promote environmental awareness and to encourage training. However, in terms of resources, the employer organisations felt that finances should be granted to industry by central or regional government. We give below three examples of the developing role of employer organisations in Italy.

6.5.1   Confindustria

Confindustria is the largest of the employer organisations in Italy. Confindustria is divided by industrial sector and by region. The priority given to environmental issues, and training in particular, varies both between sectors and regions. The Chemical Association for example, is the most active having run a number of conferences on environmental issues relating to the chemical industry. Policies are formulated at Headquarters which also functions as a central information point for the Regional divisions. Training is carried out by the Regional divisions.

Confindustria is currently focusing on three aspects of environmental education and training. The first is education in schools. It has recently produced a book for teachers to use in environmental teaching. The second is encouraging the formation of links between industry and universities. This reflects a general concern, which was expressed in the majority of interviews, over the gap that exists between the current research that is carried out in universities and its application to industry. Thirdly, Confindustria is involved in developing training courses.

Currently Confindustria is setting up an Institute of the Environment in Milan. The objective is to provide a central point for environmental issues for industry. This reflects a growing awareness in industry of the need to respond to increasing environmental demands. Currently, there is no such facility and it is evident from our discussions with training providers that such a facility is necessary.

6.5.2 Assolombardo

Within Confindustria it is the Regional divisions which are generally responsible for undertaking training. Assolombardo is the Lombardy Regional branch of Confindustria. Assolombardo, like Confindustria, is divided by industry sector. Its main functions are representing the political interests of its members and providing administrative assistance and technical advisory services. Assolombardo provides a number of environmental courses. These are either held in-house, or at Assolombardo offices. Courses are generally 32 hours in length and approximately 15 places are available. The courses cost £500.00 per capita. Course content covers: fire prevention, water pollution, waste and chemical impact. The courses are attended mainly by employees of SMEs.

Assolombardo identified the issue of resource constraint within SMes as a major inhibitor to the up-take of training. Labour constraints, for example, mean that SMEs are unable to allow personnel time off work for training. Hence Assolombardo, in recognition of this, is planning to arrange classes on the environment on Saturday and in the evenings. Regarding the financial constraints faced by SMEs, Assolombardo identified the need for SMEs to receive grants from the Region or from Central Government emphasising that employer organisations do not have the resources to allocate to this.

Assolambardo views the employer organisations as having a vital role to play in training provision. The discussion emphasised the need for the formulation of a national programme by Central Government but believed that such a programme would be most effectively administered through local employer organisations. The main strength of employer organisations is that they are in touch with the requirements of industry and that they have its trust.

6.5.3 Confapi

Confapi is an employer organisation for small companies which aims to protect the interests of its members against the political interests of large companies by parliamentary lobbying. It also campaigns for the provision of financial incentives for its members.

Confapi currently does not have a formal environmental training programme. However it expressed concern over the low emphasis placed on environmental management by small firms. Confapi considers training to be an effective means by which to increase the level of environmental awareness. It considers that the Government should implement a **national** training programme which should be administered through the employer organisations who understand the needs of industry and who have established regional networks through which such a programme could be effected.

Confapi has recently formed an agreement with the Trade Unions regarding a two year training programme for school leavers. Similar agreements, between Trade Unions and employer organisations, within the framework of a national programme, are considered to be an effective mechanism for promoting environmental training.

6.6 Regulatory Agencies

The role of regulatory agencies is one which is likely to vary significantly between Member States, depending upon a range of factors, particularly the relationship which the Agencies have with industry. The experience differs between Member States and is constantly evolving. Two broad types of relationship exist; the "policeman" role and the "teacher" role. In the policeman role the Agency adopts a strictly independent and objective enforcement role which reduces the degree to which the Agencies can co-operate and assist SMEs to develop environmental management responses through informal information and advice. In the teacher role, which has been the more typical and traditional role of Agencies, the Agencies play an important role in the exchange of information, between firms, on the most appropriate technical responses. They also provide direct advice and assistance to SMEs when applying for licenses and permits, and on monitoring and analytical procedures to measure compliance with the agreed standards and regulations.

This distinction in the role played by Regulatory Agencies is particularly evident between Member States. In Northern Member States (eg, Denmark, Germany) regulatory agencies adopt a more formal process of enforcement against agreed standards and regulations. In Southern Member States (Italy, Spain) there is a less formal relationship, reflecting the comparatively limited environmental legislation which has been developed. Agencies, particularly the national enforcement agencies, are likely to develop along the lines experienced in, for example, Germany, and adopt the "policeman" role. However, whilst this trend may be associated with less informal provision of training and advice the Agencies will still have an important formal role in communicating to industry advice on technical responses, particularly in the context of the growing adoption of BATNEEC. The Regulatory Agencies commission research and advise industry on the findings relating to the best available technologies.

Other factors which will affect the role of the Agencies include the degree to which the Agencies operate through a decentralised system of pollution control, the degree to which enforcement agencies have the resources and commitment to implement environmental regulations and develop industry responses, and the extent to which the Agencies themselves have trained personnel capable of liaising with, and advising, companies.

6.6.1 Regulatory Agencies in Italy

The potential role for regulatory agencies to provide informal advice and training has been examined with respect to the Agencies operating in Italy, and their characteristics. In Italy there is a highly regionalised system of enforcement, which has resulted in the respective enforcement responsibilities of the Ministry of Environment, the Regions, the Provinces and muncipalities, being poorly defined. This has lead to a situation where industry inspections and visits are sporadic and may be carried out by a number of organisations: the Ministry inspectors, the inspectors of the environmental departments of the Region or, more commonly, by local health units or the Police.

A further problem is that many of the Regional Departments have a very poor understanding of the environment and often incorporate environmental issues into Health and Safety considerations. The wide variation in environmental standards between the Regions is an area of grave concern to the Ministry, in term of how rigorously they carry out their Regulatory functions.

The potential training role is considered with respect to both the central Ministry of Environment and the Regional Departments.

6.6.1.1 The Ministry of Environment

The Ministry of Environment is not directly involved in the provision of formal training to industry. However it does commission a large volume of training and research programmes. It is very difficult to gain an overview of the work that is being carried out in the area of environmental education and training because, several departments have an interest in education and no one department has overall responsibility. Programmes within the Ministry are thus unco-ordinated with one department being unaware of what another is doing. This results in resources being used wastefully and ineffectively. There are a number of contributory factors. Firstly, the Ministry has only recently become operational (1986) and is currently facing pressing issues associated with the tightening of EC legislation and concerns over regulatory enforcement. Hence the machinery is not yet in place to implement an effective and co-ordinated education and training programme. Secondly, with regard to the need for co-ordination within the Ministry, the Mission highlighted the fact that specialists working in the respective departments often lack the general awareness which is essential to a more integrated, co-ordinated approach to environmental research and training. There would appear to be a need for general awareness within the despatch of the Ministry.

The consultations held during the Mission indicated that the Ministry of Environment could undertake the following roles:

i) the development of a national environmental training programme
ii) the provision of a central information point (the Ministry is currently investigating the setting up of an environmental database);
iii) the provision of finance, to encourage the uptake of training particularly to SMEs.

The consultees did not seem to think that the Ministry should be directly involved in provision of training, indicating that training is more effectively executed at a regional/local level.

6.6.1.2 <u>The Regions</u>

The Regions (local government) in Italy function independently of central government. Whilst the Regions are required by central Government to establish an environmental department which has responsibility for implementing environmental regulations, the extent to which this has been implemented varies from Region to Region. Lombardy Region, for example has established a large environmental department whereas other Regions have only a very limited number of staff with responsibility for the environment. The extent to which the Region becomes involved in the provision of training also varies considerably. We have explored the potential role through discussion with representatives of Lombardy Region, recognising that this is a Region which has given particular emphasis to its environmental responsibilities.

The Assesorate Ambiente in Lombardy Region (the environmental department) is very active in environmental training. It's activities are divided into the following subject areas:

- water
- air
- waste
- land reclamation.

Courses generally take the form of day release courses. Finance is sometimes provided by the Region itself. However the Region is of the view that there should be more finance available from central government.

The environmental department also runs an educational programme which is targeted at schools. A large number of resources are allocated to producing publications on environmental themes. The department carries out research and produces publications about the environment for teachers. The department also initiated an educational programme in the region called "Man and Nature". This programme was aimed at promoting environmental awareness within the community and was run in conjunction with Universities in Milan.

The discussion above highlights a number of issues for the development of informal training by regulatory agencies. Firstly, there will be, in a decentralised structure, variations in the extent of environmental training provision. Greater co-ordination by the central agency and recommendations to emmulate best practice would ensure a more uniform and extensive level of provision. Secondly, the Agency has a legal and professional stature which makes it well placed to exhort the value of improved environmental performance and training to SMEs and encourage environmental education. Thirdly, since training is not the primary responsibility of the Agency, funding of places and of SMEs would support greater provision and take-up of training services. Fourthly, the activities in Lombardy Region do provide evidence of the possibilities for an informal training role combined with regulatory responsibilities and represent an example for other regulatory agencies.

6.7 Health and Safety Agencies

Many environmental management practices are performed as part of the health and safety practice of the plant. Furthermore, health and safety agencies have been responsible for advising on the required competences and practices of industry and encouraging training to maintain health and safety standards. To the extent that the development of environmental management can been seen as directly analagous to the development of health and safety practices, these agencies can be seen as potential sources of advice on the development of training. However, such agencies are unlikely to be training providers. The health and safety responsibilities exercised in the workplace by trade unions is discussed in Section 6.9.

6.8 Research Institutions

A range of research institutions advise on the environmental impact of industry and have a detailed appreciation of the industrial processes which can give rise to pollution and the need for environmental management. They are also active in technical programmes to demonstrate new techniques for recycling and pollution control. However, this knowledge is diffuse amongst the different institutions and traditionally they have no remit, and therefore have not generally developed the requisite skills, to diffuse this research and to advise firms directly. To the extent that they can offer specialist and highly focused advice these institutions might be able to perform a consultancy role and to develop specialist courses.

6.8.1 Research Institutions in Italy

The importance of research institutions playing a role in the provision of environmental training was highlighted in consultations undertaken during the Mission. The Federation of Scientific and Technical Association (FAST) is an independent non-profit research institute which was founded in 1898 in Milan. FAST undertakes research in the fields of energy and resources, biotechnology, ecology, environmental training and professionalism. FAST was one of the first organisations in Italy to be involved in environmental training. The first course, run in 1982, was entitled "Managers and the Environment" and was targetted at personnel from the Public administration. It's general aim was to promote environmental awareness amongst managers. FAST has recently established the Association Analisti Ambientali (AAA) which is an inter-disciplinary group which aims to promote an inter-disciplinary approach to the environment. The AAA held a conference in 1989 on the need for an inter-disciplinary approach and has scheduled another one for 1991.

The courses provided by FAST cover a wide range of environmental subjects. Specifically, tailored courses are provided if requested by industry. The courses are attended mainly by employees from the Public Administration and large companies, although employees from SMEs also attend. Courses are generally tailored for managerial personnel. The number of places available depends on the content of the course. Courses on general environmental awareness offer a larger number of places, 30-35, whereas more technical courses average 21-30 places. Courses are provided either on-site or in-house at FAST's offices. The "Environment" and Information Technology is a new theme which is receiving increasing emphasis in courses. FAST also provides an advisory service on a range of environmental issues.

The Italian Society for the Environment (Castalia) is a research institution which was set up by the IRI group to faciliate collaboration between the State and the Public Administrations with regard to the protection and management of the environment.

Castalia focus on three activities:

- national resource management;
- industrial waste management;
- training and research.

Castalia founded an environmental school in 1987 which provides courses for personnel of the IRI group, private and public sector industries and research institutions. Castalia provides courses on a wide variety of subjects. The courses provided by Castalia are mainly of the FP type and are generally 4-5 weeks in duration. The primary subject area is water pollution although courses are provided on a wide range of environmental subjects: information technology and the environment; information technology for environmental analysis; environmental impact assessments; and management of natural resources.

These examples serve to show the potential of research institutions to play an important role in developing environmental training. They have a number of particular attributes. Firstly, because of the research base behind many of its courses and the professional experience of the training providers, courses are likely to have an up-to-date and high quality subject content. Secondly, because the research institutions are active in promoting research applications in industry the courses are likely to reflect the needs and requirement of industry for environmental management. Thirdly, because the research institutions have a high level of credibility they are likely to be attractive providers for SMEs. Fourthly, because the research institutions are not overtly commercial the costs of attending courses or providing materials is likely to be less than when using private sector consultants.

6.9   Trade Unions

As Social Partners the trade unions are able to perform the same types of functions as the employer organisations, discussed in Section 6.5. Of particular value is their ability to identify the training needs of the work force, particularly of technical and operative staff. Unions have played a major role in encouraging and demanding improved health and safety standards and there is evidence in this study that they are beginning to develop a similar role in stimulating improved environmental management. Direct training provision is not a likely role for trade unions. Moreover, trade unions have, generally, yet to fully respond to the requirement for environmental training; to recognise the environmental responsibilities of the workforce, and to encourage improved environmental performance in SMEs. This is evident from discussions with the trade unions in Italy.

There are three main Trade Unions in Italy: CGIL, CISL and UIL. Of these CGIL is the largest, with a membership of 5 million members. CISL has 3.5 million members and UIL 1.7 million members. These trade union organisations were united until a few years ago when they separated for political reasons. Each union is now politically affiliated.

The unions are structured to reflect the character of different industrial sectors and agencies. The structure of the Unions is such that the chemical association of one Union may form agreements with its counterpart in another Union. The Unions also unite for both the formulation of agreements with employer organisations and for the formulation of union policy. For example, they have recently formed agreements with the employer organisations regarding the level of training in industry (Law 46 in Italy stipulates that at least 10% of an employees time at work should be spent in education).

Consultation with CGIL, which is the only Trade Union in Italy to have established an environmental division, indicates that the majority of its activities relate to safety at work and industrial risk. However, the need for a national training programme was emphasised. CGIL is currently working on a proposal for a national programme for environmental training, in conjunction with the employer organisations. However the CGIL considers that this should be the responsibility of the Government as any agreement need to be universally accepted and enforced.

The role of Trades Unions, suggested by this study and recognised, for example, by the International Confederation of Free Trade Unions, is extensive and includes :

- recognition that in the long term only environmentally sound employment is going to be secure employment;

- pressure to act upon the direct experience of workers who are in daily proximity to environmental management problems, and who are well placed to identify particular problems and solutions;

- encouragement of the view that the environment is as much a part of work place responsibilities as health and safety, and exploitation of the existing health and safety structures, joint committees etc, to secure improved environmental preformance;

- support for regular plant inspections and environmental audits and assistance with the development of corporate environmental responses.

Thus trade unions have the potential to: raise the awareness of company management of the environmental responsiblity of the company; provide support for the necessary environmental responses; and assist to articulate the required skills and competences to which training provision needs to respond.

6.10 Business Support Channels

Traditionally, banks and other financial advisors have been a source of advice for SMEs. Moreover, public sector initiatives designed to improve the financial performance of SMEs, e.g., through funding technical, financial and marketing advice to firms, may also play a role in encouraging new environmental management practices. Such initiatives may include finance to investigate changes in the production process in order to minimise waste and finance for the use of training services directed at improving the range and level of competences of SMEs. To the extent that these channels are well developed this may obviate the need to develop new channels for advice and assistance. In the context of this study we have focused upon the potential for international networks; these are discussed in Section 5.2. However, there is growing interest in, for example, the UK, in examining ways of encouraging the take-up of cleaner and low waste technologies using existing regional and national programmes designed to stimulate business development and technology transfer, with environmental training as an integral element in the programme.

6.11 Co-operation Between SMEs and Regulatory Agencies

The scope for co-operation between SMEs and regulatory agencies exists to stimulate the take-up and provision of environmental training. The potential for greater co-operation exists particularly at the regional, rather than the national, level. However, the regulatory agencies, because it is not their central responsibility, encounter difficulty in financing the development of environmental training beyond their existing informal information and advisory role. Moreover, personnel in regulatory agencies are primarily trained in the management and execution of pollution control procedures rather than in the wider, multi-disciplinary skills required to shape corporate environmental management responses.

This section has shown the wide range of national and regional organisations which have a role to play in stimulating the take-up and provision of environmental training and the effect which institutional traditions and developments have on the precise role which the different organisation can play. One needs to be careful, therefore, of identifying common roles and solutions for particular organisations. The process of policy development should, therefore, focus on securing co-operation between SMEs and all national and regional organisations with the responsibility and commitment to secure improved environmental performance.

7.0 CONCLUSIONS

7.1 The Need for Improvements in Environmental Education and Training

This study confirms the view that inadequacies exist in the skills and competences of personnel concerned with environmental issues relating to industry. The existing level of education and training provision is deficient. SMEs, particularly, are unaware of their need for training manifested in a lack of demand for environmental education and training services. The absence of expressed demand for environmental education and training provision does not imply the absence of a need for such provision. Thus the policy response must not exclusively focus on the supply of such services but must also incorporate responses designed to stimulate the awareness of SMEs and the demand for education and training services.

The rationales for seeking improvements in the demand for, and supply of, environmental education and training services, (Section 2.7), are summarised prior to a discussion of conclusions which have emerged from this study relating to the types of improvements which should be considered.

- First, the provision and take-up of environmental education and training services are fundamental in ensuring the effective and efficient implementation of environmental policy and the meeting of environmental standards and regulations. Research in this, and other studies, demonstrates that there are insufficient numbers of trained personnel, in regulatory agencies and SMEs to implement current or proposed policies. Improvement in the delivery and take-up of environmental education and training services is essential to ensure that there are sufficient personnel with appropriate skills and competences to prepare, implement and enforce, current and emerging environmental legislation.

- Secondly, the take-up of environmental education and training services underpins diffusion and adoption of the scientific and technological change which is an integral part of developing improved and more sophisticated environmental management practices. Education and training related to the application of clean and low waste environmental technologies and procedures is essential if regulatory agencies and SMEs are to adopt preventive rather than reactive environmental management practices.

- Thirdly, the take-up of environmental education and training services assists SMEs in meeting integrated economic development and environmental quality objectives. The integration of these objectives is a prerequisite for achieving sustainable development. Such services are essential in areas of the Community which are characterised by fragile physical environments and/or degraded and damaged environments and where there is a parallel need to secure economic development objectives in order to reduce regional economic disparities. Developing and enhancing these services would then complement EC objectives which promote regional economic development.

- Fourthly, both provision and take-up of environmental education and training should be seen, in the light of the comments above, as central links between the various components which include: the preparation, monitoring and enforcement of environmental policy, legislation and programmes; and the development and adoption of new cleaner technologies and environmentally sensitive management practices in industry. Improvements in education and training services cannot be viewed in isolation from the development of sound, sustainable economic and environmental policy.

7.2 The Training Needs of Regulatory Agencies

Regulatory agencies, as discussed in Section 6.0, vary markedly between Member States and between regions in their characteristics and responsibilities. It is, therefore, difficult to summarise the detailed training needs of personnel in these agencies. However, broad areas of need have been identified in this study:

- training in monitoring and analysis of waste streams, involving measuring, analytical, and laboratory based tasks;

- training in emerging environmental legislation and the operation and enforcement of environmental standards, involving awareness and technical skills;

- training in the range of industry responses to environmental regulations and the assessment of the best technological and commercial response of the company, involving, technical, engineering, environmental and commercial skills.

Critical determinants of the relative emphasis to be given to each of these three areas in different agencies, include the nature of responsibilities for enforcement, the nature of the environmental problems and SME responses which are handled, and the nature of the agency's role with respect to industry, ie., "teacher" or "policeman".

7.3 The Training Needs of SMEs

The training needs of SMEs vary significantly between companies depending upon a range of circumstances including:

* environmental sensitivity of the area;
* environmental standards/regulations;
* enforcement practices;
* company size and activity;
* level of sophistication of management;
* current training provision.

The study has made a clear distinction between training needs and the demand for training, recognising that in many SMEs there is little recognition of the need for environmental training, which results from scarce management resources, and leads to a depressed level of expressed demand. Thus the paramount education and training need is to make senior managers in SMEs aware of their environmental responsibilities and to demonstrate, wherever possible, the commercial benefits of adopting improved environmental management practices and technologies and of the commercial costs of a "do nothing" response.

The study has examined the requirement for training in Sections 2.0 and 3.0. In summary the main requirements are for:

- training in emerging environmental legislation and its implications in terms of environmental standards, enforcement practices and the need for company wide environmental strategies;

- training in the necessary scientific, technological and engineering skills to ensure compliance with environmental standards and regulations, including measuring and monitoring of waste streams and the design and operation of pollution control and cleaner production techniques;

- training in the use of environmental audits, and the conduct of environmental impact and risk assessments. These techniques will be increasingly required, even by relatively small companies, to ensure improvements in environmental performance;

- education in the recognition and acceptance of corporate environmental responsibilities.

- education and training for all levels of personnel, from directors through to operatives. SMEs require existing personnel to develop new competences in environmental management.

- requirements exist both in the short-term and the long-term with an immediate requirement to improve the level of environmental awareness in SMEs.

7.4 Environmental Education and Training Responses

The discussion above (Sections 7.2 and 7.3) has identified the broad areas where training responses are required. It has to be recognised that the detailed training response will be influenced by a host of different factors, which vary between Member States and between regions. The development of training responses must recognise these local factors. However, a number of common elements in the training response have been identified in this study:

- Firstly, the training response must recognise the need to raise the level of awareness and engage SMEs in the task of recognising environmental responsibilities and the positive benefits of developing corporate environmental management responses.

- Secondly, the training response must recognise the need of SMEs and local/regional regulatory agencies for information as to the sources of environmental education and training. The diffuse sources of information and training provision make it difficult for SME's and local regulatory agencies to identify the most appropriate and helpful source of provision.

- Thirdly, the training response, tailored to the specific requirements of SMEs and regulatory agencies, has to serve different levels of personnel requiring different types of information and competences. For example, directors and senior managers require information about environmental legislation and policies and advice in formulating appropriate management responses. Technical managers require information and advice on compliance with environmental standards including specific training in appropriate technological and engineering skills. Operatives require technical information to induce them to implement better process control and good housekeeping measures.

- Fourthly, training responses need to recognise that effective environmental management responses depend essentially upon the appropriate application and efficient operation of pollution control technologies. Both SMEs and regulatory agencies require a knowledge of the techniques relevant to specific industrial processes and their performance in use. The training response has, therefore, to be highly focussed and specific to particular processes whilst, at the same time, ensuring that lessons relating to the successful implementation and use of pollution control technology in one industrial sector can be passed on to other sectors. The education and training response must recognise that there are generic pollution control technologies which can be applied to a range of environmental management requirements. Information on the availability, and expertise in the use, of these technologies would remove significant barriers blocking the adoption of cleaner and low waste technologies.

- Fifthly, the training response must recognise the range of different methods of delivery which exist, ranging from "in-house" and "on-the-job" training using back-up materials and facilities, to short course provision which responds to specific management and technical requirements for information and skills, and distance learning techniques. The method of delivery will vary according to the existing infrastructure which is available to deliver training to SMEs and regulatory agencies in each Member State. The delivery of provision therefore must maximise the use of existing channels of delivery of training services. Furthermore, information channels which exist between SMEs and less formal training organisations eg., Trade Unions, Chamber of Commerce, etc, must be utilised.

- Sixthly, the appropriate methods of delivery differ according to the type and level of training. However, this study has identified the value of short, highly focused and targeted courses which are available in local colleges and training centres, in stimulating better environmental management by SMEs. The use of distance learning packages has also been highlighted as an effective method of delivery.

- Finally, the training response must ensure that it addresses longer term needs as well as the immediate requirements of SMEs and regulatory agencies. In particular, there is a need to integrate environmental subjects into vocational training programmes and university degree courses in the traditional disciplines such as engineering, chemistry and also computing and electronics. In addition environmental education in schools and colleges should be seen as vital in developing a broader environmental awareness and a set of values and attitudes which encourage the acceptance of environmental responsibilities in industry.

7.5 The Possibilities for Co-operation Between SMEs and Regulatory Agencies

The relationship between regulatory agencies and SMEs is determined by a range of factors. The primary factor is the legislative remit under which the agency operates. The study has identified two modes of operation, reflecting different remits. The first mode is that of "teacher" where the agency advises on and negotiates with SMEs as to the most effective pollution control and environmental management response. This relationship will often embrace informal training as well as information exchange, designed to secure the co-operation of SMEs in the most effective manner. This mode tends to be operated by local and regional agencies.

The second mode is that of "policeman" where the agency may advise on the required environmental standards but, as the enforcement agency, is reluctant to develop informal links with SMEs preferring to maintain a detachment and independance. The move to more formal and stricter environmental standards is likely to lead to an increasing emphasis on this latter mode of operation. This mode tends to be operated by the national enforcement agencies.

The possibility for co-operation, where policy choices allow, should embrace centrally the need to improve the diffusion and take-up of cleaner and low waste technologies. The enforcement by regulatory agencies of BATNEEC, within the Community, places increasing emphasis on the take-up of improved production and pollution control technologies and procedures. Moreover, these improved techniques provide SMEs with the required flexibility to respond to changing and increasing environmental standards. More traditional "end-of-pipe" techniques, developed in response to a given environmental standard, lack the necessary flexibility.

7.6 The Involvement of the Social Partners

There are a large range of training responses which have value in promoting improved industrial environmental management. The success of a number of responses depends, on the actions of the Social Partners (see Sections 5.0 and 6.0). The detailed role of the Partners varies between Member States depending, in part, upon the way in which their respective responsibilities hav evolved. However, there are a number of fundamental training responses with respect to SMEs which the Social Partners have a role in developing. The relative emphasis to be placed on the role of employers organisations in environmental training and trades unions will of course vary between Member States.

- First, there is an emerging need for agencies which are capable of evaluating the required company wide environmental management response. The role of the agency would embrace the requirement to develop information and expertise on the use of cleaner, waste minimising production and pollution control technologies and to secure their diffusion and take-up by SMEs. This emergent role becomes more important if co-operation between SMEs and regulatory agencies is limited by a move towards a "policeman" role for regulatory agencies. The potential for Social Partners to clarify and develop this role, discussed in Section 6.0, represents an important new area of activity for the Partners.

- Secondly, the urgent need to engage SMEs in, and to communicate the positive corporate benefits of improved environmental management may be met by the Social Partners using their existing channels of communication with SMEs to encourage and demonstrate the value of accepting and responding to corporate environmental responsibilities. Key elements of the response by Social Partners would include the dissemination of information on the implications for corporate members of environmental legislation and the demonstration, using case studies of SMEs, of the corporate benefits.

- Thirdly, the research, reported in Section 3.0, highlighted the importance of preparing specific training services for particular industrial sectors. Social Partners at a sectoral level can advise on the specific, focused training services required by their members.

- Fourthly, the Social Partners can respond to the longer term underlying need to develop values and attitudes amongst managers and the workforce and the development of a corporate "environmental ethic". The Social Partners can develop environmental education provision aimed at highlighting the requisite environmental responsibilities to achieve improved environmental standards.

7.7 General Comments on Improvements in the Provision of Services

The range of improvements in education and training which are necessary, to ensure that environmental improvements are realised, is broad; covering, for example:

* the diffusion of the commercial benefits of environmental management;
* the diffusion of existing education and training sources;
* new education and training provision;
* new institutions and institutional responses;
* the clearer definition of the role of the regulatory agencies;
* the clearer definition of the role of the Social Partners.

Detailed comments on the types of training responses which are required are provided, see Section 7.4. We conclude here with a number of general observations:

- Improved environmental education and training is instrumental in the performance of environmental management and the improvement of environmental standards in industry.

- The provision of environmental education and training needs to be tailored to the particular circumstances in Member States and different regions therein. Specific circumstances to be considered include:

    * the role of the regulatory agency;
    * the nature of SMEs (size, activity);
    * the type of environmental problem (capacity, activity);

* the quantity and quality of existing education and training provision;
* the available infrastucture for new provision.

- Responsibility for developing environmental education and training lies, in different forms, with a wide range of international and national organisations and agencies. The contribution of these organisations represents a valuable resource for improving environmental education and training. Clarification, co-ordination and development of the specific roles and responsibilities would improve the value of this resource.

- Environmental regulations and standards will continue to rise throughout the Community. The ability of SMEs and regulatory agencies to comply with these regulations and standards varies between different parts of the Community. Southern Member States in particular, have to achieve a relatively greater improvement in environmental performance in order to meet new environmental regulations. Thus priorities attached to the development of environmental education and training provision must reflect the need for a relatively greater improvement in environmental performance in SMEs in Southern Member States, compared with SMEs in Northern Member States.

- The improvement in environmental education and training depends upon the environmental education and expansion of training services. This study indicates that the numbers of qualified trainers is limited and is insufficient to respond to increases in expressed demand. This, therefore, raises an important requirement for future trainers, to be trained particularly those employed in SMEs and those providing consultancy services to SMEs and regulatory agencies. Moreover, there is a requirement to organise networks of individuals and organisations capable of providing the appropriate skills, in order to efficiently harness and market available skills for the benefit of SMEs and regulatory agencies.

- Finally, the take-up of environmental education and training and the subsequent impact on environmental standards is ultimately determined by the extent to which managers of SMEs perceive significant commercial advantage from improving environmental management performance and the commercial risks of a "do nothing" strategy. This requirement must be recognised in any programme designed to provide environmental education and training for SMEs and, indeed, a fundamental element of any provision must be a "marketing" element aimed at securing take-up.

ANNEXES

CONTENTS

Annex A :	References	135
Annex B :	Consultees	143
Annex C :	Survey Instruments	191
Annex D :	The International Workshop	231
Annex E :	Industry Case Studies	239
Annex F :	The Italian Mission	253
Annex G :	A Review of Environmental Training Provision in the UK	257
Annex H :	An Overview of Environmental Policy	269

ANNEX A

REFERENCES

BIBLIOGRAPHY

1. Anagritur, 1983 Training Requirements in the Environmental Fields in the Italian Agricultural Sector. Proposals of training schemes at professional level and their resulting new job opportunities.

2. Boutwood H, Bell J and Macrory R, (1984) Imperial College of Science and Technology (1984) : Training for Pollution Control in Industry. Commission of the European Communities

3. Balafoutas (1985) Descriptive Analysis of Requirements in Respect of Environment Specialists to Work for Greek Muncipalities Synoposis : Final Reports

4. CBI (1989) : Report on Skills Training Survey : Managing the Skills Gap

5. CBI (1990) : Industrial Trends Survey Quarterly, Full Results. Number 115

6. CBI (1990) : Waking up to a Better Environment

7. CEC (1989) : Preparing Small and Medium Sized Enterprises for Europe 1992 Experimental Training Schemes

8. CEC DG XII (1990) : Enterprises in the European Community

9. Chamber of Commerce (1990) : Environmental Guidelines for World Industry

10. Cogliati V (1988) : Professione Ambiente (Environmental Training)

11. Deloitte, Haskins and Sells (1989) : Management Challenge for the 1990s : The Current Education, Training and Development Debate. Training Agency

12. Department of the Environment Welsh Office (1990) : Waste Management The Duty of Care : A consultation paper and draft Code of Practise under the Environmental Protection Bill

13. Department of the Environment/Welsh Office (1988) : Integrated Pollution Control. A Consultation Paper

14. Department of the Environment/Welsh Office (1988) : Waste Disposal Law Amendment. A Consultation Paper : decision following public consultation

15. Department of the Environment/Welsh Office (1988) : Waste Disposal Law Amendment. Follow Up, Consultation Paper

16. ECOTEC Research and Consulting Ltd (1985) : Training and Advice Requirements in the Environmental Field in the European Community : Final Report

17. ECOTEC Research and Consulting Ltd (1985) : Potential Economic Benefits from Integrating Environmental and Pollution Control Measures into Industrial Processes. A Series of Concrete Examples

18. ECOTEC Research and Consulting Limited (1989) : The UK Pollution Control Industry : The Strengths and Weaknesses of UK Suppliers of Pollution Control. Department of Trade and Industry

19. ECOTEC Research and Consulting Limited (1989) : Training in the Environmental Field. Commission of the European Communities

20. ECOTEC Research and Consulting Ltd (1989) : Industry Costs of Pollution Control. Department of the Environment

21. ECOTEC Research and Consulting Limited (1990) : Education and Training of Personnel Concerned with Environmental Issues Relating to Industry : European Foundation for the Improvement of Living and Working Conditions

22. ECOTEC Research and Consulting Limited (1990) : Developing a Framework of National Vocational Qualification, for the Environmental Sector : The Training Agency

23. ECOTEC Research and Consulting Ltd (1990) : Training in the Environmental Field. Final Report prepared for the Commission of the European Communities (DG XI)

24. ECOTEC Research and Consulting Ltd (1990) : The Impact of Environmental Management on Skills and Jobs. Final Report to the Training Agency

25. ECOTEC Research and Consulting Ltd (1990) : Occupational and Qualification Structure in the Field of Environmental Protection

26. ECOTEC Research and Consulting Ltd : Developing a Framework of National Vocational Qualifications for the Environmental Sector. Final Report

27. Elkington J (1990) : The Environmental Audit : A Green Filter for Company Policies, Plants, Processes and Products. World Wide Fund for Nature

28. Employment Committee (1990) : Third Report, Employment Training. Report Proceedings of the Committee and Minutes of Evidence

29. Employment Committee (1990) : Employment Training. Third Report. Report Proceedings of the Committee and Minutes of Evidence

30. ENI (1984) : Descriptive Analysis of Requirements in Environmentally Specialised Resources in respect of Regulations at Community, National and Local Level. Final Report

31. Euroconsult Ltd (1984) : Skilled Labour Requirements and New Job Descriptions in the Sewage Sludge Sector

32. European Chemical Industry Federation (CEFIC) (1988) : CEFIC Guidelines for the Communication of Environmental Information to the Public

33. European Trade Union Confederation (1986) : Environment Programme

34. European Trade Union Confederation (1990) : The Environmental Dimension if 1992 Environmental Working Group, Brussels, 23rd May 1990. Document ENV

35. European Trade Union Confederation (1990) : The Internal Market and the Environment. Arguments in Favour of Developing Economic Investments

36. Eurostat (1990) : Basic Statistics of the Community

37. Incentive (1984) : Definition of a Research Project/Proposed Training Scheme for the New Job of "Industrial Ecologist"

38. International Labour Office (1989) : ILO Contribution to Environmentally Sound and Sustainable Development

39. International Labour Office (1990) : Environment and the World at Work, Labour Conference 77th Session

40. ISFOL (1989) : Occupazione Ambiente Figure Professionali e bisagni formation

41. Johnson B and Coxelle G : The Environment Policy of the European Communities

42. Jones B and Scott P (1989) : Occupational Structure and Vocational Training Provision in the Office Sector in the United Kingdom. European Centre for the Development of Vocational Training

43. Jones W (1990) : The Delegate Report of Seminar Proceedings on "Management Training - The Environmental Dimension"

44. Kogan Page (1989) : British Qualifications. 20th Edition

45. Kormondy J (1989) : International Handbook of Pollution Control

46. Labour Office (1989) : Employment and Training Implication of Environmental Protection in Europe

47. Le Centre de Formation et du Documentation sur l'Environnement Industriel (1984) : Les Besoins de Formation pour les Responsables du Contrôle de l'Environnement dans l'Industrie Française

48. Lee N, University of Manchester (1984) : Training for Environmental Impact Assessment

49. Macrory R and Withers S : Waste Management in the United Kingdom : Research Professorship Environmental Policy Science Center, Berlin

50. Mathrani S, Council for Environmental Education (1987) : Environmental Education and Training in Industry. Department of the Environment

51. Ministerio dell'Ambiente (1989) : Relzione sullo stato dell' Ambiente (Report on the State of the Environment)

52. Ministry of Universities and of Scientific and Technical Research Natural Programme of Research and Training for the Environment

53. National Council for Vocational Qualification and Training Agency (1990) : National Vocational Qualifications Information and Guidance Notes

54. National Council for Vocational Qualifications (1988) : Developing a National System of Credit Accumulation and Transfer. Leaflet No. 1

55. National Council for Vocational Qualifications (1989) : National Vocational Qualification. Criteria and Procedures

56. OECD : Centre pour la Recherche et l'Innovation dans l'Enseignement

57. Organisation for Economic Co-operation and Development : The Impact of Environmental Measures on Employment. Issue Paper

58. PA Consultancy Group and the CBI (1990) : Waking up to a Better Environment

59. Pollution Prevention Management, French Ministry of Environment : Employment and Environment

60. The Hazardous Waste Inspectorate (1988) : Professionalisation and Training in Waste Management. Third Report

61. The International Confederation of Free Trade Union (1990) : Trade Unions and the Environment. Proposals for Action

62. The Manchester Area Pollution Advisory Council (1989) : Monitoring Report

63. The World Commission on Environment and Development (1987) : (The Bruntland Report) Our Common Future

64. University of Amsterdam (1985) : Promotion of Clean Technologies in Small Enterprises : Interim Report

65. Wallenberg P, International Chamber of Commerce, Addition to the Conference on Environmental Protection - A Global Business Challenge

66. Winter G (1988) : Business and the Environment

67. Wood C (1987) : The Utility of UK Pollution Panels in Achieving Integrated Pollution Control

68. Institute for Social Research and Progress (1984) : Descriptive analysis of requirements in respect of environment specialist in energy and waste: Final Report

69. Ineral (1984) Environnement, emploi, formation en region Provence Alpes - Cote d'Azur : Interim Report.

70. European Federation for Environment Defense (1984) : Descriptive Analysis of requirements in respect of training for environment specialist in the treatment of toxic waste

71. EUROCONSULT Ltd (1984) : Skilled labour requirements and new job descriptions for the waste management sector.

72. ECONPUBLICA (1984) : Descriptive Analysis of requirements in respect of specialist environmental resources in the public sector at regional level : A case study of Italy

73. Cellenno R. (1985) : Preliminary summary of studies carried out in Italy for the Commission of the European Communities on environment and employment. Requirements for training of environmental workers

ANNEX B

CONSULTEES

Ministère de l'Environnement et du Carde de Vie
(Ministry of the Environment)
14 boulevard du General-Leclerc
F-92524 Neuilly-sur-Seine
FRANCE

Service de l'Hydraulique
(Water Resources Service)
19 avenue de Maine
F-75732 Paris
FRANCE

Centre International de Recherche sur
l'Environnement et de Développement (CIRED)
(International Research Center on Environment
and Development)
54 boulevard Raspail No. 311
F-75270 Paris Cedex 06
FRANCE

Ministerio de Obras Publicas y
Urbanismo - Dirección General de Medio
Ambiente (DGMA)
(Ministry of Public Works and Urban Planning -
General Directorate for the Enviornment)
Paseo de la Castellana 67
E-28071 Madrid
SPAIN

Bundesministerium für Umwelt
Naturschutz und Reaktorsicherheit
(Federal Ministry for the Environment,
Nature Conservation, and Reactor Safety)
Abteilung N
Postfach 120629
D-5300 Bonn 1
GERMANY

Bundesministerium für Wirtschaftliche
Zusammenarbeit (BMZ)
(Federal Ministry for Economic Cooperation)
185 Kaiserstrasse
D-5300 Bonn
GERMANY

Ministry of Physical Planning, Housing,
and the Environment
Environment Directorate
Pouliou 8
GR-115 23 Athens
GREECE

Ministry of Energy and Natural Resources
Zalokosta 1
GR-106 71 Athens
GREECE

Department of Forest Research and Education
Terma Alkmanos Ilisia
GR-115 28 Athens
GREECE

Panellhnio Kentro Ockologiken Ereynon
(PAKOE)
Sufliou Street
Ampelokopi
GR-115 27 Athens
GREECE

Ministére de l'Environnement
et des Eaux et Forêts
(Ministry of the Environment,
Water and Forests)
5a rue de Prague
Luxembourg

Ministerie van Landbouw en Visserij
(Ministry of Agriculture and Fisheries)
Department for Nature Conservation
Environmental Protection and Wildlife Management
Postbus 20401
NL-200 EK
The Hague
NETHERLANDS

Ministerie van Volkshuisvesting
Ruimtelijke Ordening en Milieubeheer
(Ministry of Housing, Planning,
and the Environment)
Postbus 20951
NL-2500 EZ
The Hague
NETHERLANDS

Ministerio do Plano e da Administracao
do Territorio (Ministry of Planning and
Land Management)
Rua do Seculo
51-20, P-1200 Lisbon
PORTUGAL

Secretaria de Estado do Ambiente e
dos Recursos Naturais (Secretariat of State
for Environment and Natural Resources)
Rua do Seculo
51-20
P-1200 Lisbon
PORTUGAL

Ministerio dell'Ambiente
(Ministry of the Environment)
Servizio per la Prevenzione degli
Inquinamenti ed il Risanamento Ambientale
Piazza Venezia II
00187 ROMA

Egidio Zavattiero
Istituto Superiore di Sanitá
Reparto Igiene del Suolo
(Department of Soil Hygiene)
Viate Regina Elena 299
00161 Roma
ITALY

Ente Nazionale per le Energie Alternative
ENEA (National Institute for Alternative Energies)
Dipartimento Protezione Ambiente e Salute
(Department of Environment and Health Protection)
Piazza Morandi 2
20121 Milano
ITALY

Direccao Geral do Saneamento
Bàsico (Basic Sanitary)
Rua Antero de Quental
44 1 100 Lisboa
PORTUGAL

SCK/CEN Environmental Programm
Boeretang 200
B-2400 MOL
BELGIUM

Association pour la Prevention
de la Pollution Atmospherique
58 rue du Rocher
75008 Paris

Room A. 508
HM Inspectorate of Pollution
Romney House
43 Marsham Street
LONDON
SW1P 3PY

Comitato di Studio per
l'Inquinamento Atmosferico
within Associazione Termotecnica Italiana
C/O ISMAR
Via Assarotti 15/8
16122 Genova
ITALY

J G Papaioannou
President
Hellenic Association on
Environmental Pollution (ERYEA)
Xenofondos 14
105.57 Athens
GREECE

M. V Alexandre
Ministére de la Région Wallonne
avenue du Prince de Liége 7
5100 Jambes
BELGIUM

Directeur Général de
l'Institut Bruxellois pour la Gestion
de l'Environnement
Avenue Louise 149 Bte 18
1050 Bruxelles
BELGIUM

OVAM
Kan. De Deckerstraat 22-26
2800 Mechelen
BELGIUM

AROL
Coppernicuslaan 1
2018 Antwerpen
BELGIUM

W M Z
Bondgenotenlaan 140
Leuven
BELGIUM

Ministry of Public Works
12 Varvaki Street
GR-114 74 Athens
GREECE

Ministry of the Interior
Directorate for Planning and Studies
27 Stadiou Street
-101 83 Athens
GREECE

Consejero Obras Publicas y Ordenacion del Territorio
Gabriel Alomar y Villalonga, 33
E-07006 Palma de Mallorca
SPAIN

Dtor General Medio Ambiente y
Conservacion de la Naturaleza
Avda de Anaga, 15-7
Edificio Multiple
E-38001 STA Cruz Tenerife
SPAIN

Director General de Urbanismo y Medio Ambiente
C/Francisco Suarez 2
E-47000 Valladolid
SPAIN

Director General Medio Ambiente
c/Cervantes 12
E-28006 Merida (Badajoz)
SPAIN

Director Regional Medio Ambiente
E-26003 Logrono
SPAIN

Director Gabinete Medio Ambiente
Consejero Orbas Publicas,
Urbanismo y Transportes
Avda Blasco Ibanez, 50-3
E-46004 Vålencia
SPAIN

Dtor Agencia Medio Ambiente
Avda Eritana 1
E-41013 Sevilla
SPAIN

Dtor Agencia Medio Ambiente
Plaza General Ordonez, 1-7°
E-33007 Oviedo
SPAIN

Director Agencia de Medio Ambiente
Juan de Herrera, 14
E-39002 Santander
SPAIN

Environmental/Training Dept
Agence pour la Qualite de l'Air
Tour Gran
Cedex 13
92082 Paris La Defense 2
FRANCE

Miliostyrelsen
Copenhagen
DENMARK
Environmental/Training Dept
VRM (Ministerie van Volkshuisvesting)
Postbus 20951
The Hague
2500 EZ
NETHERLANDS

Environment/Training Directorate
VROM
Postbus 450,2260 MB
Leidschendam
NETHERLANDS

Environment/Training Dept
Ministere de Sante Publique et Environment
Rue da la Loi 56
Brussels 1040
BELGIUM

Ministere de la Solidarite
de la sante et de la Protection Sociale
1 Place de Fontenoy
75700 Paris
FRANCE

Environment/Training Dept
Ministete de l'Environment
5A Rue dec Prague
LUXEMBOURG 2918

Environment/Training Dept
Agence Financiere de Basin Seine-Normandie
51 Rue Salvador-Allende
Naterre
Paris F-92027
FRANCE

A N R E D
2 Square la Fayette
BP 406
Angers
F-49004 Cedex 01
FRANCE

Environment/Training Dept
Ministerio de Industria y Energia
Edificio Cuzco IV
Po Castellana 141, PTA 13
Madrid
E-28046
SPAIN

Training Dept
Department of Environment
O'Connor
Bridge House
D'Olier Street
Dublin 2
EIRE

Director General Ordencion del Territoria
Urbanismo y Medio Ambiente
Laverde Ruiz, s/n
Edificio San Cayetano
E-Santiago de Compostela
SPAIN

Dtor de los Servicios Metropolitanos
de la Corporacion Metropolitana
c/62, No 420, Sector A
Zona Franca
E-08004 Barcelona
SPAIN

Ilmo Sr D Juan Jose Otamendi
Viceconsejero de Medio Ambiente
c/Samaniego 2
E-01008 Vitoria
SPAIN

Alfredo Bonet 6 do
E-07003 PLMA De Mallorca
SPAIN

Vereinigung
Osterrcichischer Industrieller
Rue Joseph 11,40/bte 10
B-1040 Bruxelles
BELGIUMS

Ministry of the Enviornment
National Environmental
Research Institute
Thoravej B, 3rd Floor
DK-2400 Copenhagen NV
DENMARK

Ministry of the Enviroment
The National Agency for
Physical Planning
Haraidsgade 53
DK-2100 Kobenhavn
O DENMARK

Ministry of the Environment
The National Agency of
Environmental Protection
Strandgade 29
DK-1401 Copenhagen K
DENMARK

Ministry of Housing,
Physical Planning and
Environment
State Inspectorate for
Public Health
PO Box 450
2260 MB Leidschendam
NETHERLANDS

Central Council for the
Environment (CRMH)
PO Box 90740
2509 LS The Hague
NETHERLANDS

H W de Boer
Ministry of Agriculture
and Fisheries
General Inspectorate
PO Box 234
6460 AE Kerkrade
NETHERLANDS

Ministry of Transport and
Public Works
Transport Inspectorate
PO Box 20906
2500 EX The Hague
NETHERLANDS

Royal Netherlands
Meteorological Institute (KNMI)
PO Box 201
3730 AE Bilthoven
NETHERLANDS

Directorate General for
Environment
PO Box 450
2260 MB Leidschendam
NETHERLANDS

HM Industrial Air Pollution Inspectorate
Pentland House
47 Robbs Loan
Lothian
EDINBURGH
EH14 1TY

HM Industrial Pollution
Inspectorate for Scotland
27 Perth Street
Lothian
EDINBURGH
EH3 5DW

HM Inspectorate of Pollution
Room A103
Romney House
43 Marsham Street
LONDON
SW1P 3PY

HM Inspectorate of
Pollution
Room B553
Romney House
43 Marsham Street
LONDON
SW1 3PY

National Rivers Authorities
Rivers House
30 - 34 Albert Embankment
LONDON
SE1 7TL

HM Industrial Pollution
Inspectorate
27 Perth Street
EDINBURGH
EH3 5RB

Alkali and Radio Chemical
Inspectorate
23 Castle Place
Belfast BT1 1FY
NORTHERN IRELAND

Hazardous Waste
Inspectorate
27 Perth Street
EDINBURGH EH3 5RB

Environmental Protection
Scottish Development Dept.
27 Perth Street
EDINBURGH
EH3 5RB

Rhône-Méditerranée-Corse
31 rue Jules Guesde
Pierre Bénite - 69310
Lyon
FRANCE

Agence Fancaise pour
la Maîtrise de l'Energie
27 rue Louis Vicat
75015 Paris
FRANCE

Agence pour la Qualité
de l'Air
Tour GAN - Cedex 13
92082 Paris La Defense
FRANCE

Nederlandse Vereungung
voor Reingingsdirekteuren
(NVRD) (Dutch Institute
for waste management)
Postbus 348
3300 AH Dordrecht
NETHERLANDS

Ministére de l'Industrie,
des P & T et du Tourisme
101 rue du Grenelle
75007 Paris
FRANCE

Ministére de l'Intérieur
Direction Générale des
Collectivités Locales
4 - 12 rue d'Aguesseau
75800 Paris
FRANCE

Direction de la Qualité
44 Boulevard de Grenelle
75732 Paris Cedex 15
FRANCE

Ministére des Affairs
Sociales et de l'Emploi
Direction Générale de la
Santé
1 place Fontenoy
75700 Paris
FRANCE

Der Bundesminister für
Umwelt-Naturschutz und
Reaktorsicherheit
5300 Bonn 1
Adenauerallee 139-141
GERMANY

Federal Environmental Agency
Umweltbundesamt
1000 Berlin 33
Bismarckplatz 1
GERMANY

Baden- Württemberg Minister Für Umwelt
Keruerplatz 9
7000 Stuttgart 1
GERMANY

Bayern, Staatsmimster für
Landesentwicklung und
Umwelt
Rosenkavalierplatz 2
8000 München 80
GERMANY

Institut de L'Hygeine
l'Epidemiologie
rue Juliette Vytfmar 14
1050 Bruxelles
BELGIUM

Berlin Senatorin für
Stadtentwicklung und
Umweltschütz
Lindenstrasse 20-25
1000 Berlin 61
GERMANY

Direccao Da Qualidade Do Ambiente
Secretaria De Estado Do Ambiente
Rua Do Seculo 57
P 1200 Lisbon
PORTUGAL

Direccion General del Medio Ambiente
Ministerio de Obras Publicas
y Urbanismo
Paseo Castellana 67
E-28071 Madrid
SPAIN

Department of Environment
Environment Policy Section
Custom House
Dublin 1
EIRE

Chargé de Mission
Inter-Environnement Wallonie (IEW)
Federation des associations d'environnement
Rue du Luxembourg 20
1040 Bruxelles
BELGIUM

Associaçào Portuguesa para
Estudos de Saneamento Bàsico
Rua Antero de Quental 44
1100 Lisboa
PORTUGAL

Internationales Institut
für Umwelt und Gesellschaft
Forschungsschwsrpunkt
Umweltpolitik
1000 Berlin 30
Potsdsmerstr 58
GERMANY

Royal Society of Arts
(Environmental Secretary)
8 John Adam Street
LONDON WC2

Confédération Nationale
du Déchet (C N D) et
Fédération Nationale des
Activitiés du Déchet (FNAD)
72 rue d'Amsterdam
75009 Paris
FRANCE

Syndicat Nationale des
Industries du Déchet (SNID)
10 rue de Washington
75008 Paris
FRANCE

Union Nationale des
Exploitants de Décharges
(UNED)
3 rue Alfred Roll
75017 Paris
FRANCE

N V Vuilafvoer Maatschappij
(VAM)
PO Box 5380
1007 AJ Amsterdam
NETHERLANDS

AVR Chemie
Prof. Gerbrandyweg 10
3197 KK Rotterdam-Botlek
NETHERLANDS

ATEGRUS - Technique Association
for the Management of Urban Solid Wastes
Múgica y Butrón 10
48007 Bilbao
SPAIN

Associazione Nazionale di Ingegneria
Sanitaria ed Ambientale
Piazza Sallustio 24
00187 Roma
ITALY

Unione Imprese Difesa Ambiente
Piazza Diaz 2
20123 Milano
ITALY

Confederazione Italiana dei Servizi
Pubblici degli Enti Locali
Piazza Cola di Rienzo 80
00192 Roma
ITALY

Assorecuperi
Corso Venezia 47/49
20121 Milano
ITALY

European Council of Chemical
Manufacturers' Federations
Avenue Louise 250
Bte 71
B-1050 Brussels
BELGIUM

International Group of National
Associations of Manufacturers of
Agrochemical Products (GIFAP)
Avenue Albert Lancaster 79a
B-1180 Brussels
BELGIUM

International Iron and Steel Institute
(IISI)
Rue Col Bourg 120
B-1140 Brussels
BELGIUM

International Petroleum Industry
Environmental Conservation Association
(IPIECA)
College Hill
1st Floor
LONDON   EC4 2RA

International Primary Aluminium
Institute (IPAI)
New Zealand House
9th Floor
Haymarket
LONDON

Lead Development Association (LDA)
Berkeley Square 34
LONDON
W1X 6AJ

Bureau International de la Recuperation
(BIR)
Place du Samedi 13
Bte 4
B-1000, Brussels
BELGIUM

Business and Industry Advisory Committee
to OECD (BIAC)
Chausée de la Muette 13/15
F-75016 Paris
FRANCE

Bundesdeutscher Arbeitskreis für
umweltbewuBtes Management eV (BAUM)
Christian-Förster-Str 19
2000 Hamburg 20
WEST GERMANY

Institute of Environmental Sciences Ltd
14 Princes Gate
Hyde Park
LONDON
SW7 1PU

Society of British Gas Industries
36 Holly Walk
Leamington Spa
Warwickshire
CV32 4LY

United Kingdom Petroleum Industry
Association (UKPIA)
9 Kingsway
LONDON
WC2B 6XH

Klon
Ingenieurs - KIVI
Prinsegracht 23
2514 AP Den Haag
NETHERLANDS

Training Department
European Water Pollution
Control Association
EWPCA Secretariat
Markt 71
St Augustin 1
D-5205
GERMANY

TÜV Rheinland eV
Institut für Materialprüfung
und Chemie
5000 Köln 91
Am Grauen Stein/
Konstantin-Wille-Str 1
GERMANY

Institut für Energietechnik
und Umweltschutz
6000 Frankfurt aM 1
DLG
Zimmerweg 16
GERMANY

Dachverband wissenschaftlicher
Gesellschaften der Agrar-,
Forst-, Ernährungs-, Veterinär-
und Umweltforschung eV
6000 Frankfurt aM 1
DLG
Zimmerweg 16
GERMANY

Ausschuß für Umweltpolitik
Bundesverband der Deutschen
Industrie eV
5000 Köln 51
PF: 510548
Gustav-Heinemann-Ufer 84-86
GERMANY

Thermo Prozess und
Abfalltechnik
6000 Frankfurt aM 71
PF: 710864
Lyoner Str. 18
GERMANY

Bund für Umwelt und
Naturschutz von
Deutschland eV
5300 Bonn1
in der Raste 2
GERMANY

Bundes v Bürgerinitiativen
Umweltschutz eV
5300 Bonn 1
Friedrich-Ebert-Allee 120
GERMANY

Verenging van Leveranciers
van Milieuapparatuur
Dutch Environmental Trade
Association
Bredewater 20
Postbus 190
2700 AD
Zoetermeer
NETHERLANDS

Secretary General
UNICLIMA (Trade Association
for Mechanical Engineering)
10 Avenue Hoche
Paris 75382
FRANCE

European Confederation of
Pulp, Paper and Board
Industry (CEPAC)
Rue Washington 40
Bte 7 B-1050 Brussels
BELGIUM

Syndicat National des
Industries du Déchet (SNID)
10 rue de Washington
75008 Paris
FRANCE

Office communautaire et régional de la
formation professionnelle et de l'Emploi
(FOREM)
Bd de l'Empereur 7
B-1000 Bruxelles
BELGIUM

Manpower Employment Organisation
Parakis 8
GR-16610 Athens
GREECE

Greek Productivity Centre (ELKEPA)
2 Parnasscy Str
15124 Kifissia
Athens
GREECE

Ministry of Labour
Dir of Working Conditions (E2)
40 Pirgos Str
10182 Athens
GREECE

Greece faithfully Asso Dioikema
40125 Bologna
Palazzo Isolani
Via Santo Stefano 16
ITALY

General Manager
Hellenic Management Association
36 Amalias ave
Athens
Greece

Greek Productivity Center
28 Kapodistriou str
Athens
Greece

Vlaamse Dienst voor Arbeidsbemiddeling
en Beroepsopleiding (VDAB)
Keizerslaan 7
B-1000 Bruxelles
BELGIUM

Undervisningsministeriet
Frederiksholmskanal 21
DK-1220 Kobenhavn K
DENMARK

Bundesinstitut für Berufsbildungsforschung
(BIBB)
Fehrbelliner Platz 3
D-1000 Berlin 31
GERMANY

Bundesanstalt für Arbeit
Regensburgerstr 100
D-8500 Nürnberg
GERMANY

Landesregierung Baden-Württemberg
Minister für Kultus und Sport
Neues Schloss
D-7000 Stuttgart 1
GERMANY

Landesregierung Bayern
Staatsminister für Unterricht und Kultus
Salvatorplatz 2
D-8000 München 2
GERMANY

Landesregierung Berlin
Senator für Schulwesen
Berufsausbildung und Sport
Bredtschneiderstr 5
D-1000 Berlin 19
GERMANY

Landesregierung Bremen
Senator für Bildung
Wissenschaft und Kunst
Rembertiring 8-12
D-2800 Bremen
GERMANY

Landesregierung Hamburg
Behörde für Schule und Berufsbildung
Hamburgerstr 31
D-2000 Hamburg 76
GERMANY

Landesregierung Hessen
Kultusminister
Luiseplatz 10
D-6200 Wiesbaden
GERMANY

Landesregierung Niedersachsen
Kultusminister
Schiffgraben 12
D-3000 Hannover
GERMANY

Landesregierung Nordrhein-Westfalen
Kultusminister
Völklingerstr 49
D-4000 Düsseldorf
GERMANY

Landesregierung Aheinland-Pfalz
Kultusminister
Mittlere Bleiche 61
D-6500 Mainz
GERMANY

Landesregierung Saarland
Minister für Kultus
Bildung und Wissenschaft
Hohenzollernstr 60
D-6600 Saarbrüken 1
GERMANY

Landesregierung Schleswig-Holstein
Kultusminister
Düsternbrooker Weg 64-66
D-2300 Kiel
GERMANY

Instituto Nacional de Empleo (INEM)
Ministerio de Trabajo y Seguridad Social
Condesa de Venadito 9
E-28027 Madrid
SPAIN

Ministerio de Educaciòn y Ciencia
Alcala 34
E-28014 Madrid
SPAIN

Ministére de l'Education Nationale,
de la Jeunesse et des Sports
110 rue de Grenelle
F-75007 Paris
FRANCE

Ministére du Travail de l'Emploi
et de la Formation Professionnelle
127 rue de Grenelle
F-75007 Paris
FRANCE

Ministére de Travail
de l'Emploi et de la Formation
professionnelle
Délégation á la Formation Professionnelle
50-56 rue de la Procession
F-75015 Paris
FRANCE

Agence Nationale pour l'Emploi (ANPE)
4 rue Galilée
F-93198 Noisy-le-Grand Cedex
FRANCE

Association Nationale pour la Formation
Professionnelle des Adultes (AFPA)
13 Place de Villiers
F-93108 Montreuil Cedex
FRANCE

Centre pour le Développement de l'Information
sur la Formation Permanente
(Centre INFFO) Tour Europe Cedex 07
F-92080 Paris la Défense
FRANCE

OAED (Hellenic Manpower Employment &
Training Organisation)
Thrakis 8
Glyfáda
GR - 16610 Athen
GREECE

Ypourgio Ethnikis Pedias kai Thriskevmaton
(Ministery of National Education and Religion)
Mitropoleos 15
GR - 10185 Athen
GREECE

FAS - The Training and Employment Authority
27-33 Upper Baggott Street
IAL - Dublin 4
IRELAND Vocational Education Committees
Head Office
Florence Road
Bray
Co. Dublin
IRELAND

Istituto per lo Sviluppo della Formazione
Professionale dei Lavoratori (ISFOL)
Via Bartolomeo Eustachio 8
I-00161 Roma
ITALY

Regione Sardegna
Giunta Regionale
Assessore alla Formazione Professionale
Via Trento 69
I-09100 Cagliari
ITALY

Regione Sicilia
Assessore alla Formazione Professionale
Pal. d'Orleans
Piazza Indipendenza
I-90129 Palermo
ITALY

Regione Valle d'Aosta
Giunta Regionale
Assessore alla Formazione Professionale
Piazza Albert Deffeyes
I-11100 Aosta
ITALY

Regione Trentino-Alto Adige
Giunta Regionale
Assessore alla Formazione Professionale
Via Gazzoletti 2
I-38100 Trente
ITALY

Regione Friuli-Venezia Giulia
Giunta Regionale
Assessore alla Formazione Professionale
Piazza Oberdan 6
I-34122 Triesta
ITALY

Regione Abruzzo
Giunta Regionale
Assessore alla Formazione Professionale
Via Colle Pretara
I-67100 L'Aquila
ITALY

Regione Basilicate
Giunta Regionale
Assessore alla Formazione Professionale
Via Pretoria 277
I-86100 Potenza
ITALY

Regione Calabria
Giunta Regionale
Assessore alla Formazione Professionale
Viale De Filippis
I-88100 Catanzaro
ITALY

Regione Campania
Giunta Regionale
Assessore alla Formazione Professionale
Via 6. Lucia 81
I-80132 Napoli
ITALY

Regione Emilia Romagna
Giunta Regionale
Assessore alla Formazione Professionale
Viale Silvani 6
I-40122 Bologna
ITALY

Regionae Lazio
Giunta Regionale
Assessore alla Formazione Professionale
Via della Pisana 1301
I-00163 Roma
ITALY

Regione Liguria Giunta Regionale
Assessore alla Formazione Professionale
Via Fieschi 15
I-16121 Genova
ITALY

Regione Lombardia
Giunta Regionale
Assessore alla Formazione Professionale
Via Fabio Filzi 22
I-20124 Milano
ITALY

Regione Marche
Giunta Regionale
Assessore alla Formazione Professionale
Via Gentile da Fabriano
I-60100 Ancona
ITALY

Regione del Molise
Giunta Regionale
Assessore alla Formazione Professionale
Via XXIV Maggio 130
I-66100 Campobasso
ITALY

Regione Piemonte
Giunta Regionale
Assessore alla Formazione Professionale
Piazza Castello 165
I-10122 Torino
ITALY

Regione Puglia
Giunta Regionale
Assessore alla Formazione Professionale
Via Estramurale Capruzzi 212
I-70124 Bari
ITALY

Regione Toscana
Giunta Regionale
Assessore alla Formazione Professionale
Palazzo Budini-Gottai
Via de' Servi 51
I-50123 Firenze
ITALY

Regione dell'Umbria
Giunta Regionale
Assessore alla Formazione Professionale
Piazza Italia 1
I-06100 Perugia
ITALY

Regione Veneto
Giunta Regionale
Assessore alla Formazione Professionale
Palazzo Balbi-Dorsoduro 3901
I-30123 Venezia
ITALY

Chambre des Métiers du Grand-Duché
de Luxembourg
41 rue Glesener
L-1631
LUXEMBOURG

Ministerie van Onderwijs en Watenschappen
Postbus 25000
NL - 2700 LZ Zoetermeer
NETHERLANDS

Contractcentrum Onderwijs Arbeid (COA)
Limburg
Sint Pieterskade 7
NL - 6212 JV Maastricht
NETHERLANDS

Instituto do Emprego e Formascao
Profissional (IEFP)
Rua das Picoas 14, 9°
P - 1000 Lisboa
PORTUGAL

Ministério de Educascao
Av. Miguel Bombarda 20
P - 1093 Lisboa Codex
PORTUGAL

Training Agency
Moorfoot
Sheffield
S1 4PQ
GREAT BRITAIN

Secretaria General de Medio Ambiente
MOPU
Paeso Catellana 67
28071 Madrid
SPAIN

Instituto Agronómico
Mediterrâneo de Zaragoza
Ctra de Montañana 177
50080-Zargoza
SPAIN

Instituto de Salud
Pública de Navarra C/Leyre 15
31003 - Pamplona
SPAIN

Instituto Catalán de Tecnologia
(ICT) Via Layetana 39 4o
08003 - Barcelona
SPAIN

Fundacion Universidad-Enipresa
Serrano Jover 5
28015-Madrid
SPAIN

Escuela de Organizaciò-Industrial
Gregorio del Amo 6
28040-Madrid
SPAIN

CEDEX (Centro de Estudios y Experimentaciòn
de Obras Pùblicas)
C/Alfonso XII 3
28014-Madrid
SPAIN

Instiuto de Estudios de la Energia
Avda Complutense, 22
28040-Madrid
SPAIN

Medio Ambiente Asesores
C/Evaristo San Miguel, 20
28008-Madrid
SPAIN

European Environmental Bureau
Maison Europeene de l'Environment
Rue du Luxembourg 20
Brussels B-1040
BELGIUM

Environmental/Training Dept
Warren Spring Laboratory
Gunnelswood Road
Stevenage
Herts
SG1 2BX

Greek Productivity Center (Elkepa)
2 Parnassey STR
15124 Kifissia
Athens
GREECE

Ministry of Labour
Dir. of Working Conditions (E2)
40 Pirgos STR
10182 Athens
GREECE

Institut National de la Statistique et des Etudes
Economiques (INSEE)
18 Boulevard Adolphe Pinard
75675 Paris
Cedex 14
FRANCE

Instituto Nacional de Estatistica
Avenida Antonio José de Almeida
Lisboa 1
PORTUGAL

Ministére de l'Education Nationale
de la Jeunesse et das Sports
110 rue de Grenelle
F-75007
Paris
FRANCE

Ministére du Travail
de l'Emploi et de la Formation
Professionnelle
127 rue de Grenelle
F-75007 Paris
FRANCE

Instituto Nacional de Estatistica
Avenida Antonio José de Almeida
Lisboa 1
PORTUGAL

Institut National de Statistique
Rue de Louvain 44
1000 Bruxelles
BELGIUM

Office National de l'Emploi (ONEM)
7 Boulevard de l'Empereur
1000 Bruxelles
BELGIUM

Danmarks Statistiks
Sejrogade 11
2100 Kobenhaven O
DENMARK

Institut National de la Statistique
et des Etudes Economiques (INSEE)
18 Boulevard Adolphe Pinard
75675 Paris
Cedex 14
FRANCE

Ministére du Travail
1 Place de
75700 Paris
FRANCE

Bundesanstalt für Arbeit
Regensburger Strasse 104
8500 Nürnberg
GERMANY

Institut der Deutschen Wirtschaft
Gustav-Heinnemann-Ufer 84-88
5000 Koln 51
WEST GERMANY

Statistisches Bundesamt
Gustav-Stresmann-Ring 11
62 Wiesbaden 1
WEST GERMANY

National Statistical Service
14-16 Lycourgou Street
Athens
GREECE

Central Statistics Office
Ardee Road
Rathmines
Dublin 6
IRELAND

Department of Labour
Davit House
50-60 Mespil Road
Dublin 4
IRELAND

Mespil House
Mespil Road
Dublin 4
IRELAND

Istituto Centrale di Statistica
Via Cesare Balbo 16
00100 Roma
ITALY

Ministero del Lavoro e della
Previdenzo Sociale
6 Via Flavia
Roma
ITALY

Administration de l'Emploi
34 Avenue de la Porte Neuve
LUXEMBOURG

Central Bureau voor de Statistiek
Prinses Beatrixlaan 428
2270 AZ Voorburg
Den Haag
NETHERLANDS

Ministerie van Social Zaken
en Werkgelegenheid
Zeestraat 73
Den Haag 2500 EV
NETHERLANDS

International Labour Office (ILO)
CH-1211 Geneva 22
SWITZERLAND

Office National de l'Emploi (ONEM)
7 Boulevard de l'Empereur
1000 Bruxelles
BELGIUM

Union des Villes et Communes Belges
rue d'Arlon 53 (bte 4)
B-1040 Bruxelles
BELGIUM

International Union of Local Authority
Wassenaarseweg 41
NL-2596 CG Den Haag
NETHERLANDS

Amrsradsforening
Landemaerket 10
DK 1119 Kobenhavn V
DENMARK

Kommunernes Landsforening
Gyldenlavesgade 11
DK 1600 Kobenhavn V
DENMARK

Deutscher Landkreistag
Adenauerallee 136
D-5300 Bonn 1
WEST GERMANY

Deutscher Stadtetag
Lindenallee 13-17
D-5000 Koln 51
WEST GERMANY

Deutscher Stadte-und Gemeindebund
Kaiserwertherstrasse 199-201
D-4000 Düsseldorf 1
WEST GERMANY

Union des Villes et Pouvoirs Locaux
15 rue de Richelieu
F-75001 Paris
FRANCE

Union of Muncipalities and
Communities of Greece
8 Akadimias and Genadiou
GR Athinai 141
GREECEE

Irish Public Bodies
Mutual Insurance Limited
Westmoreland Street 1-2-3
IRL-Dublin 2
IRELAND

Associazione Nazionale dei Comuni Italiani
Via dei Prefetti 46
I-00186 Roma
ITALY

British Section of IULA
12 Old Queen Street
LONDON
SW1H 9HP

Convention of Scottish Local Authorities
16 Moray Place
EDINBURGH
EH3 6DL

Association of County Councils
Eaton House
66a Eaton Square
LONDON
SW1W 9BH

Greater London Council
The County Hall
LONDON SE1 7PB

Association of Metropolitan Authorities
36 Old Queen Street
LONDON
SW1H 9JE

National Association of Local Authorities
108 Great Russell Street
LONDON
WC1B 3LD

Association of District Councils
25 Buckingham Gate
LONDON
SW1E 16LE

London Boroughs Association
Westminster City Hall
Victoria Street
LONDON   SW1E 6QW

Hellenic Association on
Environmental Pollution (ERYEA)
Xenofondos 14
105.57 Athens
GREECE

Comitato di Studio per
l'Inquinamento Atmosferico
within Associazione Termotecnica Italiana
C/O ISMAR
Via Assarotti 15/8
16122 Genova
ITALY

Local Government SA (EETAA)
19 Omirou Street
Athens 10672
GREECE

Dr Karl Ahrens, MdB
Verband Kommunaler Unternehmen e V
5000 Köln 51
Brohler Str 13
WEST GERMANY

Verband Kommunaler
Stadtereinigungsbetriebe eV
5000 Köln 51
PF 510620 Lindenallee 13/17
WEST GERMANY

Verband Privater
Stadtereinigungsbetriebe e V -
Bundesverband-Arbeitgeberverband
5000 Köln 90
PF 90 08 45
Haupstrasse 305
WEST GERMANY

Vereniging van Nederlands
Gemeenteen (VNG)
De Willemshof
Nassaulaan 12
2514 JS Den Haag
NETHERLANDS

Municipality of Thebes
Dimarhion Thivas
Normos Viotias
Thebes
Greece

Municipality of Kalamata
Kalamata Town Hall
Kalamata
GREECE

FGTB - Federation Generale du Travail de Belgique
rue Haute 42
B-1000 Bruxelles
BELGIUM

CSC- Confederation des Syndicats Chretiens
de Belgique
rue de la Loi 121
B-1040 Bruxelles
BELGIUM

LO - Landsorganisationen i Danmark
Rosenorns Alle 12
DK 1970 Kobenhavn
DENMARK

FTF radet for Danske Tjenestemands-og
Funktionarorganisationer
Vesterport
Trommesalen 2a
DK-Kobenhavn
DENMARK

GB Bundesvorstand
Hans Bockler Strasse 39
Postfach 2601
D-4000 Dusseldorf 30
WEST GERMANY

UGT - Union General de Trabajadores de Espana
San Bernardo 20-5
E-Madrid 8
SPAIN

STV-ELA Solidaridad de Trabajadores Vascos
Av Isabell 11, 21-1
E-San Sebastian
SPAIN

CGT-FO Confederation Generale du Travail
Force Ouvriere
198 av du Maine
F-75680 Paris Cedex 14
FRANCE

Secretaire Confédéral
CFDT - Confederation Francaise
Democratique du Travail
4 bd de la Villette
F-75955 Paris Cedex 19
FRANCE

GGCL - Greek General Confederation of Labour
69 rue du 28eme Octobre
GR-Athinai
GREECE

ICTU - Irish Congress of Trade Unions
Raglan Street 19
Ballsbridge
IRL Dublin
IRELAND

CISL - Confederazione Italiana Sindacati Lavoratori
Via Po 21
1-00198 Roma
ITALY

CGIL - Confederazione Generale Italiana del Lavoro
Corso d'Italia 25
1-00198 Roma
ITALY

Secrétaire National
Central Générale des Syndicats Libéraux de Belgique
Koning Albertlaan 95
BELGIUM

VBO/FEB Fédération des Entreprises de Belgique
Rue Ravenstein 4
BELGIUM

NCMV Nationaal Christelikj
Middenstandsverbond
De Heer Petrus THYS -
Algemeen Secretaris
Spastraat, 8
Brussels

BOERENBOND
De Heer Hinnekens - Voorzitter
Miderbroederstraat, 8
3000 Leuven
BELGIUM

Solidaridad de Trabajadores Vascos
(ELA-STV)
Consulado, 8 - bajo
Apartado 971
20080 San Sebastian
SPAIN

Greek General Confederation of Labour
(GSEE)
Odos 28 Octovriou 69
GR - 104 Athens
GREECE

Uniao Geral de Trabalhadores
(UGT-Portugal)
Rua de Buenos Aires 11
P-1200 Lisboa
PORTUGAL

UGT-P Delegaciòn
Rue Grétry 11 (Boite 21)
B-1000 Bruxelles
BELGIUM

UCM/Union des Classes Moyennes
Avenue des Gaulois, 32
B-1040 Bruxelles
BELGIUM

Uniòn General de Trabajadores
C/Hortaleza 88
E-28004 Madrid
SPAIN

Oficina de la UGT en Bruselas
Rue Grétry 11-5°-2
B-1000 Bruxelles
BELGIUM

UIL-Unione Italiana del Lavoro
Via Lucullo 6
I-00187 Roma
ITALY

CGTL - Confédération Générale du Travail de Luxembourg
BP 149
L-Esch sur Alzette
4002
LUXEMBOURG

LCGB - Letzbuerger Chréstleche
Gewerkschaftsbond
BP 1208
LUXEMBOURG

FNV - Federatie Nederlandse Vakbeweging
Postbus 8456
NL-1005 AL Amsterdam
NETHERLANDS

CNV - Christelijk Nationaal
Vakverbond
Postbus 2475
Ravellaan 1
NL-Utrecht
NETHERLANDS

Chamber of Commerce
Rua porasde Santo Antao 89
1194 Lisboa Codex
PORTUGAL

Chamber of Commerce
Prinses Beatrixlaan 5
PO Box 95309
2509 den Haag
NETHERLANDS

International Chamber of Commerce
Commission on Environment
Cours Albert ler 38
F75008
Paris
FRANCE

International Environmental Bureau
Route de Chene 61
CH 1208 Geneva
SWITZERLAND

Union of Industrial and
Employers' Confederation of Europe (UNICE)
Rue Joseph II 40
B-1040 Brussels
BELGIUM

Training Dept
Bundesverband der Deutschen Industrie
Gustav-Heinemann-Ufer 84-88
Koln D-5000
WEST GERMANY

Training Dept
Umweltbundesamt
1 Bismarkplatz
Berlin 33
D-1000
WEST GERMANY

Training Dept
Vereinigung Deutscher Electrizitatswerke EV
Stressemannalle 23
Frankfurt 70
D-6000
WEST GERMANY

Training/Environment Dept
Verband der Chemischen Industrie
Karlstrasse 21
Postfach 111943
Frankfurt-am-Main 2
D-6000

WEST GERMANY Training/Environmental Dept
Union Des Industries Chimiques
Avenue Marceau 64
Paris F-75008
FRANCE

Vereniging van de Nederlandse
Chemische Industrie
Vlietweg 14
Postbus 443
Leidschendam
2260 AK
NETHERLANDS

Training Dept
Confederation of British Industry
Centre Point
103 New Oxford Street
LONDON
WC1A 1DU

Training Dept
Federation des Industries Chimiques
de Belgique
Square Marie-Louise 49
Brussels B-1040
BELGIUM

Environment/Training Dept
Industriraadet (Federation of Danish Industies)
H C Andersons Boulevard 18
Copenhagen V
DK-1596
DENMARK

Training Dept
Federation des Entreprises de Belgique
4 Rue Ravenstein
Brussels B-1000
BELGIUM

Training Dept
Confederation des Employeurs Espagnols
Diego de Leon 50
Madrid 6
SPAIN

Training Dept
CNPF - Conseil National du Patronat Francais
31 Av Pierre ler de Serbie
BP 15/16
Paris F-75784
FRANCE

Training Dept
Confederation of Irish Industry
Confederation House
Kildare Street
Dublin 2
EIRE

Training Dept
CONFINDUSTRIA
Viale dell'Astronomia 30
Rome I-00144
ITALY

Training Dept
Federation des Industriels Luxembourgeois
7 Rue Alcide de Gasperi
Plateau de Kirchberg
LUXEMBURG

Training Dept
Verbond van Nederlands Ondernemingen
PO Box 93093
Princes Beatrixlaan 5
The Hague
NL-2509
NETHERLANDS

Training Dept
Confederacao da Industria Portugesa
Ave 5 de Outubro 35-1
Lisbon P-1399
PORTUGAL

Office of the Danish Employer's
Confederation and the Federation of
Danish Industries
Rue Joseph 11, 40/bte 5
B-1040 Bruxelles
BELGIUM

Confederation Espanola de
Organizationcs Empresariales
Square de Meeus 30/bte 5
B-1040 Bruxelles
BELGIUM

Dr Ing K Grefen
Nerein Deutscher Ingenieure
VDI Kommission Reinhaltvng
Graf-Recke Strasse 84
Postfach 11 39
Dusseldorf D-4000
WEST GERMANY

International Confederation of
Free Trade Unions
34-51 Rue Montagne aux Herbes Potageres
Bruxelles 1000
BELGIUM

International Organization of Employers
98 Rue de St Jean
Geneva
SWITZERLAND

Federation of Greek Industry
5 Xenofontos str
Athens
GREECE

Chambre de Commerce et d'Industrie d'Avignon
et de Vaucluse
46 Cour Jean Jaurès
84.000 Avignon
FRANCE

European Trade Union Institute
Boulevard de l'Imperatrice
Bruxelles B-1000
BELGIUM

Chamber of Commerce
Rue des Sols 8
B-1000 Brussels
BELGIUM

Chamber of Commerce
9 Boulevard Malesherbes
75008 Paris
FRANCE

Chamber of Commerce
Börsen
DK-1217
Kobenhavn K
DENMARK

Chamber of Commerce
Kolumbastrasse 5
Postfach 10-04-47
5000 Köln 1
GERMANY

Chamber of Commerce
27 Kaningos Street
Athens 10682
GREECE

Verband Deutscher Maschinen und
Analagenbau e.v.
Lyoner Strasse 18
Postfach 71 08 64
Frankfurt 71
d-6000
WEST GERMANY

Conseil National du Patronat Francais
Délegation aupres des
Communautes Européennes
Rue Jospeh II, 40/bte 12
B-1040 Bruxelles
BELGIUM

Federation of Greek Industries
Rue Joseph II, 40/bte 9
B-1040 Bruxelles
BELGIUM

Confindustria - SII sa
Avenue de la Joyeuse Entrée, 1
B-1040 Bruxelles
BELGIUM

Irish Business Bureau
Avenue de Cortenberg 66/bte 9
B-1040 Bruxelles
BELGIUM

Verbond van Netherlandse
Ondernemingen
Rue Jospeh 11 40/bte 11
B-1040 Bruxelles
BELGIUM

Associacao Industrial Portuguesa
Avenue Louise 430/bte 13
B-1050 Bruxelles
BELGIUM

Confederacao da Industrial Portuguesa/
Camara de Comercio Industria Portuguesa
Rue Joseph 11, 40.bte 15
B-1040 Bruxelles
BELGIUM

Bundesvereinigung der Deutschen
Arbeitgeberverbande eV
Gustav-Geinimann-Ufer 72
Postfach 51 05 08
D-5000 Köln 51
WEST GERMANY

European Trade Union Institute
Boulevard de l'Imperatrice 66
Bruxelles B-1000
BELGIUM

Chamber of Commerce
7 Clare Street
Dublin 2
IRELAND

Chamber of Commerce
Via Xx Steeembre No 5
IT-00187 Roma
ITALY

Chamber of Commerce
7 Rue Alcide de Gasperi
B P 1503
L-2981
LUXEMBOURG

Chamber of Commerce
Rua Portas de Santo Antao 89
1194 Lisboa Codex
PORTUGAL

Chamber of Commerce
Avinguda Diagonal
452-454, 08006 Barcelona
SPAIN

Chamber of Commerce
Centre Point
103 New Oxford Street
London
WC1A 1QB

Dr. Antionio Libri,
Ente Nazionali Idrocarbaure (ENI),
Piazzale Enrico Mattell, 1,
I-001 44 Roma.

Professor E. Gerelli,
ECONPUBLICA, Centre for Research on the Public Sector Economy,
University of Pavia,
Corso Carlo Alberto, 5,
I-27100 Pavia.

General Manager,
Greek Productivity Centre,
28, Kapodistriou str.,
Athens,
Greece.

Mr. Deliyiannnis,
Federation of Greek Industry,
5, Xenofontos str.,
Athens,
Greece.

General Manager,
Hellenic Management Association,
36, Amalias Ave,
Athens,
Greece.

Dr. Lino Raffaele,
Institute for Social research and Progress,
Via Capecelatro, 5,
I-20148 Milano.

Professor George Balafoutas,
LIDEA Ltd.,
Agias Sofias, 9,
GR-546 23 Thessalonika.

MJL de Olviera E Silva Vila Lobos,
Sub Director,
Direccao da Qualidade do Ambiente,
Secretaria do Estado do Ambiente,
rua do Seculo, 57,
P-1200 Lisbon.

General Manager,
Municipality of Thebes,
Dimarhion Thivas,
Normos Viotias,
Thebes,
Greece.

President,
Centro Studi ed Informazione,
Communita Europee,
Corso Vittorio Emmanuele, 197,
I-70122 Bari.

President,
European Federation for Environmental Defence (FEDE),
Pie Monte, 39,
I-00187 Roma.

Der Senator für Arbeit/Forderwerk,
Freie Hansestadt Bremem,
Schillerstrasse, 14,
D-2800 Bremen.

General Manager Municipality of Kalamata,
Kalamata Town Hall,
Kalamata,
Greece.

Professor J.J. Fried,
European Institute of Water (EIW),
23, Boulevard d'Anvers,
F-67000 Strasbourg.

ERVET,
Servizio Ambiente-Energia,
Via Morgagni, 6,
I-40122 Bologna.

Ufficio Relazioni Esterne,
Montefluos-Montedison,
Foro Buonaparte, 31,
I-20121 Milano.

Politecnico di Milano,
Istituto di Ingegniria Sanitaria,
Leonardo da Vinci, 32,
I-20131 Milano.

Governo dell'ambiente,
University of Pavia,
I-27100 Pavia.

Professor J. Santos Oliveira,
Universidada Nova de Lisboa,
Faculdada de Ciencias e Tecnologia,
Quinta da Torre,
Monte da Caparica,
Portugal.

Dr. Paulo Estadao,
Ministerio do Ambiente,
Rua Braamcamp,
82-49 Dto,
P-1200 Lisboa.

Professor Margaris,
Egeo University,
Department of Environment,
Kanari, 9,
GR-10671 Athens.

PERPA,
Patisiou, 147,
GR-12151 Athens.

Professor Luis Toharia,
Director del Departamento,
Universidad de Alcala,
Madrid,
Spain.

Mr Kaidsas,
Directorate Secondary Curriculum Studies,
Section A,
Athens,
Greece.

Mr Pinto Patista,
International Relations,
Employment and Vocational Training Institute,
EAFB,
Instituto de Formacao Profissional,
Lisboa.

Mr E Peter-Davis,
ECO Conseil,
Institut pour le Conseil en Environnement,
7 rue Goethe,
Strasbourg,
France.

J Vigneron,
Universite de Paris VII,
c/o Department Environnement,
2 Place Jussieu,
75231 Paris,
Cedex 05,
France.

Mr J P Giraudon,
Chambre de Commerce et d'Industrie d'Avignon
et de Vaucluse,
46 Cour Jean Jaurès,
84.000 Avignon,
France.

Mr Dominique Motte,
Chargé de Mission,
Inter-Environnement Wallonie (IEW),
Federation des associations d'environnement,
Rue du Luxembourg 20,
1040 Bruxelles,
Belgium.

President,
Centre de Formation et de Documentation
sur 'Environnement Industrial,
99 Boulevard Malesherbes,
75008 Paris,
France.

A Roufagali,
Hellenic Agency for Local Development and
Local Government SA (EETAA),
19 Omirou Street,
Athens 10672,
Greece.

President,
INERAL,
Rue de Vaugirard,
75006 Paris,
France.

INCENTIVE,
Vialle Liegi 33,
00198 Roma,
Italy.

ANNEX C

SURVEY INSTRUMENTS

TRAINING ON THE ENVIRONMENT FOR PERSONNEL IN REGULATORY AGENCIES AND INDUSTRY PARTICULARLY SMALL AND MEDIUM SIZED ENTERPRISES

This study is an initiative of the European Foundation for the Improvement of Living and Working Conditions, which is being carried out by ECOTEC Research and Consulting Limited. The study aims to provide an over-view of the provision of Environmental Training, to industry (especially SME's) and regulatory agencies, in all Member States and seeks to identify gaps and areas of potential improvement in training.

Please note that this is not a questionnaire but, rather, an indication of the issues which are of relevance to the study. We would be grateful to receive your written response to the points detailed below.

A DETAILS OF THE RESPONDENT ORGANISATION

* Name of the organisation

* Address

* Name and position of the respondent

B CURRENT TRAINING PROGRAMMES

Please provide information relating to the main training programmes (not specifically environmental training) for which your Agency is responsible and indicate:

* the main purpose of each training programme
* the number of places available per annum
* the duration of courses under the programme
* the criteria for trainees to gain access to each programme (eg, age, qualifications)
* the use of managing agents (if any)
* the spatial focus (eg, regional/national)
* the industry focus (eg, engineering, manufacturing, or all).

C   CURRENT PROVISION OF ENVIRONMENTAL TRAINING

The environment, in the context of this study, relates to the environmental management practices of industry and the environmental regulatory agencies. Environmental management consists mainly of industrial pollution control but also includes waste reduction, materials recycling, and the adoption of "cleaner technologies".

Please provide details of training programmes which deal specifically with environmental issues or which contain environmental components. Answer separately for regulatory agencies and industry and indicate any special emphasis given to small and medium sized enterprises (SME's). Please provide information relating to:

* Targetting of Training - which industrial sectors; what level of personnel (management, operative); and what size of enterprise is environmental training provided for?

* Type of Training - whether in-house training, short courses, seminars/conferences or distance learning methods of training are provided.

* Content of Training - whether management or technical training is provided; details of subject area of training; and views as to the changes in emphasis given to environmental training.

* Scale of Training - details regarding the current scale of provision of environmental training (number of courses, number of places, duration of courses).

If you are aware of training programmes run by other organisations/agencies please give details?

D THE FUTURE OF ENVIRONMENTAL TRAINING

1. Please provide details of any future programmes on environmental training (if any) which you are planning or considering?

2. Please describe your views as to the requirements of industry and the regulatory agencies for environmental training and the, likely, future changes in these requirements given changes in technology and environmental legislation.

3. How do you consider environmental awareness and training may best be promoted. Please answer with reference to:

    * the requirements of the small and medium sized enterprises;
    * the role of local authorities/muncipalities, universities, trade associations, regulatory bodies;
    * and the role of the Training Agencies.

   and in recognition of the various types of initiatives available, including:

    * on-the-job training;
    * off-the-job training (short courses);
    * distance learning;
    * seminars/conferences;
    * discussions with trade unions, trade associations etc.

Please send your written response to Mr James Medhurst, Director, ECOTEC Research and Consulting Limited, Priestley House, 28-34 Albert Street, Birmingham B4 7UD, by 30th June 1990.

Thank you very much for your co-operation.

LA FORMATION A L'ENVIRONNEMENT POUR LE PERSONNEL DES AGENCES DE REGLEMENTATION ET POUR L'INDUSTRIE, EN PARTICULIER POUR LES PETITES ET MOYENNES ENTREPRISES

Cette etude, commandée par la Fondation Europeenne pour l'Amelioration de Conditions de Vie et de Travail, est réalisée par ECOTEC Research and Consulting Limited. Elle a pour but de fournir une vue d'ensemble de l'offre de formation a l'environnement destinee à l'industrie, en particulier aux PME, et aux agences de reglementation dans tous les Etats membres. L'étude tente egalement d'identifier les lacunes et les ameliorations potentielles de la formation.

Veuillez remarquer que ceci n'est pas un questionnaire, mais plutôt des indications de la portée de l'étude. Nous vous serions reconnaissants de nous faire parvenir votre réponse écrite aux thèmes elabores ci-dessous.

A DETAILS RELATIFS A L'ORGANISATION INTERROGEE

* Nom de l'organisation

* Adresse

* Nom et position du répondant

B PROGRAMMES DE FORMATION ACTUELS

Veuillez décrire les principaux programmes de formation (toutes disciplines) dont votre agence est responsable, et indiquer:

* l'objectif principal de chaque programme de formation
* le nombre de places disponibles par an
* la durée des cours de ces programmes
* les critères d'accès à chaque programme (ex. âge, qualifications)
* le recours a des specialistes (s'il y a lieu)
* le ciblage géographique (ex. régional, national)
* le ciblage industriel (ex. ingénierie, production, ou général)

C L'OFFRE ACTUELLE DE FORMATION A L'ENVIRONNEMENT

> Dans le contexte de cette étude, "environnement" fait référence aux pratiques de gestion de l'environnement de l'industrie et des agences ayant pouvoir de réglementation. La gestion de l'environnement recouvre non seulement le contrôle de la pollution industrielle, mais aussi la réduction des déchets, le recyclage des matériaux et l'adoption de "technologies douces".

Veuillez décrire les programmes de formation spécifiques à l'environnement ou comportant des éléments y ayant trait, en séparant les agences et l'industrie. Veuillez également mentionner toute attention particulière accordée aux petites et moyennes entreprises (PME). Donnez, s'il vous plaît, des informations relatives au:

* Ciblage de la formation - à quels secteurs industriels, quelles catégories de personnel (direction, production), et à quelle taille d'entreprise la formation est-elle destinée?

* Type de formation - indiquez s'il s'agit de formation interne à l'entreprise, de séries de cours, de séminaires et conférences, ou de cours par correspondance.

* Contenu de la formation - s'agit-il d'une formation technique ou à la gestion? donnez des détails sur les sujets abordés, et votre opinion sur les changements de priorités en matière de formation à l'environnement.

* Volume de la formation - décrivez le volume actuel des prestations de formation à l'environnement (nombre de cours, durée des cours, nombre de places).

Avez des informations relatives à des programmes de formation dispensés par d'autres organisations/agences? quelques précisions, s'il vous plaît.

D L'AVENIR DE LA FORMATION A L'ENVIRONNEMENT

1. Veuillez décrire les futurs programmes de formation à l'environnement que vous envisagez ou préparez (si c'est le cas) ?

2. Donnez votre opinion sur les besoins de l'industrie et des agences de réglementation en matière de formation à l'environnement, ainsi que sur l'évolution de ces besoins en fonction des changements de la technologie et de la législation relative à l'environnement.

3. Quels sont, selon vous, les meilleurs moyens d'encourager la prise de conscience et la formation à l'environnement? Donnez des détails sur:

   * les besoins des petites et moyennes entreprises
   * le rôle des autorités locales/municipalités, universités, associations et chambres de commerce, organismes de réglementation
   * le rôle des centres de formation

et, en fonction des différents types d'initiatives existants, veuillez décrire:

   * la formation continue "sur le tas"
   * cours de recyclage en entreprise
   * cours par correspondance
   * séminaires/conférences
   * discussions avec les syndicats, les associations et chambres de commerce

Veuillez retourner votre réponse à **James Medhurst, Directeur, ECOTEC Research and Consulting Limited, 28-34 Albert Street, Birmingham B4 7UD**, avant le 30 juin 1990.

Merci vivement de votre coopération

A REVIEW OF ENVIRONMENTAL EDUCATION AND TRAINING FOR INDUSTRY

Regulatory Agencies

The European Commission, through the European Foundation, has commissioned ECOTEC Research and Consulting Limited to review the need for, and provision of, education and training for personnel concerned with environmental issues relating to industry, particularly small and medium sized enterprises.

As an agency responsible for regulating industrial pollution it would be greatly appreciated if you could answer all the questions, unless otherwise indicated. Please tick the answer boxes as requested. Your answers will be treated in strictest confidence. Please give the questionnaire to another member of staff if you feel that their expertise is more relevant.

An addressed envelope is enclosed for the return of the questionnaire. Please return the questionnaire by the 30th June 1990.

Any queries regarding this questionnaire should be made to:

James Medhurst (Director), ECOTEC, England, **Tel:** (21) 616 1010

A: AGENCY DETAILS

1. Name of Agency _____

2. Address _____
   _____

3. Name and position of respondent _____

4. Name of overseeing Government Department (*if any*) _____

B: AGENCY REMIT
(*please tick the relevant answer box*)

1. Is the Agency involved in the regulation/monitoring of environmental media? YES ☐ NO ☐
   If YES, please specify.
   - (a) air   YES ☐   NO ☐
   - (b) water   YES ☐   NO ☐
   - (c) land   YES ☐   NO ☐
   - (d) noise   YES ☐   NO ☐
   - (e) waste   YES ☐   NO ☐
   - (f) other (*please specify*)
   _____
   _____

2. How many professional staff are employed by the Agency? _____

3. How many are involved in surveillance in the field (inspectors)? _____

4. Does the Agency have responsibility for the control of industrial pollution? YES ☐ NO ☐

5.   Does the Agency have direct contact with
      industry?   YES ☐   NO ☐

      If you have answered NO to question 5, go straight to Section E.

C: **CONTACT WITH INDUSTRY**

1.   What is the nature of the contact with industry?

      a)   regulation enforcement   YES ☐   NO ☐

      b)   technical advice   (i)   waste analyses   YES ☐   NO ☐
                                 (ii) control technology   YES ☐   NO ☐
                                 (iii) monitoring requirement   YES ☐   NO ☐

      c)   education (awareness) (i)   informal advice   YES ☐   NO ☐
                                 (ii) formal advice   YES ☐   NO ☐
      d)   training   YES ☐   NO ☐

      e)   other (*please specify*) _____

      _____

2.   What is the extent of annual contact with individual firms:

      a)   Average number of firms visited per annum, per inspector _____

      b)   Average length (man days) of contact per firm, per annum _____
           with the Agency.

3.   Type of Industry Visited.

      a)   Is the number of visits directly related to:

           i)   requirements of legislation   YES ☐   NO ☐
           ii)   size of firm   YES ☐   NO ☐
           iii) industrial sector   YES ☐   NO ☐
           iv)   other (*please specify*)

      _____

      b)   Please give details of industrial sectors which have the most visits.
           i)   _____

           ii) _____

           iii) _____

4.   Type of Firm Visited

      a)   Approximately what percentage of total annual visits are made to:

           i)   large firms (>500 employees)   _____ %
           ii)   medium sized firms (50 - 500 employees)   _____ %
           iii) small firms (<50 employees)   _____ %

b) Is the nature of the contact different for firms of
different sizes   YES ☐   NO ☐

c) If YES, what is the emphasis of visits to small firms (<50 employees) compared with larger firms?

    i) enforcement   more ☐   less ☐
    ii) technical advice   more ☐   less ☐
    iii) awareness   more ☐   less ☐
    iv) training   more ☐   less ☐
    v) other (*please specify*)

_____

_____ more ☐ less ☐

D: EXPERIENCE OF THE INSPECTORS

(**n.b.** inspectors are defined as those staff with direct contact with industry)

1. What is the education level attained by inspectors:

    a) Percentage with at least first degree   _____ %
    b) Percentage with at least second degree   _____ %
    c) Percentage with a specialist technical second degree   _____ %
        (eg, engineering, chemistry, biology, etc)
    d) Pecentage with broader environmental policy/technological
        experience outside the agency (eg R&D, environmental
        management, policy research)   _____ %.
    e) Percentage with specialist training in providing
        education/advice/training to industry   _____ %.
    f) Percentage with direct experience of
        working in industry   _____ %.

2. Does the Agency provide on-going training for Inspectors?   YES ☐   NO ☐

If YES, which forms of training does the Agency use?
(*please tick relevant boxes*)
    a) Off the job training in-house (provided by   ☐
        the Agency or an external trainer).
    b) Short courses.   ☐
    c) Distance learning.   ☐
    d) Films/videos/talks.   ☐
    e) Seminars/conferences.   ☐
    f) Other (*please specify*)   ☐

3. What form of training for Inspectors does the Agency consider
to be most useful for Inspectors?

_____

_____

E: ROLE OF THE AGENCY IN ENVIRONMENTAL TRAINING IN INDUSTRY

1. Do you think that the Agency could have a role to play in improving company awareness/training of personnel for environmental management, particularly in small and medium sized firms ?

    YES ☐   NO ☐

2a. If YES in what areas should the Agency be involved?

   i)   Technical advice   YES ☐   NO ☐
   ii) Management awareness   YES ☐   NO ☐
   iii) Training courses   YES ☐   NO ☐
   iv) Other (*please specify*)   YES ☐   NO ☐

2b. If NO, why not? _____

3. What methods could the Agency use to improve environmental training, particularly in small and medium sized firms ?
   (*please tick as appropriate*)

   a) Provision of verbal advice about sources of training   YES ☐   NO ☐
   b) Organisation of training seminars/conferences for industry.   YES ☐   NO ☐
   c) Provision of training courses directly by the Agency.   YES ☐   NO ☐
   d) Organisation of training courses by the Agency but delivered by external experts   YES ☐   NO ☐
   e) Provision of distance learning material.   YES ☐   NO ☐
   f) Other (*please specify*)   YES ☐   NO ☐

F: OBSERVATIONS ON POLICIES FOR ENVIRONMENTAL TRAINING

1. Do you expect changes in environmental policy and technology to increase the requirement for environmental training in industry?

    YES ☐   NO ☐

2. Do you consider the general level of environmental training and awareness in industry to be satisfactory?

                        YES ☐   NO ☐

If NO

a) Which areas are most in need of improvement (*please rank 1-4 in order of priority*)

    i) management awareness of environmental issues ☐
    ii) technical training of environmental specialists ☐
    iii) training for technicians. ☐
    iv) other (*please specify*) ☐

_____

_____

b) Which size of firm most require improved training (*please rank 1-3 in order of priority*)

    1) small (< 50 employees) ☐

    2) medium (50-500 employees) ☐

    3) large (>500 employees) ☐

c) Which of the industrial sectors that you deal with most require improved training. (*please specify and rank 1-4 in order of priority*)

    1) _____

    2) _____

    3) _____

    4) _____

3. Which organisation offers the best opportunity for improving environmental management in small and medium sized firms ? (*please rank 1-8 in order of importance*):

    a) training agencies ☐

    b) health and safety agencies ☐

    c) government research institutions ☐

    d) private sector consultants ☐

    e) regulatory agencies ☐

    f) employer organisations ☐

    g) trade union organisations ☐

    h) business support agencies (eg. banks, advisory bodies) ☐

Please return the questionnaire in the envelope provided to :

ECOTEC Research and Consulting Ltd,
Priestley House,
28-34 Albert Street,
Birmingham
B4 7UD
United Kingdom

Thank you for your co-operation

COMPTE RENDU DE L'EDUCATION ET DE LA FORMATION EN ENVIRONNEMENT DESTINEES A L'INDUSTRIE

Les agences ayant un pouvoir de réglementation

La Commission européenne, par l'intermédiaire de la Fondation européenne, a chargé ECOTEC Research and Consulting Limited de passer en revue les besoins et les prestations d'éducation et de formation du personnel concerné par les problèmes d'environnement et d'industrie, en particulier dans les petites et moyennes entreprises.

Nous vous serions reconnaissants si vous pouviez, en tant qu'agence responsable de la réglementation de la pollution industrielle, répondre à toutes les questions, sauf contre-indication. Veuillez cocher les cases réponses comme demandé. Vos réponses seront traitées dans la plus stricte confidence. N'hésitez pas à transmettre ce questionnaire à un autre membre du personnel si vous jugez que son expérience est mieux appropriée.

Vous trouverez ci-joint une enveloppe pour nous retourner le questionnaire. Veuillez avoir l'obligeance de nous le faire parvenir avant le 30 juin 1990.

Pour toute information concernant ce questionnaire, contacter:
James Medhurst (Directeur), ECOTEC, UK, Tel (21) 616 1010

A: RENSEIGNEMENTS CONCERNANT L'AGENCE

1. Nom de l'agence _____

2. Adresse _____

3. Nom et position du répondant _____

4. Nom du service gouvernemental responsable
   (*s'il existe*) _____

B: ROLE DE L'AGENCE
(Cochez la case réponse appropriée)

1. L'agence joue-t-elle un rôle dans la régulation/le contrôle d'un domaine particulier de l'environnement?

    OUI ☐   NON ☐

    Si OUI, veuillez spécifier

    (a) air ☐
    (b) eau ☐
    (c) sol ☐
    (d) bruit ☐
    (e) déchets ☐
    (f) autres *(spécifiez)* ☐
    _____
    _____

2. Combien d'employés qualifiés travaillent pour l'agence? _____

3. Combien d'entre eux participent à la surveillance sur le terrain (inspecteurs)? _____

4. L'agence a-t-elle des responsabilités en matière de contrôle de la pollution industrielle?

    OUI ☐   NON ☐

5. L'agence est-elle en contact avec l'industrie?

    OUI ☐   NON ☐

    Si vous avez répondu NON à la question 5, passer directement à la section E.

C: LES CONTACTS AVEC L'INDUSTRIE

1. Quelle est la nature de vos contacts avec l'industrie?

    a) application de la réglementation   OUI ☐   NON ☐

    b) conseil technique
        (i) analyse des déchets   OUI ☐   NON ☐
        (ii) technologie de contrôle   OUI ☐   NON ☐
        (iii) exigence en matière de controle   OUI ☐   NON ☐

    c) éducation (sensibilisation)
        (i) conseil informel   OUI ☐   NON ☐
        (ii) conseil formel   OUI ☐   NON ☐

    d) formation   OUI ☐   NON ☐

    e) autres *(précisez, s'il vous plait)*   OUI ☐   NON ☐
    _____
    _____

2. **Quelle est la fréquence annuelle de vos contacts avec chaque entreprise ?**

    a)   nombre moyen d'entreprises visitées par an, par inspecteur _____

    b)   durée moyenne (en journées de travail), par entreprise et
par an, du contact avec l'agence _____

3. **Types d'industries visitées**

    a)   la fréquence des visites est directement liée:
   - i)   aux exigences de la législation   OUI ☐ NON ☐
   - ii)   à la taille de l'entreprise   OUI ☐ NON ☐
   - iii) au secteur industriel   OUI ☐ NON ☐
   - iv) autres (*précisez, s'il vous plait*)   OUI ☐ NON ☐

   _____

   _____

    b)   quels sont les secteurs industriels que vous visitez le plus?

        i) _____

        ii) _____

        iii) _____

4. **Types d'entreprises visitées**

    a)   répartition approximative (%) du nombre total annuel de visites
   - i)   grandes entreprises (plus de 500 employés) _____ %
   - ii)   moyennes entreprises (de 50 à 500 employés) _____ %
   - iii) petites entreprises (moins de 50 employés) _____ %

    b)   la nature du contact est-elle différente   OUI ☐ NON ☐
selon la taille de l'entreprise

    c)   si OUI, quelle est la proportion de visites aux entreprises de moins de 50 employés relative aux plus grandes entreprises
   - i)   application de la réglementation   moins ☐ plus ☐
   - ii)   conseil technique   moins ☐ plus ☐
   - iii) sensibilisation   moins ☐ plus ☐
   - iv) formation   moins ☐ plus ☐
   - v)   autres (*précisez SVP*)

   _____

   _____ moins ☐ plus ☐

D: L'EXPERIENCE DES INSPECTEURS

(**N.B.** Les inspecteurs sont définis comme les membres du personnel en contact direct avec l'industrie)

1. **Quel est le niveau d'études des inspecteurs:**

   a) pourcentage ayant au moins un diplôme du premier cycle _____ %

   b) pourcentage ayant au moins un diplôme du deuxième cycle _____ %

   c) pourcentage ayant un diplôme de l'enseignement supérieur de technicien spécialisé (ex. ingéniérie, chimie, biologie, etc.) _____ %

   d) pourcentage ayant une expérience en matière de politique ou technologie de l'environnement hors de l'agence (ex. R&D, gestion de l'environnement, recherche de politiques) _____ %

   e) pourcentage ayant une formation spécialisée préparant à l'éducation, au conseil ou à la formation dans l'industrie _____ %

   f) pourcentage ayant une expérience professionnelle dans l'industrie _____ %

2. **L'agence offre-t-elle une formation continue aux inspecteurs?**

   OUI ☐   NON ☐

   Si OUI, quel est le type de formation utilisé par l'agence?
   (*Cochez la case réponse appropriée*)

   a) cours de recyclage internes ☐
      (dispensés par l'agence ou par un intervenant extérieur)
   b) courtes périodes de cours ☐
   c) cours par correspondance ☐
   d) films, vidéos, discussions organisées ☐
   e) séminaires, conférences ☐
   f) autres (spécifiez SVP) ☐

3. **Quel est le type de formation que l'agence considère comme le plus utile pour les inspecteurs?**

   _____
   _____
   _____
   _____
   _____
   _____

E. ROLE DE L'AGENCE EN MATIERE DE FORMATION A L'ENVIRONNEMENT POUR L'INDUSTRIE

1. Pensez-vous que l'agence pourrait avoir un rôle à jouer dans la sensibilisation et la formation du personnel à la gestion de l'environnement, en particulier dans les PME?

   OUI ☐   NON ☐

2a. Si OUI, dans quels domaines l'agence devrait elle être impliquée?

   i) conseil technique   OUI ☐   NON ☐
   ii) sensibilisation à la gestion   OUI ☐   NON ☐
   iii) cours de formation   OUI ☐   NON ☐
   iv) autres (*précisez SVP*)   OUI ☐   NON ☐

   _____

   _____

2b. Si NON, pourquoi?

   _____

   _____

3. Quelles sont les méthodes que l'agence pourrait adopter pour améliorer la formation dans le domaine de l'environnement, en particulier dans les PME?
   (*Cochez la case réponse appropriée*)

   a) information et conseil sur les formations disponibles   OUI ☐   NON ☐
   b) organisation de conférences et de séminaires de formation pour l'industrie   OUI ☐   NON ☐
   c) prestation de cours de formation par l'agence elle-même   OUI ☐   NON ☐
   d) organisation de cours de formation par l'agence, mais dispensés par des intervenants extérieurs spécialisés   OUI ☐   NON ☐
   e) mise à disposition de programmes de cours par correspondance   OUI ☐   NON ☐
   f) autres (*précisez SVP*)   OUI ☐   NON ☐

   _____

   _____

F. OBSERVATIONS SUR LES POLITIQUES DE FORMATION DANS LE DOMAINE DE L'ENVIRONNEMENT

1. Vous attendez-vous à ce que les changements en matière de politique et de technologie de l'environnement viennent augmenter la demande de formation de l'industrie dans ce domaine?

   OUI ☐   NON ☐

2. **Pensez vous que le niveau général de la formation et de la sensibilisation de l'industrie à l'environnement soit satisfaisant?**

   OUI ☐   NON ☐

   Si NON

   a) Quels sont les domaines qui nécessitent une intervention particulière
   (*classez, SVP, de 1 à 4 par ordre de priorité*)

       i) sensibilisation à la gestion des problèmes d'environnement ☐

       ii) formation technique de spécialistes de l'environnement ☐

       iii) formation de techniciens ☐

       iv) autres (*précisez SVP*) ☐

   _____

   _____

   b) Quelle est la catégorie d'entreprises ayant le plus besoin d'améliorer leur formation
   (*classer, SVP, de 1 à 3 par ordre de priorité*)

       1) petite (moins de 50 employés) ☐

       2) moyenne (de 50 à 500 employés) ☐

       3) grande (plus de 500 employés) ☐

   c) Quels sont, parmi les secteurs industriels avec lesquels vous travaillez, ceux qui ont le plus besoin d'améliorer la formation (*spécifiez de 1 à 4 par ordre de priorité*)

       1) _____

       2) _____

       3) _____

       4) _____

3. **Quels sont les organisations qui offrent les meilleurs possibilités d'amélioration de la gestion de l'environnement dans les PME** (*classer, SVP, de 1 à 8 par ordre d'importance*)

       a) centres de formation ☐

       b) agences de contrôle santé/sécurité ☐

       c) centres nationaux de recherche ☐

       d) consultants du secteur privé ☐

       e) agence ayant un pouvoir de réglementation ☐

       f) organisations patronales ☐

       g) organisations syndicales ☐

       h) agences d'assistance aux entreprises (ex. banques, organismes de conseil) ☐

Veuillez, sil vous plait, retourner ce questionnaire dans l' enveloppe fournie à :

> ECOTEC Research and Consulting Ltd.
> Priestley House
> 28-34 Albert Street
> Birmingham
> B4 7UD
> Royaume Uni

Merci de votre coopération

A REVIEW OF ENVIRONMENTAL EDUCATION AND TRAINING FOR INDUSTRY

The European Commission, through the European Foundation, has commissioned ECOTEC Research and Consulting Limited to review the need for, and provision of, education and training for personnel concerned with environmental issues relating to industry, particularly small and medium sized enterprises.

It would be greatly appreciated if you could answer all the following unless otherwise indicated. Please tick the answer boxes as requested. Your answers will be treated in strictest confidence. Please give the questionnaire to another member of staff if you feel that their expertise is more relevant.

Please return the questionnaire in the addressed envelope provided, by the 31st July 1990.

If you have any queries regarding this questionnaire please do not hesitate to contact :

James Medhurst (Director), ECOTEC, England, **Tel:** (21) 616 1010

SECTION A: DETAILS OF ORGANISATION

1. Name of Organisation _____

2. Address of Organisation _____

3. Name and position of respondent _____

4. Does your organisation represent:

Employers	YES ☐	NO ☐
Employees	YES ☐	NO ☐
Commerce generally	YES ☐	NO ☐
Other (*please specify*)	YES ☐	NO ☐

5. **Which industrial group(s) does your organisation represent**

Tick Group(s) Represented

a)	Agriculture, forestry and fishing	YES ☐ NO ☐
b)	Energy and water supply industries	YES ☐ NO ☐
c)	Extraction of minerals and ores other than fuels; manufacture of metals, mineral products and chemicals	YES ☐ NO ☐
d)	Metal goods, engineering and vehicle industries	YES ☐ NO ☐
e)	Other manufacturing industries	YES ☐ NO ☐
f)	Construction	YES ☐ NO ☐
g)	Distribution, hotels and catering repairs	YES ☐ NO ☐
h)	Transport and communication	YES ☐ NO ☐
i)	Banking, finance, insurance, business services and leasing	YES ☐ NO ☐
j)	Other services	YES ☐ NO ☐
k)	All manufacturing industries	YES ☐ NO ☐
l)	All industries	YES ☐ NO ☐

Please specify, if appropriate, more precisely the industrial group(s) your organisation represents.

_____

_____

_____

6. **Approximately what percentage of your member companies are:**

a)	Small (<50 employees)	_____	%
b)	Medium (50 - 500 employees)	_____	%
c)	Large (>500 employees)	_____	%
	Total	100	%

7. **What is the role of your organisation?**
   (*Please tick as appropriate*)

Function	Primary Role	Other Role(s)
a) Promotion of national industry overseas	☐	☐
b) Provision of Business Services	☐	☐
c) Issue of Guidelines on Best Practise for Industry	☐	☐
d) Provision of Information on: policy/legislation	☐	☐
health/safety	☐	☐
environmental issues	☐	☐
e) Lobbying of government on members' behalf	☐	☐
f) Provision of training	☐	☐
g) Promotion of environmental good practice	☐	☐

SECTION B: AWARENESS OF ENVIRONMENTAL MANAGEMENT

8a. Has your organisation established an environmental committee / action group ?

        YES ☐   NO ☐

If YES, please give details:

_____

_____

_____

8b. **If YES, what are its major functions:**
(*Please tick as appropriate*)

   i) Dissemination of information on environmental legislation/policy ☐
   ii) Advice on environmental good practice ☐
   iii) Promotion of environmental awareness ☐
   iv) Provision of training on environmental issues ☐
   v) Policy making on environmental issues ☐
   vi) Other (*please specify*) ☐

_____

_____

9. Do you think there has been an increase in 'environmental awareness' amongst your members?

        YES ☐   NO ☐

10. To your knowledge, are your members introducing measures to address environmental management issues?

        YES ☐   NO ☐

If YES, what measures are they introducing?
(*Please tick as appropriate*)

   a) Development of in-house awareness ☐
   b) Attendance at seminars/conferences ☐
   c) Use of consultants ☐
   d) Identification of senior management responsibility ☐
   e) New management strategies ☐
   f) New marketing activities ☐
   g) New production and technological methods ☐

11. **If production and technological changes are occuring which of the following developments are being adopted by your members?**
    (*Please tick as appropriate*)

    a) Use of cleaner technologies ☐
    b) Integrated pollution control ☐
    c) End-of-pipe technology ☐
    d) Material substitution ☐
    e) Recycling of waste products ☐
    f) Management and disposal of pollutants ☐
    g) Changes in the production process ☐
    h) Changes in the final product ☐

SECTION C: LEVEL OF COMPANY INVOLVEMENT WITH ENVIRONMENTAL MANAGEMENT

12. **Please indicate which personnel in your member companies have some responsibility for environmental management tasks?**
    (*Please tick as appropriate*)

    i) Chairman/Partner ☐
    ii) Managing Director ☐
    iii) Marketing Manager ☐
    iv) Training Manager ☐
    v) Production/Technical Manager ☐
    vi) Plant Manager ☐
    vii) Works Manager ☐
    viii) Laboratory Staff ☐
    ix) Technicians/Fitters ☐
    x) Other (*please specify*) ☐

    _____
    _____

13. **Is there any evidence to suggest that there has been any change in the skills requirement of your member companies, due to changes in environmental management requirements?**

    YES ☐   NO ☐

    If YES, please give details:
    _____
    _____
    _____
    _____

14. **Have member companies created specific senior management post(s) to address environmental management requirements?**

    YES ☐   NO ☐

15. **Have member companies expanded existing senior management positions to include responsibility for environmental issues?**

    YES ☐   NO ☐

    If YES, which existing senior management positions now take responsibility for environmental issues?
    (*please tick as appropriate*)

    a) Managing Director ☐
    b) Marketing Director ☐
    c) Finance Director ☐
    d) Technical Director ☐
    e) Personnel Director ☐
    f) Other (*please specify*) ☐

    _____

    _____

16. **Have member companies created specific post(s) to address production and technical aspects of increased environmental management?**

    YES ☐   NO ☐

    If YES, please indicate the type of job which has been created
    (e.g. job title, degree of management responsibility, type of technical functions).

    _____

    _____

    _____

SECTION D : TRAINING NEEDS OF INDUSTRY

17. **Is there, generally, adequate education and training for those responsible for environmental management in your member companies?**

    YES ☐   NO ☐

    If NO

    a) Which areas are most in need of improvement (*please rank 1-4 in order of priority*)

    1) management awareness of environmental issues ☐
    2) technical training of environmental specialists ☐
    3) training for technicians. ☐
    4) other (*please specify*) ☐

    _____

    b) Which size of firm most requires improved training (*please rank 1-3 in order of priority*)

    1) small (< 50 employees) ☐
    2) medium (50-500 employees) ☐
    3) large (>500 employees) ☐

c) For those organisations whose membership includes more than one industry please indicate which industrial sectors most require improved training ?
(please specify and rank 1-4 in order of priority)

1) _____
2) _____
3) _____
4) _____

18. **Are there any specific skill shortages affecting the level/quality of environmental management amongst your member companies?**

    YES ☐   NO ☐

    If YES, please give details

    _____
    _____
    _____
    _____

19. **Which of the following do your member companies tend to look for in recruiting employees for environmental management?**
    (Please tick as appropriate)

    1) Graduates, with specific environmental management training. ☐
    2) Technically competent graduates to be trained appropriately in-house. ☐
    3) Technically competent workers/managers to be trained appropriately in-house. ☐

20. **Please indicate which of the following formal environmental training methods are used by your member companies ?**
    (Please tick as appropriate)

    a) In-house, off the job training courses (either provided by the company or an external training provider) ☐
    b) Induction courses ☐
    c) Short courses provided by external institutions ☐
    d) Day/block release ☐
    e) Evening classes ☐
    f) Distance learning ☐
    g) None of these ☐
    h) Other *(specify)* ☐

    _____
    _____

21. **Please indicate which of the following informal training methods are used by your member companies ?**
    (*please tick as appropriate*)

    a) On-the-job experience ☐
    b) Films/videos/talks ☐
    c) Seminars/conferences ☐
    d) Educational campaigns ☐
    e) Leaflets/circulars/publications ☐
    f) Discussions with external organisations ☐
    g) None of these ☐
    h) Other (*please specify*) ☐

    _____

    _____

    _____

22. **Which of the training methods itemised in questions 20 and 21 are most appropriate for training for environmental management?** (*please rank 1 - 3 in order of preference*)

    1) _____

    2) _____

    3) _____

23. **To your knowledge are any of the environmental regulatory agencies involved in providing training in pollution control to your member companies ?**

    YES ☐   NO ☐

    If YES, please indicate which agencies and the nature of the training they provide.

    _____

    _____

    _____

    _____

SECTION E: TRAINING FUNCTION OF THE ORGANISATION

24a. **Does your organisation provide/arrange training on environmental issues ?**

    YES ☐   NO ☐

24b. If YES, what type of training is provided ?
   (*please tick as appropriate*)

   i)   Promotion of in-house training ☐
   ii) Provision of short courses ☐
   iii) Provision of distance learning materials ☐
   iv) Organisation of seminars/conferences ☐
   v)   Other (*please specify*) ☐

   _____
   _____
   _____

24c. For whom is training provided ?
   (*please tick as appropriate*)

   i)   Chairman/Partner ☐
   ii)   Managing Director ☐
   iii) Marketing Manager ☐
   iv)   Training Manager ☐
   v)   Production/Technical Manager ☐
   vi)   Plant Manager ☐
   vii) Works Manager ☐
   viii) Laboratory Staff ☐
   ix)   Technicians/Fitters ☐

25. Have there been any recent changes in your involvement in environmental education and training ?
   (*please tick as appropriate*)

   a) Increased involvement ☐
   b) Decreased involvement ☐
   c) No change ☐

   If there has been a change, please indicate the reason(s)
   (*Please tick as appropriate*)

   i)   Increased environmental awareness ☐
   ii) Legislative changes ☐
   iii) Policy changes ☐
   iv) Technology changes ☐
   v)   Other (*please specify*) ☐

   _____
   _____
   _____

26. Do you anticipate that your involvement will change in the future?

   Yes ☐
   No ☐
   Unsure ☐

If YES, why is this?
(*please tick as appropriate*)

i) Increased environmental awareness ☐
ii) Legislative changes ☐
iii) Policy changes ☐
iv) Changing technology ☐
v) Other (*please specify*) ☐

_____
_____
_____

27. **Do you consider that your organisation has an important role to play in promoting environmental awareness amongst your member companies?**

    YES ☐   NO ☐

    If YES, please indicate the means by which this objective may best be achieved.

_____
_____
_____
_____
_____
_____

Please return the questionnaire in the envelope provided, by the 3 Ju 1990, to :

ECOTEC Research and Consulting Ltd.
Priestley House
28-34 Albert Street
Birmingham
B4 7UD

Thankyou for your co-operation

COMPTE RENDU DE L'EDUCATION ET DE LA FORMATION EN ENVIRONNEMENT DESTINEES A L'INDUSTRIE

La Commission européenne, par l'intermediaire de la Fondation européenne, a charge ECOTEC Research and Consulting Limited de passer en revue les besoins et les prestations d'éducation et de formation du personnel concerné par les problèmes d'environnement et d'industrie, en particulier dans les petites et moyennes entreprises.

Nous vous serions reconnaissants de bien vouloir repondre a toutes les questions, sauf contre-indication. Veuillez cocher les cases reponses comme demandé. Vos reponses seront traitées dans la plus stricte confidence. N'hésitez pas à transmettre ce questionnaire a un autre membre du personnel si vous jugez que son experience est mieux appropriee.

Vous trouverez ci-joint une enveloppe pour nous retourner le questionnaire. Veuillez avoir l'obligeance de nous le faire parvenir avant le 30 juillet 1990.

Pour toute information concernant ce questionnaire, contactez:
James Medhurst (Directeur), ECOTEC, UK, Tel (21) 616 1010

SECTION A: RENSEIGNEMENTS CONCERNANT L'ORGANISATION

1. Nom de l'organisation _____

2. Adresse _____

3. Nom et position du repondant _____

4. Votre organisation represente-t-elle?

les employeurs	OUI ☐	NON ☐
les employés	OUI ☐	NON ☐
le secteur industriel	OUI ☐	NON ☐
autres (*précisez SVP*)	OUI ☐	NON ☐

5   Quelles sont les secteurs représentés par votre organisation ?

   a) agriculture, forêt et pêche   OUI ☐   NON ☐
   b) industries de production d'énergie et d'eau   OUI ☐   NON ☐
   c) extraction de minéraux et minérais autres que   OUI ☐   NON ☐
      combustibles; métallurgie, produits minéraux et chimiques
   d) produits métalliques, ingéniérie et industrie automobile   OUI ☐   NON ☐
   e) autres industries de production   OUI ☐   NON ☐
   f) construction   OUI ☐   NON ☐
   g) distribution, hôtels et restauration   OUI ☐   NON ☐
   h) transports et communications   OUI ☐   NON ☐
   i) banque, finance, assurance, services commerciaux   OUI ☐   NON ☐
      et credit-bail
   j) autres services   OUI ☐   NON ☐
   k) toutes les industries de production   OUI ☐   NON ☐
   l) ensemble du secteur industriel   OUI ☐   NON ☐

Veuillez spécifier plus précisément, si nécessaire, les secteurs industriels représentés par votre organisation

_____

_____

_____

6. Répartition approximative (%) des entreprises affiliées

   a) petites entreprises   (moins de 50 employés)   _____ %
   b) moyennes entreprises   (de 50 à 500 employés)   _____ %
   c) grandes entreprises   (plus de 500 employés)   _____ %
      Total   ___100____ %

7. Quel est le rôle de votre organisation?
    (Prière de cocher la case appropriée)

    Fonction   rôle principal   autres rôles

    a) promotion de l'industrie nationale à l'étranger   ☐   ☐
    b) services aux entreprises   ☐   ☐
    c) comptes rendus pour l'industrie sur les meilleures   ☐   ☐
       pratiques
    d) diffusion d'informations sur:
                     politiques et législation   ☐   ☐
                     santé et sécurité   ☐   ☐
                     problèmes d'environnement   ☐   ☐
    e) pression du gouvernement sur le comportement des   ☐   ☐
       membres
    f) prestation de formation   ☐   ☐
    g) promotion des technologies non-polluantes   ☐   ☐

SECTION B: SENSIBILISATION A LA GESTION DE L'ENVIRONNEMENT

8a. Votre organisation a-t-elle créé un comité ou groupe d'action en faveur de l'environnement?

OUI ☐   NON ☐

Si OUI, veuillez donner des détails.

_____

_____

_____

_____

8b. Si OUI, quelles sont ses principales fonctions
(Prière de cocher la case appropriée)

- i) diffusion d'informations concernant la législation et les politiques relatives a l'environnement ☐
- ii) conseil en technologies non-polluantes ☐
- iii) sensibilisation a l'environnement ☐
- iv) prestation de formation aux problèmes d'environnement ☐
- v) élaboration de politiques relatives a l'environnement ☐
- vi) autres *(precisez SVP)* ☐

_____

_____

9. Pensez-vous qu'il y ait eu une intensification de la prise de conscience de l'environnement parmi vo membres?

OUI ☐   NON ☐

10. A votre connaissance, les membres de votre organisation ont-ils introduit des mesures pour repondr aux problèmes de gestion de l'environnement?

OUI ☐   NON ☐

Si OUI, quelles mesures ont-ils introduit ?
(Prière de cocher la case appropriée)

- a) sensibilisation interne à l'entreprise ☐
- b) participation à des cours/séminaires ☐
- c) recours à des consultants ☐
- d) identification de la responsabilité de la direction ☐
- e) nouvelles stratégies de gestion ☐
- f) nouvelles activités de marketing ☐
- g) nouvelles méthodes de gestion et technologies ☐

11. **Dans le cas de changement de technologie ou de methode de production, quelles ont été les solutio adoptées par vos membres?**
   (Prière de cocher la case appropriée)

   a) utilisation de technologies moins polluantes ☐
   b) contrôle intégré de la pollution ☐
   c) technologies en aval ☐
   d) matériaux de substitution ☐
   e) recyclage de déchets ☐
   f) gestion et élimination des agents polluants ☐
   g) modification du processus de production ☐
   h) modification du produit fini ☐

SECTION C: DEGRE D'ENGAGEMENT DES ENTREPRISES DANS LA GESTION DE L'ENVIRONNEMEN

12. **Parmi vos membres, quelles sont les catégories de personnel responsables de la gestion d l'environnement ?** *(Prière de cocher la case appropriée)*

    i) president/associe ☐
    ii) directeur general ☐
    iii) directeur des ventes ☐
    iv) directeur de la formation ☐
    v) directeur technique/de la production ☐
    vi) directeur du site ☐
    vii) directeur des travaux ☐
    viii) personnel de laboratoire ☐
    ix) techniciens/monteurs ☐
    x) autres (précisez SVP) ☐

    _____
    _____

13. **Avez-vous constaté une évolution des compétences demandées dans vos sociétés membres en raison des changements des exigences de la gestion de l'environnement?**
    OUI ☐   NON ☐

    Si OUI, veuillez donner des détails:
    _____
    _____
    _____

14. **Les sociétés membres ont-elles créé des emplois spécifiques pour répondre aux exigences de la gestion de l'environnement?**
    OUI ☐   NON ☐

15. Les sociétés membres ont-elles étendu les fonctions de la direction pour y inclure la responsabilité problèmes d'environnement?

    OUI ☐   NON ☐

    Si OUI, quels sont les postes de direction responsable aujourd'hui de la gestion de l'environnem
    (Prière de cocher la case appropriée)

    a) directeur général   ☐
    b) directeur des ventes   ☐
    c) directeur financier   ☐
    d) directeur technique   ☐
    e) directeur du personnel   ☐
    f) autres (précisez SVP)   ☐

    _____

    _____

16. Les sociétés membres ont-elles créé des emplois spécifiques pour repondre aux aspects techniques de production liés au caractère plus strict de la gestion de l'environnement?

    OUI ☐   NON ☐

    Si OUI, veuillez indiquer le type d'emplois créés
    (ex. description du poste, degré de responsabilité dans la gestion, aspects techniques)

    _____

    _____

    _____

SECTION D: BESOINS DE FORMATION DE L'INDUSTRIE

17. En général, l'éducation et la formation des responsables de la gestion de l'environnement de vos sociétés membres est-elle adaptée?

    OUI ☐   NON ☐

    Si NON,

    a) Quels sont les domaines requiérant une amélioration? (classez SVP de 1 à 4 par ordre de priorité

        1) sensibilisation à la gestion des problèmes   ☐
           d'environnement
        2) formation technique de spécialistes de   ☐
           l'environnement
        3) formation de techniciens   ☐
        4) autres (précisez SVP)   ☐

    b) Pour quelle taille d'entreprise est-il nécessaire d'améliorer la formation?
       (classez SVP les propositions de 1 à 3 par ordre de priorité)

        1) petites entreprises (moins de 50 employés)   ☐
        2) moyennes entreprises (de 50 à 500 employés)   ☐
        3) grandes entreprises (plus de 500 employés)   ☐

c) pour les organisations ayant des membres appartenant a plusieurs industries, veuillez indiquer secteurs industriels necessitant une meilleure formation ?
   (*veuillez specifier et classer de 1 à 4 par ordre de priorité*)

   1) _____

   2) _____

   3) _____

   4) _____

18. Constatez-vous, parmi vos sociétés membres, une insuffisance des qualifications spécifiques affectant le niveau ou la qualité de la gestion de l'environnement?

    OUI ☐   NON ☐

    Si OUI, veuillez preciser.

    _____

    _____

    _____

    _____

19. Quelles catégories de personnel vos sociétés membres recherchent-elles lors de leur recrutement en matière de gestion de l'environnement ? (*classez, SVP, de 1 à 3 par ordre de préférence*)

    1) des diplômés du supérieur ayant une formation spécialisée en gestion de l'environnement. ☐
    2) des diplômés du supérieur ayant une competence technique et à qui l'entreprise assurera une formation spécifique ☐
    3) des travailleurs ou gestionnaires ayant une competence technique et à qui l'entreprise assurera une formation spécifique ☐

20. Quelles sont les méthodes formelles de formation dans le domaine de l'environnement utilisées par vos sociétés membres ?
    (*Prière de cocher la case appropriée*)

    a) cours de formation interne à l'entreprise (organisés par la société ou un organisme de formation) ☐
    b) cours d'initiation ☐
    c) courtes périodes de cours dispensés par des institutions extérieures ☐
    d) formation intermittente ☐
    e) cours du soir ☐
    f) cours par correspondance ☐
    g) aucune de ces formations ☐
    h) autres (*précisez SVP*) ☐

    _____

21. Quelles sont les methodes informelles de formation dans le domaine de l'environnement utilisées ¡ vos sociétés membres
    (Prière de cocher la case appropriee)

    a) expérience aquise en entreprise ☐
    b) films, videos, discussions organisees ☐
    c) séminaires, conférences ☐
    d) campagnes éducatives ☐
    e) brochures, circulaires, publications ☐
    f) discussions avec des organisations exterieures ☐
    g) aucune de ces formations ☐
    h) autres *(précisez SVP)* ☐

    _____
    _____
    _____

22. Quelles sont, parmi les methodes de formation enumerees dans les questions 20 et 21, celles qui vou paraissent les plus appropriées ?
    (veuillez classer vos choix de 1 à 3 par ordre de péférence)

    1) _____
    2) _____
    3) _____

23. A votre connaisance, exite-t-il des agences de réglementation dans le domaine de l'environnement qui offrent a vos sociétés membres des formations en matière de contrôle de la pollution ?

    OUI ☐   NON ☐

    Si OUI, indiquez les agences et les types de formation qu'elles proposent.

    _____
    _____
    _____
    _____

SECTION E: LE ROLE DE L'ORGANISATION EN MATIERE DE FORMATION

24a. Votre organisation dispense ou organise-t-elle pour les sociétés membres des formations sur le thème de l'environnement?

    OUI ☐   NON ☐

24b. Si OUI, quel type de formation offre-t-elle?
   (Prière de cocher la case appropriée)

   i) promotion de la formation au sein de l'entreprise ☐
   ii) prestation de cycles courts ☐
   iii) mise à disposition de cours par correspondance ☐
   iv) organisation de séminaires et de conférences ☐
   v) autres *(précisez SVP)* ☐

   _____

   _____

24c. A qui la formation est-elle destinée?

   i) président/associé ☐
   ii) directeur général ☐
   iii) directeur des ventes ☐
   iv) directeur de la formation ☐
   v) directeur technique/de production ☐
   vi) directeur du site ☐
   vii) directeur des travaux ☐
   viii) personnel de laboratoire ☐
   ix) techniciens/monteurs ☐

25. Votre participation à l'éducation et à la formation en environnement a-t-elle changé récemment?

   a) participation accrue ☐
   b) participation réduite ☐
   c) pas de changement ☐

   S'il y a eu un changement, veuillez en indiquer les raisons
   (Prière de cocher la case appropriée)

   i) intensification de la sensibilisation à l'environnement ☐
   ii) changements législatifs ☐
   iii) changements de politiques ☐
   iv) modifications de technologie ☐
   v) autres *(précisez SVP)* ☐

   _____

   _____

26. Pensez-vous que votre participation va s'intensifier dans le futur ?

   a) oui ☐
   b) non ☐
   c) incertain ☐

Si OUI, pourquoi?

    i)   intensification de la sensibilisation à l'environnement ☐
    ii)   changements législatifs ☐
    iii) changements de politiques ☐
    iv) modifications de technologie ☐
    v)   autres (*précisez SVP*) ☐

_____
_____
_____

27. Pensez-vous que votre organisation ait un rôle important à jouer dans la promotion de la prise de conscience des problèmes d'environnement par vos sociétés membres?

                                  OUI ☐   NON ☐

Si OUI, veuillez indiquer les meilleurs mesures a prendre pour atteindre cet objectif.

_____
_____
_____
_____
_____
_____

Veuillez, sil vous plait, retourner ce questionnaire dans l'enveloppe fournie à :

```
ECOTEC Research and Consulting Ltd.
          Priestley House
        28-34 Albert Street
            Birmingham
              B4 7UD
           Royaume Uni
```

Merci de votre coopération

ANNEX D

AN INTERNATIONAL WORKSHOP ON EDUCATION AND
TRAINING OF CATEGORIES OF PERSONNEL
CONCERNED WITH ENVIRONMENTAL ISSUES
RELATING TO INDUSTRY

AN INTERNATIONAL WORKSHOP ON EDUCATION AND TRAINING OF CATEGORIES OF PERSONNEL CONCERNED WITH ENVIRONMENTAL ISSUES RELATING TO INDUSTRY

1.0 PURPOSE OF THE WORKSHOP

The workshop was intended to be a forum for the exchange of information and ideas on the need for environmental education and training in the EC and effective ways or responding to this need. It focused, in particular, on the needs of SMEs and regional and local regulatory agencies in the South European Member States, including the practical and technical problems facing the SMEs and regulatory agencies in this area.

The workshop was organised as part of the project on the above-mentioned theme, undertaken by the Foundation in 1989-1990, in support of the extensive work of the Commission on environmental education and training and as one of several studies included under the heading "the firm in its local environment" in the Foundation's four-year programme 1989-1992. ECOTEC Research and Consulting Limited, the organisers of the workshop, carrying out this project have reviewed existing research findings and surveyed a full range of agencies in the Community with an interest in this area. The preliminary findings of the project were presented to the workshop as the basis for comments and discussion.

The following three issues were addressed by the workshop:

- the current and future education and training needs of industry, particularly SMEs, and regulatory agencies for environmental management;

- the existing nature of environmental education and training services, particularly in the South European Member States;

- the character of environmental education and training services in the future with reference to the different roles to be played by the organisations and agencies represented at the workshops.

The workshop, therefore, served three functions:

- to inform and validate the findings of the current research project;

- to provide a forum for the exchange of ideas and opinions, on environmental training, between participants with a wide range of interests;

- to provide a basis for the longer term development of policies in this field.

The meeting brought together representatives of governments, regulatory agencies, training agencies, the social partners, industry, the Commission, and ILO.

2.0 PARTICIPANTS AT THE WORKSHOP

Ms. Ana Cristina Aleixo
Secretàrio Nacional
Uniâo Geral de Trabalhadores
Rua Buenos Aires 11
1200 Lisbon
Portugal

Mr Nigal Blackburn
International Chamber of Commerce
38, Cours Alber 1er
75008 Paris
France

Prof. Francis Cambou
Université Paul Sabatier de Toulouse
(Expert à la Task Force Ressources Humaines,
  Education, Formation et Jeunesse
  Commission des Communautés Européennes)
Centre d'études spatiale des rayonnements - C.N.R.S.
9 Avenue Colonel Roche
31400 Toulouse
France

Mr Troy Davis
Bundesdeutscher Arbeitskreis für
umweltbewußtes Management (BAUM)
Sillenstraße 36
2000 Hamburg 20
Federal Republic of Germany

Mr François Desrentes
CCIAV
46, Cours Jean Jaurès
84000 Avignon
France

Mr Antonio Garcià Alvarez
Jefe de Servicio de Educaciòn Ambiental
Ministerio de obras Públicas y Urbanismo
Paseo de la Castellana 67
28071 Madrid
Spain

Mr Jean-Pierre Giraudon
CCIAV
46, Cours Jean Jaurés
84000 Avignon
France

Ms Hanne Hansen
European Foundation for the Improvement of
Living and Working Conditions
Loughlinstown House
Shankill, Co. Dublin
Ireland

Mr James Medhurst
ECOTEC Research and Consulting Limited
28-34 Albert Street
Birmingham
B4 7UD
United Kingdom

Mr Michel Miller
European Trade Union Confederation
Rue Montagne aux Herbes Potagères, 37
1000 Brussels
Belgium

Dr Armando Occhipinti
Ufficio Istruzione e Formazione
CONFAPI
Confederazione Italiana Piccola e Media Industria
Via Della Colonna Antonina 52
00186 Rome
Italy

Mr Jorn Pedersen
European Foundation for the Improvement
of Living and Working Conditions
Loughlinstown House
Shankill, Co. Dublin
Ireland

Mr Peter Plett
ILO
4 Route des Morillons
1211 Geneva 22
Switzerland

Mr Claudio Stanzani
SINDNOCA-CISL
Via Buon Compagni 19
00187 Rome
Italy

Mr Jean-Yves Terrier
Union of Industrial and Employers
Confederation of Europe
Rue Joseph II, 40
1040 Brussels
Belgium

Mr Hugh Williams
ECOTEC Research and Consulting Limited
28-34 Albert Street
Birmingham
B4 7UD
United Kingdom

3.0 THE WORKSHOP AGENDA

9.00 - 9.20   Registration

9.20 - 9.30   Opening of the workshop, by Jorn Pedersen. European Foundation for the Improvement of Living and Working Conditions.

9.30 - 9.45   Introduction by Hugh Williams, ECOTEC Research and Consulting Limited.

9.45 - 10.50   Session I : Environmental education and training needs: A review of the current and future needs of industry and regulatory agencies.

10.50 - 11.10 Coffee/tea break

11.10 - 12.25 Session II : Environmental education and training provision: A review of the existing provision of services in Europe.

12.25 - 13.55 Lunch

13.55 - 15.25	Session III : Key actors in the provision of environmental education and training. A consideration of the roles of regulatory agencies, training agencies, industry, the social partners and other actors.
15.25 - 15.40	Coffee/tea break
15.40 - 16.35	Session IV : Future approaches to environmental education and training: A discussion to inform policy developments
16.35 - 16.45	Conclusions and closure of workshop, by Jorn Pedersen

ANNEX E

INDUSTRY CASE STUDIES

CASE STUDY C1

Case Study C1 presents a chemical company which is a division of a large multinational corporation. The company employs 270 people and has been operating for almost 100 years.

The company produces a range of chemical products including agricultural chemicals (herbicides and insecticides), synthetic latex and polystyrene foams. Manufacturing generates large quantities of waste, the largest component of which is liquid waste (1000 cubic metres per day) which is treated at an on-site facility. Solid wastes are exported off-site and disposed of to landfill and waste-water is discharged to a river.

The company is subject to NRA control and must comply with consents for discharge to the river. The company is also required, under the Control of Industrial Major Accidents Hazards Regulations 1984 (CIMAH) to prepare and submit a report on on-site emergency plans and the likely impacts on man and the environment of a serious accident.

The company complies with the Corporation waste minimisation scheme, the objective of which is to reduce the amount of waste generated. This is achieved by both changing the processes involved in manufacturing and by incorporating recycling and re-use into the manufacturing process. Many corporate projects under this scheme have had payback periods of less than one year.

The company must comply with the corporate environmental policy. Environmental issues are given a high priority by the company.

Responsibility for training lies with each plant manager. Training is primarily carried out formally in-house or informally on-the job. Short courses are used as appropriate. Environmental training is provided to all staff in that all are aware of the objective of the waste minimisation scheme. More specific environmental training is provided as required by an individual's job.

The company employs a Manager for environmental affairs who allocates 100% of his time to environmental management tasks. A further 15 members of staff allocate approximately 25% of their time to environmental management tasks.

The case study presents an occupational analysis of three jobs: Environmental Manager; Plant manager; and Plant Process Manager.

Occupational Analysis

	Environmental Manager	*Plant Manger*	*Plant Process Engineer*
Tasks	policy and strategy development; advising plant managers; knowledge of legislation; appreciation of corporate requirements; liaising with regulatory authorities; liaising with corporate environmental managers; chairing company waste management committee.	developing company environmental policy; ensuring that discharge consents are met; awareness of applicable legislation; awareness of corporate requirements; providing training; liaising with waste treatment plant staff; supervising staff.	responsibility for waste management; implementation of waste minimisation projects; supervising operatives/fitters; producing documentation detailing waste arisings; audits and disposals; responsible for accident/spillage planning; implementing training programmes; member of the waste management committee.
Skills and Competences	good scientific grounding; a broad understanding of environmental issues; ability to produce reports; understanding of occupational health issues; supervisory skills; negotiating skills.	experience of other corporation sites perhaps outside the UK; financial management skills; technical skills ie a good understanding of the manufacturing process; man-management skills; awareness of environmental issues..	good understanding of manufacturing processes; good understanding of waste management /pollution control, waste treatment technologies; a good knowledge of legislation.
Education and Training	degree in a traditional science discipline ; at least six years industrial experience. The post-holder is not required to be a specialist in environmental science. However post-entry environmental training will be provided both in-house and using short courses.	degree in engineering; experience of working at other sites ouside the UK. No formal pre-entry training in the environment is required. However, post-entry training will be provided mainly in-house by the Environmental Manager or using corporate expertise.	degree in chemical or process engineering. Formal training in environmental science is not required ; post-entry environmental training will be provided relating to waste management technologies and developments in legislation.

CASE STUDY C2

Case Study C2 presents a medium-sized chemical manufacturing company which is a subsidiary of a large multinational corporation. The company produces a range of chemical products for a number of industries including the rubber, pharmaceutical and herbicide industries.

A number of wastes are produced, the largest component of which is waste-water which is treated on-site at the waste-water-treatment-unit. Waste-water is discharged to a Class 1A river and the company is thus subject to unusually strict consents.

The company's parent company considers itself to be pro-active in its environmental management. It has a written environmental policy which details environmental targets which are often beyond the legislative requirements of the countries in which the subsidiaries operate.

The company does not have a formal education and training policy. Training is provided as and when required and is provided informally, on-the-job, or formally in-house. Personnel of all categories would be sent on short courses if they were relevant to the operations of the company. The company considers environmental awareness among its staff to be important and considers all personnel to have some responsibility for environmental management.

The main changes that have occured as a result of increased environmental management activities have been an increase in the level of monitoring and an increase in the level of company liaison with external bodies. The company is planning to increase the provision of training across all categories of staff.

The case study presents an occupational analysis of three jobs: Operative, waste treatment unit; Supervisor, waste-treatment-unit; and Manager, Health and Safety.

Occupational Analysis

	Operative (w.w.t.u.)	Supervisor (w.w.t.u.)	Manager Health and Safety
Tasks	monitoring incoming and out-going waste streams; operating micro-processor controls; operating testing equipment.	providing technical advice on the waste water treatment unit; responsibility for maintaining the unit; providing training to operative staff; ensuring quality contol.	keeping up-to-date, and ensuring compliance with legislation; liaising with regulatory bodies; providing advice to external policy makers; promoting environmental best practice;responsibiltiy for training.
Skills and Competences	knowledge of the operation of the plant; knowledge of materals used in manufacturing; knowledge of consents; knowledge of environmental policy	knowledge of plant operations; knowledge of manufacturing; knowledge of consents and company regulations; interpretation skills; appreciation of environmental issues and consents, pollution control technology.	detailed understanding of the chemical and engineering processes;detailed knowledge of legislation; knowledge of pollution control technology; understanding of the environmental impacts of processes; strong interpersonal skills.
Training	No formal pre-entry training is required. Post-entry training is provided primarily on-the-job.	No formal qualifications are required; experience as a laboratory technician Post-entry will be provided primarily in-house.	Chemistry or Engineering degree; environmental expertise can be acquired post-entry on- the -job or through formal external and in-house training.

CASE STUDY C3

Case Study C3 presents a medium-sized chemical manufacturing company which is a subsidiary of a large multinational corporation. Chemical manufacture occurs at two sites. The company produces a range of fine chemicals as intermediate products for a number of industries including the pharmaceutical, agro-chemical and dye-stuffs industries.

Manufacturing produces a number of wastes including: solid waste residues; aqueous wastes containing inorganic substances and organic contaminants; and gaseous wastes, carbon dioxide, sulphur dioxide and volatile aromatic gases.

The company has an environmental policy which is incorporated into its Health and Safety policy. To date, the main focus of the company's environmental management activities has been the treatment of aqueous wastes. However as a result of the detection of phenol contaminated soil and ground-water on-site and in response to increasing pressure from the parent company to produce emission statistics, the company is currently undertaking an extensive monitoring and analysis programme.

The company does not have a formal education and training policy. Training is provided primarily in-house although management may be sent on short courses. There is no environmental training policy. However, an estimated 75% of personnel are assessed to have received environmental training awareness in the past two years.

The case study presents an occupational analysis of three jobs: the Effluent Plant Operative; the Energy/Effluent Manager; and the Senior Chemist for the Environment.

Occupational Analysis

	Effluent Plant Operative	Energy/Effluent Manager	Senior Chemist
Tasks	operation of the effluent plant: temperature, flow rate and nutrient control; analytical testing, sampling and analysis of in-coming and out-going waste streams	running the boiler house; responsibility for waste disposal; liaising with regulatory bodies; management of operative staff; providing technical input to research on waste disposal methods	developing sampling and analytical techniques; improving efficiency of biotreatment plant; process research regarding waste minimisation; research into new methods of treating waste streams; supervision of laboratory staff; auditing and quantification of emissions
Skills and Competences	numeracy/literacy, knowledge of consents, process limits ie temp and max feed-rate; knowledge of the drainage system in order to contain spillages, deal with accidents	understanding of the manufacturing processes; detailed knowledge of waste disposal legislation and legislation governing levels of discharge; knowledge of energy issues; knowledge of waste disposal technologies; background in environmental issues; man-management skills	understanding of micro-biology; strong skills in analytical chemistry; understanding of the manufacturing processes carried out at the site; knowledge of pollution control, waste-treatment and monitoring technologies.
Training	No formal qualifications are required. Post entry training is provided primarily on -the-job	degree in chemistry or engineering; ten years experience in chemical waste management, water or energy indusrties. Post-entry training will be provided primarily in-house. The post-holder may be sent on short courses on waste management	degee in chemistry; ten years experience as an industrial chemist. Formal training in environmental science is not required although a background in the subject is useful

CASE STUDY C4

Case study C4 presents a chemical company which is the dye-stuffs and chemicals division of a large multinational corporation. The company employs 200 staff and has an annual turn-over of £60 million.

The company functions as a distribution site, providing warehouse facilities for storage and re-packing. The company receives deliveries of chemicals, dye-stuffs and pigments from the corporation's UK and European manufacturing sites. These are stored in the warehouses before delivery to customers by road. Some of the chemicals are re-packed at the the site. The dye-stuffs and chemicals are mainly used in the leather and textile industries.

The main solid waste is packaging which has been returned to the company by customers. There is an increasing expectation on the part of customers that suppliers should dispose of waste on their behalf. The packaging is washed at the site and is then disposed of to landfill. Some packaging is returned to the manufacturing plant for re-use. Liquid wastes constitute the main waste component. Approximately 20 tonnes of liquid waste chemicals are exported off-site for incineration. Waste-water is discharged to sewer and is subject to a series of consents governing pH, metals, particulates, fats and greases.

The majority of pollution control equipment installed relates to hazard prevention; the control of spillages and the prevention of fire.

The company must comply with the Group environmental policy which details a commitment to safeguarding the environment by incorporating environmental protection into the corporation's mainstream activities.

The company has a formal training policy which is governed by corporate policy. Environmental isssues are included in the company's education and training policy, both because of the demands of legislation and because of the benefits to the company. Increasingly customers expect suppliers of chemicals to assist them with pollution problems that may arise from the use of their products. Hence environmental management activities are being promoted on-site and 'downstream'. Company personnel are therefore being provided with environmental training both in-house and through the use of short courses, in order to provide advice and training to customers.

The case study presents occupational analyses of two jobs: Health, Safety and Environmental Protection Manager; and the Warehouse and Distribution Manager.

Occupational Analysis

	Health Safety and Environmental Manager	*Warehouse and Distribution Manager*
Tasks	liaising with water company over consent levels; ensuring compliance of discharges with legislation; responsibility for waste disposal; providing product safety data to the customer (handling procedures and known hazards); advising on environmental, health and safety matters; attendance at health and safety and environment meetings	responsibility for the prevention and control of spillages; responsible for ensuring product segregation; training staff; testing systems to ensure correct functioning
Skills and Competences	knowledge of health and safety legislation relating to chemicals; knowledge of waste disposal legislation; broad knowledge of chemicals; knowledge of consents; knowledge of environmental impacts of chemicals; report writing/ presentation skills; man-management skills	experience in the industry; a high level of man-management skills; knowledge of hazardous characteristics of chemicals; knowledge of legislation regarding health and safety and the transportation of chemicals.
Education and Training	degree in chemistry or physics; ten years industrial experience; experience in laboratories; post-holder will attend short courses and seminars.	no formal qualifications are required for the job; work experience and experience relating to the transportation of chemicals are essential.

CASE STUDY M1

Case Study M1 presents a medium-sized aluminium foundry in the West Midlands. The company employs 500 employees and has a turn-over of £20 million. The company is currently a subsidiary of a large European manufacturing company.

A variety of aluminium alloys are purchased, melted, cast and subjected to a variety of finishing and surface treatment processes before being dispatched by road to customers. The company produces approximately 20 tonnes of aluminium components per day for the automotive, aerospace and defence industries.

Manufacturing produces large quantities of waste: contaminated sand which is sold to a contractor; aluminium swarf; liquid treatment chemical wastes; and amine and metal contaminated air. There are no consents on waste water discharged to sewer.

The company has not undertaken specific pollution control measures. It intends to phase out the use of CFCs and is currently investigating means by which to avoid using methanol as a surface treatment chemical in consideration of worker safety. The main factors contributing to the limited level of environmental management at the company were cited as being: the lack of regulatory control; the lack of internal or external financial support; lack of knowledge of available education and training; lack of customer demand for the company to incorporate environmental objectives into its activities; and the lack of perceived financial or "public image" benefits.

The company has not developed a formal environmental policy. Overall responsibility for the environment lies with the Board of Directors. However, environmental policy is devised by the Personnel and Training Manager who is assisted by the Personnel and Training Officer. To date, environmental policy has not been implemented, hence the role of managers, foremen, operatives and trade unions in relation to environmental management has not yet been determined.

Training is provided primarily on-the-job and supplemented by more formal means of in-house training. External consultants are used infrequently. The company's training policy incorporates Health and Safety but not the Environment.

The company intends to increase its environmental management activities as it expects to be subject to increasingly tight regulatory controls (requiring it to invest in monitoring and pollution control equipment). The company also aims to improve the level of environmental awareness amongst its staff. Formal in-house training and on-the-job training will be the main method of training for non-managerial staff and internal seminars will be the main method of management training.

The case study presents two occupational analyses: Personnnel and Training Manager; and the Personnel and Training Officer.

Occupational Analysis

	Personnel and Training Manager	*Personnel and Training Officer*
Tasks	devising overall environmental policy; responsibility for providing training and for identifying the training needs of staff; keeping up-to-date with environmental and Health and Safety legislation	assisting with policy development; informing managers about relevant issues and legislation; providing training seminars for managers, supervisors and shop-stewards. These tasks constitute an estimated 3% of the officer's time.
Skills and Competences	responsibility for the environment has been incorporated into personnel tasks. The current post-holder has a qualification in personnel management and is a member of the Institute of Personnel Management (IPM). Currently no scientific or technical skills are required.	Background in personnel combined with a first degree in a scientific discipline; membership of IPM
Education and Training	The manager has attended short courses relating to Health and Safety. To date, the post-holder has not received any formal environmental training.	The officer has not received any formal training on environmental management. Self motivation and general environmental awareness has resuited in the individual actively promoting environmental management within the company.

CASE STUDY M2

Case Study M2 presents a medium-sized metal manufacturing company which is a subsidiary of a large multinational corporation.

The company carries out non-ferrous smelting and refining and the main products include copper, lead and antimony. Manufacturing produces large volumes of waste. Slag is stored on-site, or where possible, sold locally for road-fill material. Liquid wastes are discharged to the river after treatment: heavy metals are precipitated out and recycled. Lead and sulphur dioxide are the two main gaseous discharges.

The company is a registered lead works and is thus subject to strict HMIP control. The NRA monitors discharge to the river. The company receives visits from HSE and the Local Authority responsible for licensing waste storage on-site. The company has invested a large amount of capital in pollution control equipment

The company is currently preparing a formal written environmental policy. The company does not have a formal education and training policy but gives high priority to training. Operative training is generally carried out on-the-job or using more formal in-house or group training. Training provision for managers includes short courses. There is no environmental training policy.

The company expects to increase its environmental activities both in terms of investment in pollution control equipment and in the provision of formal more specialised environmental training. However, there is concern on the part of the company that industry may not be able to meet the financial effects of tighter legislation and the continual downward revision of emissions targets.

The case study presents an occupational analysis of four jobs: Effluent Plant Operative; Group Manager; Environmental Scientist and Technical Manager.

Occupational Analysis

	Effluent Plant Operative	*Group Manager*	*Environmental Scientist*	*Technical Manager*
Tasks	monitoring and analysis; maintaining levels of chemicals; carrying out routine cleaning and checking tasks; checking pH levels.	overall responsibility for production; implementing health and safety legislation; responsibility for the achievement of environmental targets; reporting on monitoring results.	sampling and monitoring; maintaining sampling equipment; liaising with regulatory bodies and operating managers; presenting monitoring figures; providing technical advice to production managers.	overall technical responsibility; liaising with environmental scientist on process development responsible for implementing company responses to changes in legislation.
Skills and Competences	knowledge of pH control, metals solubility and consents levels; a background knowledge in environmental issues is required.	knowledge of metallurgy, environmetnal legislation. ability to analyse and interpret figures; diplomacy skills	strong background in analytical chemistry; knowledge of: legislation; consents, pollution control, technology, statistics; man-management skills	Knowledge of the operation of the plant. detailed knowledge of environmental legislation; knowledge of pollution control technology; man mangement. report writing and negotiating skills.
Training	No formal qualifications required. Post entry training is provided primarily on-the-job although some formal in-house training is provided	Degree in chemistry or metallurgy. No formal environmental qualifications are required.	Degree in chemistry and five years experience or an employee who has acquired sufficient in-house experience; membership of the Royal Society of Chemistry.	Degree in metallurgy, physics or chemical engineering and ten years experience is required. The post-holder will attend seminars and short courses, particularly in relation to legislation.

CASE STUDY M3

Case Study M3 presents a large metal manufacturing company which is part of a Group operating in the UK.

Manufacturing produces large volumes of solid waste, the majority of which is disposed of to landfill on-site. Ammonia vapour is incinerated on-site and slag from one of the industrial processes is sold for re-use. Aqueous wastes are discharged to the estuary.

The Group has produced an environmental brochure detailing the measures which have been undertaken to safeguard against environmental damage. At company level the impetus for improved environmental awareness is driven by senior management. The company has recently taken steps to increase environmental awareness and good practice at operative level. For example, a bonus scheme has been implemented whereby incentive payments are awarded for the achievement of environmental targets.

The company has a formal education and training policy which is determined by Group policy. A system of Total Quality Performance has been implemented which contains a commitment to training and overall improvement in standards. The company has allocated a large budget to training and actively encourages staff at all levels to undertake some form of post-entry training.

There is no formal environmental training provided. However a series of modules have been produced on the environment and increasingly environmental aspects are being incorporated into Health and Safety and Management courses.

The company expects to increase its provision of training on general environmental awareness. Increasingly environmental issues will be incorporated into supervisory, professional and managerial courses run in-house. The company is of the view that the management structure is the best mechanism for promoting environmental awareness.

The case study presents an occupational analysis of three jobs: Tar and liquor attendant, Tips Contoller; and Environmental Services Engineer.

Occupational Analysis

	Tar and Liquor Attendant	Tips Controller	Environmental Services Engineer
Tasks	maintaining and operating the system; operating recovery and separating equipment; operating the stills: supervising incineration of ammonia; monitoring pH nitrates and temperature.	supervising operatives; hiring and deploying machinery; recording types and volumes of wastes; liaising with external bodies involved with waste disposal; liasing with plant managers (ie, waste producers)	devising capital development projects; liaising with regulatory bodies and the public; monitoring; providing technical advice to plant managers; carrying out design work on plant to improve environmental performance
Skills and Competences	a thorough knowledge of process, plant equipment and control operations; understanding of the chemical processes; knowledge of the parameters within which the plant must operate.	knowledge of waste arisings; knowledge of manufacturing processes; limited engineering knowledge; operation of mobile tools; knowledge of waste disposal legislation.	competent engineer; comprehensive knowledge of the manufacturing processes: knowledge of environmental legislation; knowledge of pollution control techniques
Education and Training	No formal qualifications are required; post-entry training includes twelve weeks on-the-job training on by-product operations and the post-holder may take a City and Guilds in coal carbonising and by-products.	No formal qualifications are required; work experience including specific knowledge of mobile equipment and experience of waste disposal. Post-entry training is provided primarily on-the-job; professional journals are a useful source of information: short courses might be used if appropriate.	Chemical engineering degree or an appropriate level of experience in the industry. Post-entry training will be provided formally in-house and using external short courses.

CASE STUDY M4

Case Study M4 presents a medium-sized independent metal working company. The company employs 98 employees and has an annual turn-over of £3.5 million.

The company carries out a metal pressing and finishing operation. The main products are press parts for the motor industry eg. switch parts, buildup-units and end-caps to fuses.

The main wastes from processing include effluent sludge; scrap metal (which is sold to merchants); waste solvents and waste oils. Aqueous waste is discharged to sewer and is subject to a series of consents.

The company has not produced a formal written environmental policy. Good environmental practice is being promoted by individuals within the company rather than being determined by company policy. As a result of increased environmental awareness, the company has implemented changes in its processing methods and particularly, in the types of chemicals used. This has resulted in a substantial reduction in the volumes of waste produced with significant savings in waste disposal costs.

The company does not have a formal training policy. The main method of training provision is on-the-job. There is no provision of environmental training by the company. Overall responsibility for environmental issues at the site lies with the Works Manager. The main constraint on the up-take of environmental training and environmental good practice is economic. Senior management does not consider investment in pollution control equipment and environmental training to be a priority. A second constraint is the lack of information available to SMEs regarding all aspects of environmental management; legislation, training, pollution control technologies and clean technologies.

The company expects to continue its informal environmental management practices. The company will comply with legislation but believes that there is a need for financial incentives in order to encourage a more pro-active approach to environmental mangement.

The case study presents an occupational analysis of three jobs: Supervisor, Charge hand and Operative. Only the supervisor's jobs includes core environmental tasks.

Occupational Analysis

	Operative	*Charge Hand*	*Supervisor*
Tasks	operating all types of plant ; this involves following written instructions; taking temperature readings, recording information; following procedures for cleaning plant which involves collecting harmful solvents.	supervising operative staff; operating all types of equipment; monitoring and maintaining the level of volatile chemicals; recording information;	ensuring that chemicals comply with legislation and have no adverse environmental effects; monitoring the effluent treatment plant; providing training to operatives; liaising with Regulatory bodies; implementing Health and Safety legislation.
Skills and Competences	knowledge of the operation of all types of plant; awareness of the health and safey aspects of the chemicals; ability to follow instructions.	detailed knowledge of the operation of the plant; supervisory skills; knolwedge of legislation, consents and Health and Safety.	in-depth knowledge of the manufacturing processes; knowledge of Health and Safety legislation; knowledge of legislation governing chemicals; knowledge of consents; man-management skills
Education and Training	No pre-entry qualifications are required . Post entry training is provided on-the-job. There is no provision of environmental training.	No formal qualifications are required. Three to five years experience in the industry is required. All training is provided on-the-job.	Five to ten years experience in the industry is required or a chemistry degree and some industrial experience. Training is provided primarily on the job. The post-holder may attend conferences and seminars on environmental issues.

CASE STUDY M5

Case Study M5 presents a medium-sized lead smelting company which is a subsidiary of a multi-national corporation. The company employs approximately 200 staff.

The company produces lead ingots using lead from car batteries, scrap metal and lead which is sold as a by-product from other industries. The main wastes from manufacturing include slag from the furnaces which is disposed of to landfill off-site and aqueous waste which is discharged to the river. Gaseous emissions from the stacks include lead and sulphur dioxide. The main legislation governing the activities of the company is the Control of Lead at Work Act 1980. The company is a registered Lead Works and is thus subject to HMIP control. Discharge of aqueous wastes to the river is subject to consents and is monitored by the NRA.

The company has produced a formal written Health and Safety and Environmental plan which sets out an environmental plan for 1990, detailing environmental objectives in terms of modifications to plant and specific emissions targets to be achieved. The company must also comply with the environmental policy of the Group. Increasingly resources are being allocated to R&D into new technologies both at Group and company level.

The company has a training plan which sets out the training programme for each member of staff for the current year. Due to the nature of the industry, environmental training is provided for all new recruits. Every new member of staff is given a written training brief which outlines the environmental issues that are relevant to the operations of the company. The company does not provide on-going environmental training.

The case study presents an occupational analysis of four jobs: Smelter Operative, Environmental Chemist; Technical Manager; and Human Resources Manager.

Occupational Analysis

	Smelter Operative	Environmental Chemist	Technical Manager	Human Reource Manager
Tasks	Operating the furnaces and refining plant (operation of valves and dampeners); driving mobile equipment; cleaning/sweeping duties.	carrying out all monitoring on-site; reporting and: liaising on results; maintaining and repairing equipment; developing analysis techniques;	keeping up-to-date with legislation; responsible for overall environmental performance of the plant; aware of technical developments; liaising with regulatory bodies	Overall responsibility for environmental issues; devising an environmental strategy; carrying out a co-ordinating role between the subsidiary companies;
Skills and Competences	Numeracy, literacy; ability to follow instructions; understanding of the process operations;	chemical background; knowledge of metallurgical industries; analytical chemistry, knowledge of legislation.	knowledge of legislation; knowledge of pollution control technology; engineering knowledge; report writing/presentation skills.	experience of strategic planning; knowledge of legislation; broad understanding of metallurgy; broad understanding of environmental issues
Education and Training	No formal qualifications are required. Post-entry training is provided primarily on-the-job or on-site. Environmental training is provided as part of the induction programme but there is no further environmental training.	GCSE in chemistry. Generally the post-holder would have under-studied the post for a period of time. Training is provided primarily on-the-job	Degree in chemistry, engineering or metallurgy; no formal environmental qualifications are required.	ten years industrial experience. Currently responsibility for environmental aspects has been incorporated into a Personnel function. In the future there may be a demand for an environmental specialist.

CASE STUDY W1

The case study presents a laboratory responsible for carrying out monitoring and analyisis functions on behalf of the water company and private industry. The laboratory has been operating since 1974. It currently employs 89 staff.

The laboratory carries out chemical analysis of water, sewage and soil. The type of analysis depends largely on the source of the sample and the puposes for which it is taken. These include: operational investigation, monitoring, quality control and ensuring compliance with an increasing number of statutory requirements. The laboratory is responsible for carrying out sophisticated analysis of organics, herbicides, aqnd pesticides.

The laboratory has recently been awarded NAMAS accreditation. This refers to the National Measurement Accreditation Service which is the UK Government's unified accreditation service for calibration and testing. The work of the laboratory is therefore subject to a set of operational guide-lines. The laboratory is also subject to a series of Health and Safety legislation, particularly COSHH.

The laboratory does not have an explicit statement relating to environmental management. Quality control at the laboratory is very tight. The laboratory is committed to the provision of training for all categories of staff. In particular, emphasis is given to training inexperienced junior staff. Training is generally provided in-house by senior personnel or by external consultants. Courses provided by Water Training International are used regularly. Whilst staff at the laboratory are involved in environmental management tasks, they do not receive specific environmental awareness training.

The case study presents an occupational analyisis of three jobs: Scientific Assistant; Scientific Officer; and Senior Scientific Officer. These three examples typify the functions carried out by different categories of staff and aim to demonstrate the impact of changes in environmental legislation and practices.

Occupational Analysis

	Scientific Assistant	*Scientific Officer*	*Senior Scientific Officer*
Tasks	responsibility for undertaking all basic duties in the laboratory under the supervision of senior staff. These include; solvent extraction; sample preparation; filing; clerical duties; manipulation of samples (adding agents and treating samples for a variety of tests)	analysing extracts that are produced; reporting the results of analysis; maintenance of databases; supervison of junior staff.	responsibility for the quality of analysis and the turn-around and through-put of the analysis; responsibility for the up-keep of stocks; on 24 hour call to respond to pollution incidents; writing reports; attending management meetings; responsibility for quality control
Skills and Competences	organisational skills; initiative; communication skills; ability to follow instructions.	detailed knowledge of gas chromotography techniques;knowledge of data systems; man-management systems;knowledge of analytical methods;high level literacy and numeracy;knowledge of health and safety legislation.	strong background in chemical analysis; report writing skills; strong interpersonal / communication skills; ;dexterity with instruments; detailed knowledge of UK and EEC legislation; knowledge of new technologies; a good understanding of the Health and Safety characterisitics.
Education and Training	A Levels in science subjects are required. High priority is given to the training of junior staff. Post-entry training is provided mainly in-house using formal and on-the-job methods. These include journals, and procedure manuals. The post-holder is also encouraged to go on short courses on a variety of subjects.	Degree in chemistry. The post-holder is required to have two years laboratory experience. Training is provided primarily in-house although the post-holder will be sent on relevant short courses.	Honours Degree in Chemistry. Five years experience working in a laboratory. Limited post-entry training. However the senior chemist must keep abreast of legislative changes.

CASE STUDY W2

Case Study W2 presents the sewerage division of a regional water company which has overall responsibility for sewerage operations in the region. The work is actually carried out by the District Councils in the region, hence the water company's role is largely managerial and adminstrative.

The company does not have a formal education and training policy. Training is provided as and when required. Training requirements are identified through individual assessments of staff by managers. Training is provided primarily on-the-job. The method of training does not vary between categories of staff as the company is committed to improving quality throughout the company. The company runs a BTec course on water treatment in-house. A BTec in sewerage operations is being developed and is likely to incorporate a component in environmental awareness. Personnel are sent on short courses if appropriate. Water Training International and Sheffield Polytechnic were identified as providing useful short courses on sewerage operations and treatment.

The case study presents an occupational analysis of three jobs; Operational Maintenance Officer; Sewerage Officer; and Senior Sewerage Engineer.

Occupational Analysis

	Operational Maintenance Officer	Sewerage Officer	Senior Sewerage Engineer
Tasks	monitoring and controlling the operational maintenance for the sewerage and pumping systems; dealing with complaints; liaising with the NRA in the event of a problem; responsibility for maintaining and cleaning the pumps.	management of District Councils within the region; supervision of staff; recruitment responsibilities; developing vocational qualifications; providing advice to the District Councils; dealing with complaints; responsibility for budget control.	management of sewerage system in conjunction with the District Councils; overall responsibility for managing the physical and financial aspects of the function.
Skills and Competences	comprehensive knowledge of pumping stations and sewerage operations; knowledge of consents ; man management skills; strong interpersonal skills.	background in engineering; understanding of the operations of the District Council broad understanding of environmental legislation; high level of public responsibility	detailed knowledge of engineering, capital and strategic aspects of sewerage operations; strong management skills; good financial management skills; knowledge of environmental legislation,
Education and Training	No formal qualifications are required. Five years experience of sewerage operations. The post-holder is likely to have undertaken a B Tec in the electrical or mechanical maintenance of pumping stations and sewerage operations.	degree in engineering; membership of IWEM and five years management experience.	degree in engineering; chartered engineer with five years management experience.

CASE STUDY W3

Case Study W3 presents a regional office of a regulatory body which has responsibility for protecting and improving the water environment. One of the organisation's most important responsibilities in its role as "guardian" of the water environment is to maintain and improve the quality of controlled waters; reservoirs, lakes, estuaries and coastal waters.

The authority's mission statement (as well as the enabling Statute) clearly identifies environmental mangement as its primary objective.

The organisation has recently established a formal training and education policy. Training was previously provided on an ad hoc basis. The company has now implemented a system of staff appraisals thus providing a a more structured apprpoach to training. Training is provided using in-house expertise or external consultants. The method of training provision depends on the number of people requiring training. Personnel will be sent on short courses when only a small number require that particular course. Engineers are encouraged to gain chartered status through the Institute of Water and Environmental Management. There is no formal environmental training programme.

The case study presents an occupational analysis of four jobs; Principal Environmental Quality; Assistant Pollution Control Officer; Chartered Civil Engineer, Flood Defence; and Flood Defence Supervisor.

Occupational Analysis

	Principal Environmental Quality	Assistant Pollution Control Officer	Chartered Civil Engineer Flood Defence	Flood Defence Supervisor
Tasks	reviewing and reporting on water quality performance identifying and implementing programmes to ensure maintenance and improvements in water quality; ensuring compliance with EEC and UK legislation; negotiating consent conditions; identification of training requirements.	investigating pollution incidents; assisting in the assessment of consent applications; carrying out chemical analysis of samples; undertaking pollution surveys; carrying out routine inspections of industry; preparing and presenting evidence in legal proceedings; dealing with emergencies on 24 hour call.	design and preparation of drainage plans; carrying out pre- and post-work surveys; liaising with legal and estates section in order to prepare entry and compensation matters; undertaking cost benefit analyses; liaising with third parties (landowners).	resposibility for the workforce which carries out weed removal, bank inspections; planning the work programme; identifying day to day priorities; providing materials, plant and labour; implemeting Health and Safety; providing on-the-job training; liaising with landowners.
Skills and Competences	knowledge of legislation and directives; knowledge of environmental pollution control technology; planning skills and experience of programme implementation; policy awareness; negotiating man-managment and report writing skills	detailed knowledge of consents; knowledge of pollution control; knowledge of environmental legislation; knowledge of sampling techniques and instruments;ability to carrry out chemical analysis; strong interpersona skills; knowledge of legal proceedings.	ability to undertake a wide range of tasks; financial, contractual and engineering; negotiating skills; knowledge of legislation, particularly in relation to land drainage; economic modelling ability; man-management skills; strong interpersonal/ communication skills.	knowledge of legislation; eg, COSHH; supervisory skills; strong interpersonal skills; awareness of purchasing procedures; understanding of the operations of the organisation; good organisational skills.
Education and Training	degree in chemistry or biology and membership of theRoyal Society of Chemists or the Institute of Water and Environmental Management (IWEM).	HND/HNC in chemistry/ biology and two years experience. The post-holder is encouraged to take the IWEM qualification or a part-time degree. Training is provided primarily on-the-job However short courses will also be used.	degree in civil engineering;chartered engineer with ten years working experience. There is no provision of environmental training although conservation has recently been identified as a training requirement.	degree/HNC or five years relevant experience in the field. The post-holder wil receive post-entry training particular in the legal aspects of land drainage (Water Training International)

ANNEX F

THE ITALIAN MISSION

ITALIAN MISSION CONSULTEES

CASTALIA	Dr Guilio Rossa Crespi
PANTARCH CONSULTANCY	Art Bruno Galletta
ADN KRONUS (Press Agency)	Sn Fabba
ISFOL	Maria Teresa Palleschi
	Rita Ammassari
CONFINDUSTRIA	Dr M Leboffe
CONFAPI	Dr Armando Occhipuriti
	Dr Roberto Finesi
MINISTRY OF THE ENVIRONMENT	Dr Enrico Veneziale
ASSOLOMBARDA	Dr Vedovato
REGION OF LOMBARDY	Dr Longone
	Dr Albertoni
	Dr Meyer
	Paulo Colombo
FAST	Dr Alberto Pieri
CGIL	Luisa Benedettini
	Gloria Malaspuna
	Lizabetta Ramat
	Sig Inglese
DOCTER	Laura Cultrera
LEGA AMBIENTE	Vittorio Cogliati
	Silvana Novelli
ITALIAN EMBASSY, LONDON	Dr Raffi
CEMP	Brian Clark
BRITISH EMBASSY, ROME	Mr Evans
ITALIAN TRADE CENTRE, LONDON	Mr Wandle
CARABINIERE (Environmental Police)	Colonel Palumbo
UNIONE INDUSTRIZLE DI ROME	Mario Grecca

ANNEX G

PROVISION OF EDUCATION AND TRAINING
FOR ENVIRONMENTAL MANAGEMENT

PROVISION OF EDUCATION AND TRAINING FOR ENVIRONMENTAL MANAGEMENT

1.0 CURRENT EDUCATION PROVISION

In the light of the occupational analysis which indicates the importance of adding environmental management competences to degree level science and engineering education, this study has focussed on the provision of post-graduate rather than graduate education for environmental management. A selective survey of universities and polytechnics providing postgraduate courses in subjects relating to environmental management, using a postal questionnaire was undertaken. Seventeen courses were identified from prospectuses. Thirteen responses were received, of which three referred to courses which have recently been discontinued.

The objectives of the survey were to:

* identify the extent of provision of postgraduate courses in environmental management in the UK;
* identify the subject content of such courses;
* identify employment patterns of graduates of these courses, thereby assessing the requirements of employers for personnel trained in environmental management;
* identify the availability of short courses and distance learning packages provided for industry by the university/polytechnic sector.

1.1 Scale of Provision

In the UK there are approximately 350 places available on the 10 operating university/college courses relating to environmental management for which information was obtained. These range from general environmental management courses to courses which concentrate on specific areas of pollution control, eg, radiation, hazardous waste or water management.

Sixty four percent of places offered are on full-time courses which vary between one and two years in length. The remainder are on part-time courses which are generally two to three years in length. Virtually all currently available courses are fully subscribed. Twenty five per cent of the courses surveyed expect to increase the number of places available in the immediate future. Loughborough

University is planning to provide the opportunity for students currently undertaking the Diploma in Hazardous Waste Management to study for the MSc. Loughborough estimates that between 5 and 10 students will complete the MSc.

1.2 Course Intake

Fifty two percent of the current student in-take of the postgraduate courses surveyed have industrial experience. Often courses are targetted specifically at inter-professional level.

1.3 Course Content

The content and focus of the courses varied greatly. However, key subjects were identified in each course, although not the amount of curriculum time given to each subject, and these are summarised in Table 1.1.

TABLE 1.1: CONTENT OF UK POST-GRADUATE COURSES
FOR ENVIRONMENTAL MANAGEMENT

Subject	Percentage of Universities/Colleges Offering Subject
Environmental Technology	75
Environmental Planning/Policy	75
Environmental Legislation	88
Environmental Economics	75
Air Pollution Studies	50
Water Pollution Studies	75
Radioactive Pollution Studies	38
Solid Waste Disposal	67

SOURCE: ECOTEC Survey

Fifty per cent of courses surveyed had undergone recent changes in the content of the course. In particular, changes in EEC legislation and Directives were identified as an important source of change. For example, Environmental Impact Assessments came to the fore after the formulation of EEC Directives in this area. Environmental trends were also identified as contributing to changes in course content. The issue of global warming, for example, is currently more topical than that of oil spills therefore course content accordingly reflects this change in emphasis.

1.4 Employment of Postgraduates

Currently, Water/Local Authorities employ the highest percentage of students, see Table 1.2. However, the survey indicated that, following increased legislation in this area, the requirement of the polluting industries for personnel trained in environmental management is expected to rise. Without follow-up surveys of post-graduate employment it is difficult to suggest the extent to which post-graduates apply their education in their employment.

TABLE 1.2: EMPLOYMENT OF POSTGRADUATES FROM ENVIRONMENTAL MANAGEMENT COURSES

Employment	Percentage of Postgraduates*
Water/Local Authorities	29
Industry	20
Consultancy	14
University/Poly/Schools	13
Central Government	12
Other	12

* The percentage relates to the 350 places on operating courses.

SOURCE: ECOTEC Survey

1.5 Provision of Courses to Industry

Fifty per cent of universities surveyed which provide full-time and/or part-time courses also provide short courses to industry. Details are given in Table 1.3. The number of places available on these short courses is generally limited, ranging from 10 to 30. The number of courses run each year varies according to demand, hence it is difficult to estimate the annual provision of places on these courses. It should be noted that short courses are also available from private sector sources.

Only Loughborough University in association with Leicester Polytechnic and Surrey University prepare distance learning packages. These are targetted at waste producers and contractors and the emergency services respectively. Increasingly, universities are offering consultancy services in this area.

TABLE 1.3: DESCRIPTION OF SHORT COURSES TO INDUSTRY FOR ENVIRONMENTAL MANAGEMENT

University	Course Title
University of Birmingham	Short courses on groundwater modelling, water quality control and hydrometry
Loughborough University	Three courses twice a year on introductory hazardous waste and contaminated land
Strathclyde University	Department of Public Health and Environmental Engineering provides a number of courses, the options of which vary from year to year
University of Sheffield	Short courses on Energy Loss Prevention and Process Safety, and Energy Management in process industries
University of Surrey	A number of courses for Environmental Health Officers and MOD personnel on aspects of radiation protection and environmental monitoring
University of Manchester/ University of Stirling	Short courses, the contents of which vary from year to year

SOURCE : ECOTEC Survey

1.6   **Financing of Courses**

The survey indicated that approximately forty per cent of current student intake to these courses is financed by industry. Increasingly students are being financed through their courses by their employers as part of a Continuous Career Development programme. This is particularly true of students enrolled in part-time degree courses. Both the Science and Engineering Research Council (SERC) and the Natural Environment Research Council (NERC) are an important source of funding for students under-taking full-time or part-time post-graduate study in this field. Two types of finance are available; Advanced Course Studentships and, a limited number of Industrial Awards. In order to qualify for the latter, students are required to have obtained, usually at least, a Second Class Honours Degree and to have worked in industry for a full twelve months.

2.0   **FUTURE EDUCATION PROVISION**

The occupational analysis highlights the requirement for both general skills, including awareness, and specialist skills. To the extent that new education and training provision will be developed, the distinction between generalists and specialists requires some clarification. Education and training for environmental management is required at two broad levels; management and operative training. Management training will have a broader base, being concerned with awareness, philosophy, management attitudes whereas operative training will focus on specific technical tasks.

Higher education provision for environmental management is required for industrial managers. However, industry views technically competent graduates (eg, in chemistry or engineering) with an understanding of environmental aspects, as being preferable to "environmental scientists" who have a broad range of environmentally related skills (eg, knowledge of policy/legislation, technologies, environmental impact assessment etc). This implies that in developing education policy in this area, the emphasis should be placed in graduate education, on the need to highlight environmental issues as part of traditional disciplines; and in post-graduate education on the need to provide a multi-disciplinary environmental education for those with degrees in traditional subjects.

City & Guilds education and training is often undertaken by operatives with environmental management tasks, particularly in process engineering. The move towards a broader based City & Guilds education, away from specific craft related training, is in keeping with the requirement to add additional skills associated with environmental management to mainstream process engineering skills.

The future provision of courses in environmental management is expected to increase. Environmental management is expected to be expanded both within the framework of existing courses and to be further introduced at undergraduate level (eg, Loughborough University is developing a Chemical Engineering degree with an Environmental Management Component). Discussions with professional organisations and lead industry bodies suggest that industry would prefer to employ 'technically competent graduates' with a knowledge of environmental issues rather than specialists in environmental management. Environmental awareness was identified as an area which could be incorporated into traditional undergraduate and postgraduate courses.

3.0 CURRENT TRAINING PROVISION

Training for environmental management covers a wide range of occupational groups from operative training through to senior management training. There is a wide range of training providers, including academic institutions, lead industry bodies, trade associations, private training providers, professional institutions and company in-house facilities.

A major source of information and advice on environmental management issues is derived from contact with the regulatory agencies. However, there is increasing concern, given the introduction of IPC, that representatives of these agencies will require additional information and training. The development of new training programmes, for which Loughborough University and UMIST are bidding, specifically designed for HMIP inspectors, illustrate the requirement. Moreover, the introduction of IPC will mean that the regulatory agencies will be required to adopt an increasingly arms-length relationship with industry.

More broadly, the provision of environmental education and training is a relatively under-developed area and there has been some concern expressed in this study that there are not sufficient training providers who have the appropriate skills. This concern reflects, in part, the highly specialised nature of the training requirements, with industry requiring process specific environmental management training. The reduction in the informal information exchange which currently takes place with regulatory agencies will place greater emphasis on the requirement to develop suitable training resources.

The specific training requirements, particularly of operatives, are often met by the supplier of environmental management goods and services. This is the case where the new skills relate to new plant or production processes. Suppliers provide this training as part of the sales package. This service is important because it means that the move towards cleaner technologies is less likely to be constrained by the absence of the necessary technical skills. It also means that the reduced distinction between production and environmental management need not inhibit the acquisition of the necessary skills.

Examples of the types of delivery method which currently provide training in environmental management are:

- Distance learning;
- Lead Industry Bodies;
- Training Boards;
- Short courses;
- Seminars.

Each of these is discussed in turn.

3.1 Distance Learning

Leicester Polytechnic (Technology) Limited provides distance learning packages which focus on task specific skill training needs. The learning material consists of a number of modules which can be selected to fit individual requirements. Each module requires between 6 and 10 hours study time, depending on the student's prior knowledge of the subject. The modules provided cover: hazardous waste control; environmental management; air pollution control; water pollution control; and noise and vibration. The modules were developed in association with ICCET and Loughborough University with support from the Training Agency. Each module offers a certificate of competence, after the satisfactory completion of exercises and a postal test. This was the only training service of its type identified in the study. However, this type of service can be expected to be in demand if the modules are kept up to date.

3.2 Lead Industry Bodies

The lead industry bodies (LIB's) consulted varied in their practise of providing training services to their members. For example, the Association of the British Pharmaceutical Industry does not provide any form of training although it provides an information and referral service and has been involved in the development of NVQ's. The waste management industry training and advisory board (WAMITAB) does not provide training although it is involved in the development of NVQ's and is responsible for the development of the associated training standards. The electricity association does provide training services to the electricity industry although there are no specific courses covering environmental management. LIB's, trade associations, trade journals and trade fairs all provide informal advice and information on environmental management but generally there is no training provision for environmental management offered by LIB's.

3.3 Training Boards

Training boards were set up to deliver training services to selected industries. The engineering industry training board (EITB) delivers training services to firms in the supply industry. Discussions with the EITB indicate that whilst the EITB is involved with industry specific training it has not introduced any form of environmental management training.

3.4 Short Courses for Environmental Management

Short courses for environmental management are offered by the university/polytechnic sector, either as an academic or as a commercial activity. The nature of these courses is described in Section 1.5 above. Short courses are also being developed by the private sector. The research programme has identified two major providers of training for environmental management using this form of delivery. Water Training International specialises in providing training services to the water and associated industries. Envirotrain provide services targetted to the waste management sector at all occupational levels.

3.5 Seminars

The use of seminars to provide an opportunity for the exchange of information between the participants on environmental management issues is widespread, organised by the university sector and industry associations, such as the Environment Council. Recently, the Department of Trade and Industry has launched a programme of seminars with supporting information materials, highlighting the value of environmental management.

4.0 FUTURE TRAINING PROVISION FOR ENVIRONMENTAL MANAGEMENT

An increase in environmental management training is likely to be required as a result of a general increase in environmental awareness; the introduction of policy and legislative change, and new commercial opportunities in the market place. However, the future provision of training is an area requiring greater analysis than has been possible in the context of this study. Any assessment of future provision must take account of two major issues: the development of National Vocational Qualifications and the importance of accreditation.

4.1 National Vocational Qualifications (NVQs)

NVQs are being developed at Levels I-Level VII. This range of competences will cover occupations ranging from the basic operative to senior management. The development phase is currently concentrating on Levels I- Level III. To date, there is no specific NVQ for environmental management, but aspects of environmental management are likely to be incorporated into the following accredited schemes:

* Electricity Supply - Level III
* Electricity Generation - Levels II and III
* Engineering (Foundation) - Level I
* Engineering Maintenance - Level III
* Food Processing - Levels I and II
* Man Made Fibre, Film and Related Chemical Process Operations - Levels I and II
* Processing and Packing Chemicals - Levels I, II and III

At the above Levels the environmental management aspects are more likely to be concerned with health and safety and with awareness of what types of materials trainees/operatives are handling, rather than with environmental management of an industrial process; ie. the concern is with the immediate environment. This implies that the NVQ system is unlikely to specify the future training requirements for environmental management. The Council for Occupational Standards in Environmental Conservation (COSQUEC), the lead industry body for the environmental sector, has taken the view that it will be developing NVQ's for environmental conservation rather than for environmental management in industry.

4.2 Accreditation

The second major issue in the development of training is accreditation. Industry increasingly requires that external training courses provide some form of certification to demonstrate that an employee/trainee has successfully completed a course to a set standard. This system of accreditation has been in operation in professional institutes for a number of years. The Chilver System within the Institute of Civil Engineering, for example, requires a graduate engineer to accrue points by taking approved training courses whilst gaining work experience, prior to obtaining professional status. To the extent that industry accepts that environmental management related courses are an integral part of the training of the workforce then the demand for accredited courses will grow. How far this demand could be met and what system of accreditation would be used is not clear.

ANNEX H

AN OVERVIEW OF ENVIRONMENTAL POLICY

1.0 AN OVERVIEW OF ENVIRONMENTAL POLICY IN THE TWELVE MEMBER STATES

This Annex presents an overview of the regulatory structure and environmental policies of the twelve Member States.

For comparative purposes it is useful to present a discussion of environmental policy in terms of the priority that has been given to environmental issues in the development of national legislation.

Those countries which have developed the most comprehensive environmental policies are the Northern European countries. Denmark, West Germany and the Netherlands have formulated comprehensive environmental policies over the last two decades and have placed a high priority on the integration of environmental policies into economic and industrial policies. Belgium, France, Ireland and the United Kingdom are characterised by less rigorous environmental policies but, nonetheless have a tradition of environmental protection practices. The Southern European countries, Italy, Spain, Greece and Portugal lag behind in terms of the development of environmental policies. Spain, Portugal and Greece have only recently been admitted to the European Community and are expected to experience difficulties in complying with, increasingly stringent, EC environmental Directives. This is exemplified by requests for dispensation (eg, Portugal regarding the EC drinking water and bathing water directives).

2.0 NATIONAL PROFILES

2.1 Denmark

General Framework

The attainment and protection of environmental quality has long been a matter of high priority in Denmark. In common with other Nordic countries, Denmark has adopted an integrated approach to pollution control, largely founded on the 1983 Environmental Protection Act; this amended a previous (1974) Act and various sectoral regulations. The 1983 Act introduced comprehensive measures relating to the prevention and control of air, water, noise and soil pollution, and also provides the basis for health protection regulations and public planning policy. In addition, Denmark has a strong record of implementing EC directives, and, overall, standards of enforcement are high.

Policies regarding pollution control are formulated by the Ministry of the Environment (*Miljoministriet*), assisted by the National Agency for Environmental Protection (*Miljostyrelen*). Local authorities are largely responsible for enforcing environmental standards, although the Ministry has the powers to intervene under an appeals procedure.

Sectoral Policies

Regarding air pollution, the 1983 Law regulates the monitoring and control of industrial plant and sets up a system of authorisations for air emissions. There has also been a Rational Air Quality Monitoring Programme in force since 1981.

Water pollution policy is based on the principle of "recipient quality planning", established in the 1974 and 1983 Acts. This is a policy for the protection of groundwater and surface waters in which a standard for each body of water is determined by the Regional Councils (*Amstrad*), along with a corresponding set of water quality parameters. This is followed by the development of a master plan for sewers and sewage treatment in each catchment area to meet the water quality standards. The latter step is the responsibility of the local council (*Kommunalbesyrelsen*).

Denmark is unique in Europe in having a centralised system for the collection and disposal of hazardous waste. Under a framework law of 1972 on the "Disposal of Oily and Chemical Waste", a complete system of procedures for the management of hazardous waste has been established, covering legislation, packaging and transport, a transfer station system and a central treatment and landfill facility (known as Kommunekemi).

The prominence of environmental policy within Denmark is reflected in the recent emergence of contaminated site liability as a political and economic issue. Over the last year, the Danish government has been seeking to ensure that parties responsible for contaminating industrial sites with hazardous substances are held liable for the costs of clean-up (as is the case in the Superfund legislation in the United States) and in March 1989 achieved its first sucessful prosecution in this respect. The National Agency for Environmental Protection is now seeking further compensation from 24 firms to recover the cost of clean-up at a number of landfill sites. Thus, the principle of lasting liability, from "cradle-to-grave", has been established in Danish legislation and the contaminated land remediation market is expected to experience significant growth as a result.

Policy Instruments

The legislative controls and level of enforcement in Denmark reflect the strong committment to environmental protection. As noted above, regulations are generally implemented through a permit system for industrial discharges, set according to standards aimed at encouraging the use of the best available control technologies. Frequently, government assistance can be obtained to offset the costs of investing in clean technologies, and technical guidance may also be provided. Denmark's new environmental bill places a high priority on the adoption of clear technologies as a means of solving environmental problems. The Bill includes a programme of support for SME's to enable them to gain advice from external consultants.

There is also a strong emphasis within policy on encouraging recycling and waste minimisation strategies; this is reflected by the use of taxes on wastewater, solid waste disposal, and hazardous and chemical waste disposal as policy instruments, the revenues from which finance the clean technology scheme.

Since administrative and enforcement arrangements are relatively mature in Denmark, especially for air and water, the most significant market opportunities within environmental control will be in waste disposal and land remediation where, as indicated above, the attention of policy-makers is now being focused.

2.2 West Germany

General Framework

Environmental policies in West Germany are amongst the most demanding in the industrialised world, requiring compliance with increasingly stringent emission standards. In many respects the West German philosophy has moved on from the "command-and-control" approach to environmental policy, (i.e controlling pollution at source) to one of prevention and anticipation under the so-called *Vorsorgprinzip* (Principle of Prevention). Where prevention is not possible, environmental liability legislation is currently being strengthened.

Responsibility for environmental protection is split between federal, regional and municipal authorities. The executive function (i.e. policy-making) is executed at the national level by the Federal Ministry for the Environment,

Nature Conservation and Reactor Safety. It is assisted and advised by the Federal Agency for the Environment (*Umweltbundesamt*), which issues technical advice, provides information and commissions research.

Laws passed at the federal level provide a framework for detailed legislation passed and enforced by each of the provincial authorities (*Länder*). However, this dual legislative system has lead to some inconsistencies between the *Länder*, and more recent legislation has emphasised compliance with a series of Technical Directives (*Technische Anleitung*) as a means of standardising environmental regulations across the Federal Republic.

West Germany's record on implementing EEC directives has generally been good, although occasionally there have been conflicts in interpretation between the Federal and Länder authorities. The country's economic strength, together with its long-held concern on environmental issues, has ensured that it has remained at the forefront of discussions on Community legislation, enabling it to balance the interests of its industry and its environment.

Sectoral Policies

Legislation to combat air pollution in West Germany is based around the Federal Emission Control Act (*Bundesimmisionsschutzgesetz*) which was last amended in 1985. These general provisions are given greater clarity by the Technical Instructions on Air Quality Control of 1986 (*TA Luft*) which, amongst other matters, set out limit values for emissions to be met in industrial licences. The latest version of the Regulations require the renovation of existing plant to meet the significantly more stringent requirements for new facilities within a specific period (between three and eight years, depending on the type of equipment being used). The Regulations also enable compensation to be claimed by existing facilities. An amendment currently being debated will prescribe technical regulations for the safety and monitoring of over 200 types of industrial plant from 1990; in total about 4000 firms will be affected.

Water pollution control legislation operates around the 1976 Water Resource Policy Act (*Wasserhaushaltgesetz*). This is a framework Act which employs the concept of the "use" of the common property of water. Under the Act authority must be given for both the abstraction of water and the use of waterways for disposal purposes. The *Länder* have the responsibility of enforcing this framework law by means of Water Acts within each of the individual states. By imposing various conditions and stipulations on the use of water, including the level of effluent charges, these Acts supplement the main federal legislation.

Waste disposal law within the Federal Republic is framed around the 1972 Waste Disposal Act (*Abfallbeseitigungsgesetz*) which makes provision for defining hazardous or special waste, guidelines for waste disposal, liability for disposal and licensing of facilities and transport. This Act was revised in 1986, when, amongst other measures, regulations for the collection, recycling, burning and taxing of waste oil were incorporated into it. The most recent changes to waste disposal legislation in the Federal Republic has been the adoption in September 1989 of a revision of the Technical Instructions on Waste Disposal (*TA Abfall*) which significantly extends the definition of hazardous waste.

The Federal Government has no responsibility for implementing or enforcing the requirements of the Waste Disposal Act; this authority is devolved to the *Länder*. As in other aspects of environmental protection, each *Land* has complemented the national outline laws on waste with its own regulations, although in some cases these have caused conflict in maintaining overall environmental quality.

Policy Instruments

West Germany employs a range of environmental policy instruments. As noted above, air and water emissions are subject to a permit system and waste disposal facilities have to be licensed. A range of environmental taxes are also in force, although in some cases these apply to particular *Länder only*. *At the moment the principal tax is for wastewater discharges (the Abwasserabgabe)*, but a much wider range of tax measures is currently being proposed by parties from across the political spectrum. Therefore a more vigorous use of taxes as a policy instrument looks likely in the future.

2.3   **Netherlands**

General Framework

The Dutch have earned a formidable reputation for a progressive attitude to environmental issues, introducing in the 1970's six major statutes and a wide variety of subsidiary legislation to control all aspects of environmental pollution. This comprehensive approach has recently been formalised into a

National Environment Policy Plan covering all aspects of environmental protection, and discussed in more detail below. The wide publicity given to the Plan, including its precipitation of an early general election in June 1989, has ensured that the Dutch are now the most "environmentally aware" people in Europe. This situation has largely been forced upon them by their country's precarious physical position, sited at the mouth of two highly polluted rivers, the Meuse and the Rhine, which bring industrial pollution across its borders, and under continual threat of erosion, and even invasion, by the North Sea.

Executive responsibility for environmental policies rests with three Ministries, the most significant role being that of the Ministry of Housing, Physical Planning and Environment. Legislative and administrative powers may be delegated from the national level to local authorities (the 12 provinces and 800 municipalities); these have powers to enforce laws in individual and specific cases.

National Environment Plan

The most significant environmental policy development in the Netherlands in recent years has been the proposition of a National Environment Policy Plan (NEPP) for the period 1990-94. The Plan contains some controversial elements, but has received substantial public support and is being implemented in full following the highlighting of key requirements and additional tasks proposed in the NEPP Plus in June 1990. The Plan represents the most far-reaching environmental programme in any industrialised nation.

The Plan is founded on the principle of "Sustainable Development". As far as industry is concerned, important elements of this are the integrated management of production chains (i.e more emphasis on recycling), energy extensification (energy conservation and efficiency) and the promotion of quality of production. The Plan identifies ten "themes" - environmental and policy issues to be addressed - and seven "target groups", which will play a key role in the implementation of the Plan's objectives. The target groups are :-

- agriculture;
- transport and traffic;
- industry (including the chemical industry and refineries);
- energy;
- construction;

- water-supply and waste management;
- consumers.

The total costs of the programme over five years were estimated at FL6,650 million ($3,117 million), which will be raised by a combination of direct taxes on target groups and more general levies and fiscal measures. The aim is to improve the instruments provided by legislation, based on the principle that the polluter should pay. However, it is not yet clear how this is to be enforced, since the Netherlands has recently abandoned many of its pollution charging systems (for example those for air, noise and waste) because of difficulties in implementation and the costs of administration. The recently published NEPP Plus aims to increase environmental expenditure in the Netherlands to $8,467 million per year by 1994. The NEPP-Plus does not aim to change the strategy of the original plan fundamentally, but rather enlarges its scope and clarifies the actions required. Although the advent of the NEPP and NEPP Plus represent a more focused approach to policy, the methods of enforcement remain largely within sectoral legislation; namely sectoral Acts dealing with, amongst other issues, air, surface water, soil, noise, waste, chemical waste, environmentally dangerous substances and pesticides. The General Environmental Provisions Act (*Wet Algemene Bepalingen Milieuhygiene (WABM)*) has gradually superceded these earlier measures, all future environmental legislation being enacted as new chapters under the WABM. Currently plans are underway to ammend the General Environmental Provisions Act and establish the Environmental Management Act (EMA) in order that it be changed from a procedural Act into a regulation providing for "effective, integral protection of all aspects of the environment".

2.4 Belgium and Luxembourg

General Framework

Environmental policy in Belgium and Luxembourg is less highly developed than in the neighbouring Netherlands. In Belgium, the main reason for this has been the highly complex situation which has existed since the redrafting of the Constitution in 1980, whereby administrative and legislative powers are split between four levels: the State, the Regions, the Provinces and the Communes (municipalities). In particular, confusion over whether the adoption of proposed decrees on regional planning and environmental management is the responsibility of State or Regional government has been a major obstacle to the development of a coherent environmental policy.

This complicated constitutional situation has also made it difficult for EC Directives to be incorporated into Belgian law, and although Directives are officially adopted they are frequently not implemented.

The administration and control of most aspects of pollution control (air, water and waste) is now the responsibility of the regional authorities. Although national legislation has to be followed by the regions, regional parliaments also have authority to introduce decrees which are legally binding. This regionalisation has resulted in some variation in standards of control and enforcement within Belgium.

In Luxembourg there is a similar, but less divisive, split between national and local authorities. The Minister for the Environment has general responsibilities for environmental protection and these are enforced at a local level. The legislative structure has allowed the implementation of a wide range of EC Directives, including those covering water resources and water pollution, and waste disposal. The most important recent development has been the implementation of a material policy aimed at achieving a much higher level of waste recovery and re-use.

2.5 France

General Framework

Historically, environmental concerns have not been prominent in France. Policy formulation only became the responsibility of a separate department of State in 1986, and before this there had been continual changes in administrative arrangements dating back to 1971, reflecting the shifting priorities of various administrations. These deficiencies have now been largely corrected as a coherent system of institutions has been established.

Administration of environmental policy is now concentrated in the Ministry of the Environment (*Ministere de l'Environnement*), established in 1986, which operates via several Directorates including one concerned with pollution. The Ministry is assisted by national agencies concerned with research and information on waste and air quality, known respectively as ANRED (*Agence pour la Récuperation et l'Elimination des Déchets*) and AQA (*Agence pour la Qualité de l'Air*).

The French regulatory system operates on a principle of decentralisation. Laws passed by the central government are enforced by the regions (*Département*) and the municipalities: responsibilities include setting environmental quality objectives for the local area and issuing prior authorisations for industrial polluters. The main duties and obligations contained in EC legislation have mainly been implemented, usually in the form of administrative measures such as ministerial decrees, orders, circulars and instructions rather than specific legislation.

The draft version of the French National Environment Plan (NEP), which was published in the summer 1990, aims to integrate environmental considerations into all major political sectors. Estimates put the cost of the NEP at some $23,616 millon per year for the next ten years. The NEP is expected to establish the general guidelines and direction of environmental policy in France for the next ten years. Its objectives are to:

- establish the constitutional basis for all environmental law

- tackle the question of effective enforcement of environmental policy, inspection and monitoring

- revise individual laws so as to effect rapid and efficient action

The draft NEP deals with issues by sector and lays down a series of targets. The draft NEP also makes provision for the establishment of a National Environmental Institute which would function as a monitoring and information body and would work in close co-operation with the European Environment Agency. The draft NEP also proposes the reorganisation of existing technical agencies such as the water agencies and ANRED. The funding for the new legislation is to come from two main sources; an expansion of the "polluter pays" principle and the introduction of the "consumer pays" principle. In addition, the annual environmental budget is to be extended.

Sectoral Policies

The central instrument of environmental legislation in France is the 1976 Act on Installations Registered For Environmental Protection. This is a comprehensive Act covering air, water and noise pollution, waste management and health and safety. Activities registered under the Act, known as classified installations, are required to apply for authorisations for risks relating to the environment. As far as industrial installations are concerned, authorisations specify limit values for emissions, provisions for monitoring effluents and the ambient environment, and procedures for safe waste disposal.

There are also various sectoral regulations. For air, for example, the 1961 act on air pollution and odour abatement sets out requirements for the licensing and inspection of facilities. There is a national network of air quality monitoring, administered by AQA and financed by taxes on sulphur dioxide emissions and fuel oils. For water pollution, a Decree of 1973 lays down the technical considerations for authorising discharges into flowing waters. Once authorised by prefectoral decree, discharges are monitored by the water authorities and inspectors of classified installations.

The central law on waste is the 1975 Outline Law, which imposed responsibilities on industrial producers for disposal of the wastes they generate, and gives the government far-reaching powers to intervene in industrial processes in terms of recycling and energy recovery.

Policy Instruments

Extensive use has been made of authorisations and taxes and charges as policy instruments. Air pollution taxes have already been described. Responsibility for levying water pollution charges and using the revenue raised to provide grants for municipal and industrial treatment facilities lies with the six *Agence Financières de Bassin*. The Agences have no power to control discharges, but play a role in the co-ordination of pollution control policies. Controls over discharges to sewers are the responsibility of the local authorities (*communes*), who levy effluent treatment charges to cover the costs of operating treatment works.

2.6   **Italy**

General Framework

Environmental policy in Italy has been characterised by a fragmented structure, such issues being concentrated into a single Ministry of the Environment (*Ministero dell'Ambiente*) only in 1986. Before this, responsibilities for the management and protection of the environment were divided between eight different ministries: even after the reorganisation, there is still considerable overlap between central authorities.

The situation is complicated further by the decentralisation of many aspects of policy to the Regions, Provinces and Municipalities. The 20 Regions (*Regioni*) have acquired administrative functions regarding soil, atmospheric, water, heat and noise pollution, including public health, and have also gained powers concerning water purification and waste disposal. Many of the functions of inspecting and enforcing pollution controls have been further devolved to the 100 Provinces (*Province*) and over 8000 Municipalities (*Comuni*). This decentralised structure has given rise to a wide variation in environmental standards throughout Italy; often best and worst environmental practice exist side by side.

The final version of Italy's 3 year environmental protection plan has recently been approved. The delayed plan allocates a total of $9,760 million for a range of environmental measures over the period 1989-91. The single largest expenditure (11,767,000 million) is for soil and groundwater protection. A further 2600,000 million is to be invested for industrial waste management.

Overall, there has been a rapidly growing awareness of the environment in Italian society in recent years, witnessed, for example, by an increasing number of prosecutions under pollution control laws; rapid growth in the number of firms operating within the environmental management market; and the founding (in early 1989) of a new environmental research institute by the manufacturers organisations Confindustria and Federchemica. These trends seem set to continue.

Sectoral Policies

Air pollution legislation is largely founded on Law 615, passed in 1966, and its implementing regulations. The law contains schedules for three different sources of emission: domestic heating, industry and motor vehicles. Responsibility for enforcement, including a monitoring function, rests with local authorities and the Regional Committees on Air Pollution (the CRIA): the latter are joint bodies, with representatives from State agencies, local authorities, industry and academia. A Presidential Decree of 1971 set up a system of authorisation and control of air emissions from industrial plants: under these regulations factories must submit a report on the nature of their emissions to the local authorities. These reports are forwarded to the CIRA, which issues guidelines for each establishment, in terms of pollutants monitored at the source of production (*emissioni*) and ground concentrations around the plant (*immissioni*). This distinction is an important one, since it dictates that monitoring has a particularly important role within Italian law.

Water pollution control is based on Law 319 of 1976, (the "Merli" Law) which regulates all types of discharge into sewers or watercourses. The law also sets out general criteria on the use and discharge of water, organises public water supplies, sewers and treatment plants, provides for a general water improvement plan (based on regional plans) and the systematic monitoring of factors relating to the quality and quantity of watercourses. All discharges from industrial plant are subject to a system of authorisation, which are monitored by the local or regional authorities.

The primary legislation on wastes is the 1982 decree, which implemented several EEC Directives. The decree sets out the general framework for waste collection, transport and disposal, and defines the responsibilities of local authorities in this respect. A subsequent technical directive of 1984 sets out criteria for the classification of hazardous wastes, as well as other technical measures, including methods of sampling and analysis. Despite these improvements in the legislative structure, illegal dumping of solid wastes, including hazardous wastes, is still a major problem.

In recognition of the increasing waste problem the Italian government has recently announced that it is to allocate approximately $15.7 million for waste management research projects. These include chromium recovery from waste water and a project for an incinerator for the disposal of, for example, furans and dioxins.

Policy Instruments

As the above discussion has indicated, Italy has generally lacked the policy instruments to implement environmental policy effectively. For air and water discharges a system of authorisation has been used, monitored by a large number of local authorities; thus, there is a very diffuse enforcement system. For effluent discharges authorisation has been linked to a charging system.

2.7 Ireland

General Framework

In Ireland, environmental policy is administered by the Department of the Environment, which is assisted by the Water Pollution and Environment Councils. Within the Department, environmental protection is shared between divisions responsible for the review of environmental policy (Environmental Policy Section) and for the enforcement of legislation (Pollution Control Section). Local authorities have responsibilities for enforcing the limited pollution measures that exist, covering air and water pollution and waste disposal.

Since 1973, when Ireland joined the EEC, the laws covering environmental controls have been considerably improved, including the implementation of many EC Directives. However, the sanctions laid down by the law are relatively minimal and in certain areas, particularly waste disposal, deficiencies still remain: in practical terms there are no proper controls. Proposals for an independent Environmental Protection Agency in the Republic of Ireland have recently been approved by the government. The new Environmental Protection Agency is seen as an essential requirement in improving Irelands environmental policy framework. The Agency will have direct responsibility for licensing, monitoring and enforcement functions for classes of new development with potential for serious pollution. It will also be empowered to review licenses for existing establishments of this kind. The functions of the Agency will initially cover problems such as hazardous waste management and air and water pollution control falling into four main catagories:

- control and regulation of development likely to pose a major task to environmental quality;
- general monitoring of environmental quality;
- support, backup and advisory services; and
- environmental research.

The new Envrionmental Action Programme details the environmental policy measures of the Irish government up to the year 2000. The programme includes the provision of financial incentives for waste reduction and clean technologies in industry. Special incentives will also be introduced to encourage pollution control equipment/technology manufactures to locate in Ireland.

2.8 United Kingdom

General Framework

Environmental policy in the United Kingdom has evolved in a piecemeal manner, both in its scope and in its enforcement. A unified pollution inspectorate, Her Majesty's Inspectorate of Pollution (HMIP), was formed in 1987 to oversee aspects of air, water and waste legislation: despite this the regulatory framework is still fragmented, with many enforcement powers remaining with local authorities and the newly formed National Rivers Authority (NRA). A separate body, Her Majesty's Industrial Pollution Inspectorate (HMIPI), is the enforcement agency in Scotland; and in Northern Ireland the relevant authority is the DOE Northern Ireland.

The recently enacted Environmental Protection Act (1st November 1990) radically overhauls British pollution control systems. Part I of the Act will introduce two new industrial pollution control systems: IPC under which HMIP will regulate solid, liquid and gaseous waste from some 5000 processes and a system under which local authorities will control emissions to air from some 27,000 process. Part II of the Act amends the laws on waste disposal and restructures the Waste Disposal Authorities. The Waste Regulatory Authority will have overall regulatory responsibility and the Local Authority Waste Disposal Companies (LAWDCs) will have operational responsibility. The Act also introduces tighter environmental controls and strengthens the powers of HMIP.

These measures are discussed below in the context of the existing legislative framework.

Sectoral Policies

Air pollution control in the UK is still largely enforced by the 1906 Alkali & Works Regulation Act, which requires scheduled processes to use "best practicable means" (BPM) for preventing emissions into the atmosphere of "noxious or offensive substances". Lists of noxious or offensive substances were updated by the Health & Safety (Emissions into the Atmosphere) Regulations, 1983, passed under the Health & Safety at Work Act, 1974. All other industrial emissions are subject to control by local authorities under the Clean Air Acts of 1956 and 1968, or by the powers to abate a statutory nuisance contained in the Public Health Act of 1936.

The measures included in the Environmental Protection Act will introduce substantial changes in the enforcement of air pollution policy by establishing a system of two part scheduling. Part A scheduled processes (generally the largest and most problematic installations) will be under HMIP control, while Part B scheduled processes will be under local authority control. Part A schedules are already in force but Part B schedules will require enabling powers under the Bill since this is the first time local authorities have been given an enforcement role in air pollution control.

Increasingly, European Community Directives are influencing UK environmental legislation. In air pollution control EC measures require the introduction of Best Available Technology Not Entailing Excessive Cost (BATNEEC) to supercede BPM as the operating philosophy. Also, the emission limits to be met are increasingly those imposed in EC Directives (as for example in the recent directive on municipal incinerators) because UK legislation has remained unreformed for so long.

The UK has a well-established framework for controlling discharges of potentially polluting substances to water. This revolves around

i)   a system of environmental quality objectives (EQOs) defined in terms of water use, for different stretches of water;

ii)   controls over all discharges to and abstractions from rivers and estuaries and coastal waters under the Control of Pollution Act 1974 (CoPA) and the Water Resources Act 1963; and

iii)   controls over all discharges to sewer under the Public Health Acts 1937 and 1961.

The general principle governing the control of discharges has been the ability of the receiving waters to accommodate pollutants, without detriment to the uses specified for the waters concerned. The CoPA contains provision for the authorisation of discharges (consent agreements), the maintenance of records on these discharges and measures to combat pollution not covered by consent agreements. Consents for discharge to sewer are charged by the former water authorities but direct currently discharges to water are uncharged.

As far as water pollution control is concerned, the Environmental Protection Act is likely to complicate, rather than clarify the enforcement regime. This is because by giving HMIP control over the discharge of Red List substances to water, as proposed, the Government is compromising the powers of the NRA as laid down in the Water Act 1989. As noted above, this empowers NRA with the authority to issue consents over all discharges to sewer or to watercourses: under the Environmental Protection Act it loses its authority over the most noxious discharges but still be responsible for maintaining environmental quality standards. Hence the NRA is arguing that the Green Bill proposals will produce a fragmented and inconsistent enforcement regime as far as discharges to the aquatic environment are concerned.

The CoPA also provides a framework for waste management legislation, including the licensing of waste disposal by landfill, thermal treatment or other means. This aspect of the Act, in particular, contains many deficencies and proposals have been issued to substantially change the waste management framework in the UK, principally by the separation of local authority waste disposal and waste regulation responsibilities, and the imposition of a Duty of Care on producers for the means of disposal of the wastes they generate.

Policy Instruments

Historically, a mixture of instruments have been used within UK environmental policy. The enforcement regime is widely acknowledged to have been weak in many cases. In waste management, for example, local authorities have had a dual role (so called poacher and gamekeeper) and, until the advent of the NRA, the water environment was also policed by actors who were often major polluters (the Water Authorities). New enforcement regimes are now in force, or proposed, although in some cases (notably HMIP) evidence of a large-scale commitment of resources to enforcement is still lacking.

With the exception of effluent charges there are no environmentally related direct taxes in the UK, nor are there any formal proposals for the further use of pollution taxes as a policy instrument. Similarly, there are no product taxes in the UK, nor are any such measures under discussion. However, in a recent report to the Department of the Environment, Professor David Pearce of the London Environmental Economics Centre argued in favour of more direct taxation on air and water polluters as a policy instrument. He argued that market-based approaches were a more equitable means of enforcement than regulatory approaches because they allowed flexibility in the way firms respond in attaining compliance with the necessary standards.

The use of subsidies as a policy instrument has not found favour with a government committed to ensuring firms stand on their own feet regarding financing and investments. However, in common with most Northern European countries, grants for innovative research and demonstration projects are available under the DOE's Environmental Protection Technology (EPT) Scheme.

2.9   Greece

General Framework

The Ministry of Regional Planning, Urban Development and the Environment constitutes the central administrative body for environmental protection in Greece. This Ministry is charged with enforcing policies upheld by the National Council for Physical Planning and the Environment, and is responsible for ensuring that other Departments comply with these policies. Central government legislation, based on EC Directives, is supplemented by a system of Presidential Decrees or orders, which are addressed to particular environmental issues. Such orders provide a mechanism by which Directives on environmental legislation can be incorporated into national law.

Greece shares the problems of other Southern European EC Members in having to adjust to the pollution problems resulting from a period of rapid industrialisation. Despite an increased interest in recent years by both central and local government in restoring the environment, progress has been slow. Legislation is being promulgated and, although not yet clearly defined for the various sectors, it is expected that tighter controls will take effect and be coupled with subsidies for investment in abatement equipment.

2.10   **Portugal**

General Framework

Despite environmental concerns being given prominence in the Portuguese Constitution of 1976, a coherent environmental policy has failed to emerge. This is largely a result of the historic overcentralisation of the Portuguese state, a situation which is only now being corrected by the devolution of powers to Regional and Municipal authorities. A National Environmental Agency (*Inspeocao do Ambiente*) was set up in 1988, with help from the Dutch government, and it is proposed this will concentrate some of the responsibilities previously spread across 14 national ministries.

The most significant local authority powers are with the Municipalities (*Concelhos*), which are responsible for such aspects as water supply and sewage handling, solid waste disposal, urban and local planning and land management. In practice these authorities are often severely under-resourced, and there is a wide variation in standards applied.

Sectoral Policies

Air pollution legislation is inadequate. Many plants in the industrialised areas operate without any controls, and the local authority Air Management Committees have very few powers. There are some air quality monitoring networks, belonging either to the State or to industrial enterprises, but they are generally not adequate. In response to this, the Director General of Natural Resources (*Direção General dos Recursos Naturais*) is instigating a national air quality network in collaboration with the EEC.

Basic legislation relating to water quality and effluent standards was adopted only in 1986, and this partly aimed at implementing EEC directives. In terms of water quality monitoring, the existing network has been noted to be insufficient, so that considerable improvements in the operational database are necessary.

Waste management legislation is still in its infancy; there is a framework law, passed in 1985, but no enacting legislation.

2.11　**Spain**

General Framework

In common with other Member States where administrative powers are divided between national and regional governments, environmental policy in Spain has been fragmented and inconsistent. Most matters concerning pollution control are the responsibility of the Department of the Environment (*Direccion General de Medio Ambiente*) and the Department of Industrial Innovation and Technology (*Direccion

General de Innovacion Industrial y Tecnologia). Several other State ministries are also involved, all of these being represented on the Working Party of the Select Committee on the Environment *(Comision Interministerial del Medio Ambiente (CIMA)).*

The situation is further complicated by the devolution of powers to the 17 Autonomous Regions under the 1978 Constitution. Central government retains exclusive responsibility for promulgating laws on environmental protection, although the Regions have the authority to introduce supplementary regulations. Overall, the situation is considered unsatisfactory, and some rationalising of administrative structures is inevitable if Spain is to improve its position in line with EEC requirements. The Secretariat for the Environment has recently allocated $411.9 million in order to co-ordinate the numerous different environmental policies. The Government has also produced a plan to encourage the growth of an effective pollution control industry in recognition of the fact that Spain lacks the means by which to ensure compliance with EC environmental standards. The Government has allocated 35% of its public spending to investment in the pollution control sector.

The European Investment Bank has lent $49.8 million for environmental protection measures in Spain. The loan is to be used to bring production processes in line with European Community environmental regulations.

Sectoral Policies

Air pollution in Spain is founded on a 1972 framework law, its enforcing Regulation of 1975, and various supplementary regulations. The law makes provision for the prevention, monitoring and correction of air pollution and establishes air quality standards and acceptable emission levels. There is a sophisticated network of air quality monitoring, consisting of agencies responsible for both industrial and remote sources. Tax incentives on fuels and subsidies on investments in abatement equipment have been used as a means of implementing clean air policies.

Water pollution control is covered by a comprehensive 1985 law on water management. This introduced a procedure of prior authorisation for any activity which may cause water contamination; authorisation may be withdrawn if there is a failure to comply with the agreed conditions. Charges for emissions to sewers and surface waters were also introduced. Rates for authorised discharges are calculated on the basis of the predetermined quality of the receiving watercourse and the pollution potential of the discharge. Contravention of the regulations is subject to fines.

Waste management legislation is based on a 1975 law, amended by Decree in 1986, implementing the EC framework Directive on waste. However, uncontrolled dumping of solid waste accounts for a high proportion of waste disposal and there is still no specific legislation dealing with hazardous waste.

European Foundation for the Improvement of Living and Working Conditions

Education and Training of Personnel concerned with Environmental Issues relating to Industry

Luxembourg: Office for Official Publications of the European Communities, 1992

1992 — 300 p. — 16 cm × 23.5 cm

ISBN 92-826-4852-4

Price (excluding VAT) in Luxembourg: ECU 28.50

Venta y suscripciones • Salg og abonnement • Verkauf und Abonnement • Πωλήσεις και συνδρομές
Sales and subscriptions • Vente et abonnements • Vendita e abbonamenti
Verkoop en abonnementen • Venda e assinaturas

BELGIQUE / BELGIË

**Moniteur belge /
Belgisch Staatsblad**
Rue de Louvain 42 / Leuvenseweg 42
1000 Bruxelles / 1000 Brussel
Tél. (02) 512 00 26
Fax 511 01 84
CCP / Postrekening 000-2005502-27

Autres distributeurs /
Overige verkooppunten

**Librairie européenne/
Europese Boekhandel**
Avenue Albert Jonnart 50 /
Albert Jonnartlaan 50
1200 Bruxelles / 1200 Brussel
Tél. (02) 734 02 81
Fax 735 08 60

Jean De Lannoy
Avenue du Roi 202 /Koningslaan 202
1060 Bruxelles / 1060 Brussel
Tél. (02) 538 51 69
Télex 63220 UNBOOK B
Fax (02) 538 08 41

CREDOC
Rue de la Montagne 34 / Bergstraat 34
Bte 11 / Bus 11
1000 Bruxelles / 1000 Brussel

DANMARK

**J. H. Schultz Information A/S
EF-Publikationer**
Ottiliavej 18
2500 Valby
Tlf. 36 44 22 66
Fax 36 44 01 41
Girokonto 6 00 08 86

BR DEUTSCHLAND

Bundesanzeiger Verlag
Breite Straße
Postfach 10 80 06
5000 Köln 1
Tel. (02 21) 20 29-0
Telex ANZEIGER BONN 8 882 595
Fax 20 29 278

GREECE/ΕΛΛΑΔΑ

G.C. Eleftheroudakis SA
International Bookstore
Nikis Street 4
10563 Athens
Tel. (01) 322 63 23
Telex 219410 ELEF
Fax 323 98 21

ESPAÑA

Boletín Oficial del Estado
Trafalgar, 27
28010 Madrid
Tel. (91) 44 82 135

Mundi-Prensa Libros, S.A.
Castelló, 37
28001 Madrid
Tel. (91) 431 33 99 (Libros)
     431 32 22 (Suscripciones)
     435 36 37 (Dirección)
Télex 49370-MPLI-E
Fax (91) 575 39 98

Sucursal:

Librería Internacional AEDOS
Consejo de Ciento, 391
08009 Barcelona
Tel. (93) 301 86 15
Fax (93) 317 01 41

**Llibreria de la Generalitat
de Catalunya**
Rambla dels Estudis, 118 (Palau Moja)
08002 Barcelona
Tel. (93) 302 68 35
    302 64 62
Fax (93) 302 12 99

FRANCE

**Journal officiel
Service des publications
des Communautés européennes**
26, rue Desaix
75727 Paris Cedex 15
Tél. (1) 40 58 75 00
Fax (1) 40 58 75 74

IRELAND

Government Supplies Agency
4-5 Harcourt Road
Dublin 2
Tel. (1) 61 31 11
Fax (1) 78 06 45

ITALIA

Licosa Spa
Via Duca di Calabria, 1/1
Casella postale 552
50125 Firenze
Tel. (055) 64 54 15
Fax 64 12 57
Telex 570466 LICOSA I
CCP 343 509

GRAND-DUCHÉ DE LUXEMBOURG

Messageries Paul Kraus
11, rue Christophe Plantin
2339 Luxembourg
Tél. 499 88 88
Télex 2515
Fax 499 88 84 44
CCP 49242-63

NEDERLAND

SDU Overheidsinformatie
Externe Fondsen
Postbus 20014
2500 EA 's-Gravenhage
Tel. (070) 37 89 911
Fax (070) 34 75 778

PORTUGAL

Imprensa Nacional
Casa da Moeda, EP
Rua D. Francisco Manuel de Melo, 5
1092 Lisboa Codex
Tel. (01) 69 34 14

**Distribuidora de Livros
Bertrand, Ld.ª**
Grupo Bertrand, SA
Rua das Terras dos Vales, 4-A
Apartado 37
2700 Amadora Codex
Tel. (01) 49 59 050
Telex 15798 BERDIS
Fax 49 60 255

UNITED KINGDOM

HMSO Books (PC 16)
HMSO Publications Centre
51 Nine Elms Lane
London SW8 5DR
Tel. (071) 873 2000
Fax GP3 873 8463
Telex 29 71 138

ÖSTERREICH

**Manz'sche Verlags-
und Universitätsbuchhandlung**
Kohlmarkt 16
1014 Wien
Tel. (0222) 531 61-0
Telex 11 25 00 BOX A
Fax (0222) 531 61-39

SUOMI

Akateeminen Kirjakauppa
Keskuskatu 1
PO Box 128
00101 Helsinki
Tel. (0) 121 41
Fax (0) 121 44 41

NORGE

Narvesen information center
Bertrand Narvesens vei 2
PO Box 6125 Etterstad
0602 Oslo 6
Tel. (2) 57 33 00
Telex 79668 NIC N
Fax (2) 68 19 01

SVERIGE

BTJ
Box 200
22100 Lund
Tel. (046) 18 00 00
Fax (046) 18 01 25

SCHWEIZ / SUISSE / SVIZZERA

OSEC
Stampfenbachstraße 85
8035 Zürich
Tel. (01) 365 54 49
Fax (01) 365 54 11

CESKOSLOVENSKO

NIS
Havelkova 22
13000 Praha 3
Tel. (02) 235 84 46
Fax 42-2-264775

MAGYARORSZÁG

Euro-Info-Service
Budapest I. Kir.
Attila út 93
1012 Budapest
Tel. (1) 56 82 11
Telex (22) 4717 AGINF H-61
Fax (1) 17 59 031

POLSKA

Business Foundation
ul. Krucza 38/42
00-512 Warszawa
Tel. (22) 21 99 93, 628-28-82
International Fax&Phone
  (0-39) 12-00-77

JUGOSLAVIJA

Privredni Vjesnik
Bulevar Lenjina 171/XIV
11070 Beograd
Tel. (11) 123 23 40

CYPRUS

Cyprus Chamber of Commerce and Industry
Chamber Building
38 Grivas Dhigenis Ave
3 Deligiorgis Street
PO Box 1455
Nicosia
Tel. (2) 449500/462312
Fax (2) 458630

TÜRKIYE

**Pres Gazete Kitap Dergi
Pazarlama Dağitim Ticaret ve sanayi
AŞ**
Narlibahçe Sokak N. 15
Istanbul-Cağaloğlu
Tel. (1) 520 92 96 - 528 55 66
Fax 520 64 57
Telex 23822 DSVO-TR

CANADA

Renouf Publishing Co. Ltd
Mail orders — Head Office:
1294 Algoma Road
Ottawa, Ontario K1B 3W8
Tel. (613) 741 43 33
Fax (613) 741 54 39
Telex 0534783

Ottawa Store:
61 Sparks Street
Tel. (613) 238 89 85

Toronto Store:
211 Yonge Street
Tel. (416) 363 31 71

UNITED STATES OF AMERICA

UNIPUB
4611-F Assembly Drive
Lanham, MD 20706-4391
Tel. Toll Free (800) 274 4888
Fax (301) 459 0056

AUSTRALIA

Hunter Publications
58A Gipps Street
Collingwood
Victoria 3066

JAPAN

Kinokuniya Company Ltd
17-7 Shinjuku 3-Chome
Shinjuku-ku
Tokyo 160-91
Tel. (03) 3439-0121

Journal Department
PO Box 55 Chitose
Tokyo 156
Tel. (03) 3439-0124

AUTRES PAYS
OTHER COUNTRIES
ANDERE LÄNDER

**Office des publications officielles
des Communautés européennes**
2, rue Mercier
2985 Luxembourg
Tél. 49 92 81
Télex PUBOF LU 1324 b
Fax 48 85 73/48 68 17
CC bancaire BIL 8-109/6003/700